French Masters of the Organ

ALSO BY MICHAEL MURRAY

Marcel Dupré: The Work of a Master Organist

Albert Schweitzer, Musician

French Masters of the Organ

Saint-Saëns, Franck, Widor, Vierne, Dupré, Langlais, Messiaen

❋ ❋ ❋

MICHAEL MURRAY

YALE UNIVERSITY PRESS   NEW HAVEN & LONDON

Designed by James J. Johnson and set in Fournier type by G & S Typesetters, Inc. Printed in the United States of America.

Library of Congress Cataloging-in-Publication Data

Murray, Michael, 1943 –
    French masters of the organ / Michael Murray.
      p.   cm.
    Includes bibliographical references and index.
    Contents: Saint-Saëns — Franck — Widor — Vierne — Dupré — Langlais — Messiaen.
    ISBN 0 – 300-07291-0 (cloth : alk. paper)

    1. Organists—France—Biography.   I. Title.
ML396.M87 1998
786.5′092′244 — dc21
[B]   97-41401

A catalogue record for this book is available from the British Library.

The paper in this book meets the guidelines for permanence and durability of the Committee on Production Guidelines for Book Longevity of the Council on Library Resources.

10 9 8 7 6 5 4 3 2 1

to

Jacques Barzun

Contents

Introduction

These essays are meant to introduce the student organist to some notable creators, each a Parisian by circumstance if not by birth. I say introduce because space does not allow every opus and biographical fact to be mentioned, let alone discussed. Still, experience suggests the utility of such portraits painted in broad strokes, and the reader in search of detail may easily find it, as a glance at the Bibliography will show. There also, besides the recommended reading, I have put the occasional elaboration, the sources of quotations, and the record of my debt to colleagues, students, and friends.

I write out of love for this repertory, which for thirty years has stood at the center of my activity as performer, and out of love for my teacher. Marcel Dupré was seventy-five when we met, I eighteen. With fatherly kindliness he enlightened and guided me in countless ways, musical and other, manifesting without fail all that is admirable in the pursuit of beauty and in the life of the mind.

Decades have passed, but even the casual memories remain vivid. I can see him striding down the aisle of his music room to greet me with "Bonjour, mon p'tit." I see him on stage at the Palais de Chaillot performing with an orchestra, and to clamorous applause bowing, smiling. I see him awaiting his cue at the Saint Sulpice console of a winter morning, and giving me his hand-warmer (a felt-covered carafe of hot water) to hold for him while he plays. I see myself sitting beside him there, Sunday after Sunday, witness to the making of art so sublime the listener could scarcely credit it.

Between times I explored every corner of Paris and became her lifelong captive. The dedicated walker in those days found most districts safe at any hour, and I frequented byways whose charm was greatest just before dawn. I would stroll the empty alleys of Montparnasse or Saint Germain, relishing the silence and the soli-tude—always, it seems in retrospect, beneath a Parisian drizzle. Or I would climb Montmartre to look down at the city lights spread across the horizon. Or I would stop by an abandoned quay to pon-der the ageless drift of the Seine.

It was on weekday afternoons, when the last worshipper or tourist had departed, that I liked to revisit the churches—in silence and solitude the more easily to imagine their radiance of former days, their stones resounding with music: Saint-Saëns improvising at the Madeleine, the grace of his counterpoints at one with the grace of its Grecian colonnades; Franck performing the *Six Pièces* one long-ago evening at Saint Clotilde, the shadows of the nave adance in the candlelight; Widor at Saint Sulpice rehearsing a sym-phony lately finished, his rhythm as always imperious; Vierne at Notre Dame recording a Bach prelude and fugue, at a stately tempo which perfectly suited the grandeur of that Gothic cavern.

But not in imagination did I hear Messiaen in just as unhurried a tempo interpret Bach's "Kyrie, Gott, heiliger Geist," dwelling long on every salient phrase, long on every note, a reading that both infringed received style and fulfilled it. Nor in imagination did I hear Cochereau, Alain, Litaize, Pierre, the Duruflés, Renet, Mar-chal, and the rest. Hearing them, I heard the last representatives of a venerable tradition. Even Messiaen, whose innovations seemed daring at the time, marked not a beginning, I now believe, but a consummation. Any tradition ends, after all, when its founders' once-startling discoveries are frittered away by time and change, like the dots of a Seurat painting.

Let us begin with beginnings, however, and take as their symbol Saint Clotilde—the otherwise unremarkable parish church that Franck made famous. We do well to begin with Franck, even though Saint-Saëns preceded him in writing works that some regard as a starting point. Saint-Saëns, chronology notwithstanding, belonged to an earlier age; his music, for all its loveliness, was not epoch-making like Franck's. Franck's *Six Pièces* opened an era that closed with Messiaen's *Livre du Saint Sacrement.*

I remember Saint Clotilde as it looked on the evening I first heard and met Langlais. He played in recital the *Six Pièces,* then exactly one hundred years old. Afterward, having noted that his rendition was at odds with Dupré's, and naïvely assuming that artistic truth could be attained by compromise or meld, I decided to ask for some lessons.

The first of these and the most memorable, an hour spent on the Chorale in B Minor, took place at Saint Clotilde a few nights later. Early on, Langlais grew vexed, detecting in me too much of Dupré's restraint and too stubborn reluctance to amend; my scribbles on my score show him stopping me at almost every bar with such cries as *Tenuto!* and *Enlarge the rests!* and *More freely!* and *Make much of that!* and *This is not polyphony; don't articulate so much!* and finally, exasperated beyond endurance: *Franck is not for Dupré! Dupré is too strict!* But it was not his vexation that made the lesson memorable. On the contrary, I knew even then that great artists are necessarily intolerant, and that Langlais was a great artist. Rather, what gripped heart and mind was Franck's basilica in darkness.

Except for the organ loft Saint Clotilde was black, and the blackness was palpably alive. And susceptible as I was to the magic of an ancient city whose pavements breathed history, I was so stirred by the animate gloom I hardly cared that a great artist thought me inept, or that my master had been criticized, or that the beauties of the rebuilt Cavaillé-Coll were but a phantom of those

Franck had known. For the organ loft, the nave, the lingering smells of incense and old varnish, the echoes, the very dust—all this I knew to be Franck's own.

I was young. And yet even today I detect in Franck, and in the other French masters as well, a mystical, an otherworldly quality impossible to dismiss. I suppose it has to do with the transcendence commonly ascribed to art, a transcendence some think gives entry to a spiritual realm beyond our sensorium, and others take as a purely humanist, albeit inexplicable, phenomenon—one that rouses feelings so keen they free us for a time from our earthbound selves. But whether this quality is germane, whether or how it may put us in touch with the better angels of our nature, remains for psychology to determine.

At all events, it has long seemed desirable to have at hand in a single volume a biographical account of these composers, together with a description of their idiom and of the instrument for which they wrote, to help guide the student who wishes to play their music as it was conceived.

That student will naturally deem composers' intentions of prime importance, and will think it feasible and appropriate to discern and re-embody them. He or she will defer, that is, to the tendency of a composer's mind—that interest which dictates selection of some materials and patterns over others—and though accepting the elusive nature of intention will try to capture and convey in its fullness that essence of authorial meaning.

Not everyone will approve such a goal. Can anything definite be meant, it will be objected, by talk of composers' intentions? What concrete idea or ideas is it that we are at grips with? Is not "intention" just another of those handy words, like "baroque," "romantic," and "classic," whose utility lies in their vagueness, in their pretended exactitude? Were their meaning precise they would less conveniently express approval or scorn.

And even if "intention" can be made to stand for tangible ideas, why should anyone think a composer's intention more important than an interpreter's? The conception of fidelity to a work and duty to a creator is by no means above challenge: the *Werktreue* principle is recent, dating only from the latter nineteenth century; ought it to apply to composers who could have had no such principle in mind? And is it not based on the false belief that a work once completed is changeless, whereas musical compositions by their nature, we know, entail re-creating, hence can never be twice the same? Then too, a composer's intentions may change during the making of a work; which of multiple intentions is the interpreter to seek out and propound? What of the fact that intention more often than not falls short of achievement?

And what of renowned virtuosos who treat all music as exclusively their own? If such luminaries deem immaterial Franck's call for the timbre of an hautbois, or Vierne's for a tempo moderato, or Widor's for a measured legato, why should the student not do likewise? In sum: What if I think a flute sounds better? What if I prefer presto or staccato? Why give more weight to the marks of a score or the tenets of a tradition than to my own sense of what is fitting? There is such a thing as artistic freedom. The interpreter too has rights.

Yes. But as usual it is easy to speak first of rights and only secondarily of duties. Certainly we interpreters have rights. They derive from our artistic integrity and from the dozens or hundreds of hours spent in mastering a work. Moreover, the interpreter may— often does—reveal expressive elements of which the composer appears unaware. Take Rubinstein's recording of Rachmaninoff's Concerto in C Minor and compare Rachmaninoff's own; each performance is superb, and the composer, it seems obvious, does not invariably know best. For that matter, take Messiaen's recordings of Messiaen, which deviate markedly and eloquently from the instructions in the scores; as interpreter Messiaen appears to uncover niceties he had overlooked as composer.

Yet everyone would agree that the interpreter's preference should be thoughtful, not arbitrary. And if it is to be thoughtful, it must have a well-defined something to prefer to. This something is the composer's intentions, deviation from which cannot be arrived at intelligently without first trying to know them. Otherwise, how reasonably prefer a flute to Franck's hautbois? And this means that one must first of all search out every detail of the composer's method, and try to seize on every nuance of his thought. We must not merely attend to every mark in the score, but also, since work and score are by no means the same thing, to every scrap of biographical data and to the fine points of every tradition. Only then, when convinced that we have come as close as we can to fullness of understanding, can we in good conscience conclude that the composer could have better transmitted meaning by doing thus-and-so—and reasonably make a change. This, it seems to me, is the first of our duties as interpreters, and it is a duty if only because our acts should be ruled by mind as well as heart.

Besides, simple justice would suggest that a work belongs to the person who made it, that its creator has proprietary rights which the performer is duty-bound to respect. A work may belong to its performer secondarily, by dint of tribute paid in talent and hard labor, but the performer's rights are derivative rather than primary. This is not to belittle the performer or to contend that he or she is not essential. Music, unlike the arts that need no intermediary—painting, say, or architecture or poetry—can hardly exist without the performer; only the few hear music by reading a score, and even they necessarily construe. Except for electronic works, which literally speak for themselves, music is stillborn without the life-giving breath of personality. But at its best this personality is composite, a union of interpreter and creator the workings of which bring artistic truth to the fore that would otherwise remain undisclosed. The difficulty lies in the proportioning of self-assertion and self-effacement.

Great examples show with what results duty is fulfilled. Think of Toscanini, who in the effort to bring out the composer's meaning would add a trumpet to Beethoven's horns, or violas to Debussy's violins, but not before scrupulous study, and a degree of soul-searching that approached the Carthusian, had persuaded him that the orchestration needed clarifying. Or reflect on Landowska's deference to Bach, or Walter's deference to Mozart. Whether these artists re-created a music its author would have acknowledged, whether in fact they superimposed a later esthetics on an earlier, does not render the attitude less praiseworthy or invalidate its results.

To assume that one is competent to emend is not, of course, without risk. To take this competence for granted is to rate one's abilities on a par with the composer's. It is safer to begin by modestly assuming that the composer is probably right.

Why is it, you may ask, that faithful interpreters do not arrive at identical renditions? Toscanini's *Haffner* and Walter's differ, though each man spared no effort in trying to convey Mozart's intent. Dupré's Bach and Schweitzer's differ, though each man spent years at the most painstaking study, felt sure he played Bach as Bach desired, and made every effort to be Bach's champion. One reason is that creative genius is manifold: no single interpretation can be all-encompassing. Furthermore, the interpreter's own interest—own outlook, feelings, present-mindedness—unavoidably and rightly enters in.

A remark of Nadia Boulanger's perhaps best states the case for fidelity. In her view, interpreters who strive to be faithful not only come closest to realizing the composer's thought in its fullness, or at least a satisfactory simulacrum thereof, but in so doing bring out, as well, what is deepest and best in themselves.

They do so inadvertently, she adds, their attention being fixed on the work. They are far from regarding music-making as a vehicle for self-expression, still less a source of contentment. Indeed, in their pursuit of perfection, the contrast between their vision of a composer's intentions and their shortcomings in approaching that vision makes their life an exercise in frustration. That faithful interpreters take pains with a work is true in more than one sense: Toscanini suffered the pangs of inadequacy, and his distress is shared by all conscientious interpreters. Self-expression could not be further from their minds. It comes about spontaneously, by virtue of one's being oneself and not somebody else; one expresses one's personality because one cannot help doing so. But, says Boulanger, the process must be involuntary, or it will interfere with the work in hand.

It is plain that composers' intentions can never be wholly understood, plainer still that to try to re-create the external circumstances of a work's original performance, trusting alone to period instruments, tempos, or articulations, does not in itself suffice to reveal a composer's spirit and design. Authenticity in this benighted sense will lead us away from our goal, since the interpreter's energetic imagination can never be dispensed with. But even though artistic intent may be the thorniest of conceptions, experience would seem to prove the foregoing assertions true pragmatically, possibly because turning outward from self nearly always brings good results, in music as in life.

· 2 ·

Organists of today may find these ideals more elusive than ever before. Our profession has become isolated from the musical mainstream, and in our seclusion we have ceased to participate in what might be called, by analogy with literature, the great conversation.

To begin with, many of us, veteran and apprentice, do not often enough attend a piano or violin or song recital, or a symphony concert, or the opera, or a program of chamber music. Nor do we often enough listen to a recording by a great soloist or ensemble, heeding the subtleties of the great interpreters. And if as listeners we refuse our ears to any music but our own, likewise as players we in effect perform solely for other organists; we acquiesce in colleagues' opinions, that is, without a murmur of dissent. In our eagerness to conform to a vogue, we forget that not every work or age is equally worthy of notice, that certain scores and certain styles merit our neglect.

And we forget that the opinions of numbers of people tend to reduce to a lowest common denominator; that from this tendency neither critics nor artists are exempt; and that in no art more than in music is the allure of the mediocre pernicious. It is a truism that the organ can lend majesty to insipid melody or harmony, dignity to inept player or composer, and grandeur to the musics of other media. The facility with which it can do so should make us cling to the genuine masterworks, since art is questionable that is bought at too cheap a price.

Consider too that organists used to be trained first of all as pianists, it being taken for granted that piano technique provided an ideal foundation; we came to know, before beginning to specialize, at least one other repertory, a repertory richly diverse. Whether or not the assumption was correct is not at issue here, though we may note in passing that our French masters endorsed it to a man. Dupré voices a consensus when he says that "the organist is naïve who declines to practice octaves to develop his wrist, under the pretext that the use of detached octaves is rare at the organ."

It is in limiting our experience to our own instrument, and in submitting to habits of mind that can only be called barren, that we organists lose familiarity with artistic truths which conductors, singers, wind and string players, and pianists accept as givens. To mold a phrase by being elastic with rhythm yet unobtrusively so, to make minute adjustments of tempo in accord with texture and sonority, to attend to nuances of articulation and of timbre—in short: to apply the full powers of one's mind and sensibilities to the tones one is producing—are second nature to every competent musician but are foreign to many of us.

It may be argued in our defense that the organ is massive, mechanical, unwieldy. But this half-truth deceives. Expressiveness does not differ among instruments: what differs is the methods used to gain it. A violinist may emphasize a note by playing it more forcefully than the notes on either side, an organist by making it a shade longer; the musical result is comparable, even though one accent is achieved by dynamic means, the other by agogic. The fact is good organists command their instrument with no less eloquence than good violinists, and show that the organ can be delicately expressive. Nor does it make any difference whether one plays tracker organs or electro-pneumatic, an organ of a half-dozen stops or a hundred. Deficiency comes not from the nature of the instrument. What is lacking is the sensitive ear and the engaged intelligence. That lack must be supplied by any organist who hopes to serve the French masters, for their panoramic knowledge is inherent in their music. They knew the choral and song and chamber repertories, knew keyboard works from Haydn, Schubert, and Beethoven to Mendelssohn, Chopin, and Liszt, knew orchestration and instrumentation, knew the operas of Gluck, Rossini, Wagner, Verdi—and much else besides. No player can do them justice who does not cultivate a similar knowledge, recognizing the while that its pursuit will require a lifetime of practice and reflection.

· 3 ·

Remains a matter of definition. One often hears "romantic" used to classify each of these composers. Now it is true that by date or by predilection Saint-Saëns, Franck, Widor, and Vierne belong to the nineteenth century, a century in which, as everyone knows, a bountiful romanticism flourished. They may be so classed by reference to period, without ignoring dissimilarity of manner. But to call romantic such more recent figures as Dupré, Langlais, and Messiaen shows how muddled the term has become. Whether or not romanticist gesture can be found informing their scores, would not chronology alone insist that they be called by another name? And if "modern" is too pliant for the task, and if "neo-romanticist" begs the question, and if "avant-garde" is clearly passé, what term are we to use?

An answer will emerge in the chapters below, but we must undertake a preliminary refinement. First, "romantic" chiefly misleads not because it has come to denote many and mutually contradictory ideas—any number of useful words do the same—but because it purports to denote one style while in fact denoting many. We cannot know what synonym to infer when the tag is attached to a given object: sentimental, expressive, sensual, melodic, symphonic, heroic, undisciplined, despicable, impractical, rebellious, formless, poetic, imaginative, or—what? And we cannot in every case trust context to make meaning clear.

"Romantic" also misleads because it suggests the opposite of "classic," whereas history more accurately would let the words name the sides of a single coin. That is, together the classic and the romantic make up one idea having two main parts. It is emphasis that shifts, now to one side, now to the other. Beethoven, for instance, was either a classic-romanticist or a romantic-classicist, depending on which of his coexistent attitudes predominate in a given piece. He was never one or the other exclusively, but always both at once in proportions that varied from work to work. His style, his very epoch, is symbolized by the hyphen.

"Classic" itself misleads by being sometimes used to name a style (that of Haydn, often, and Mozart) and sometimes to name a composer who perfected a style or crowned an evolution. Chopin or Wagner is classic in this sense no less than Schubert, Palestrina, or Bach—"classic," used thus, having nothing to do with period. When, on the other hand, it does denote period (as with Haydn and Mozart) it often suggests, in Charles Rosen's words, the exemplary and normative, or what we are pleased to look back and consider exemplary and normative.

For in truth, as Walter Pater told us more than a century ago, every period and branch of art exhibits the classic and the romantic concurrently. "The romantic spirit is, in reality, an ever-present, an enduring principle, in the artistic temperament; and the qualities of thought and style which that, and other similar uses of the word *romantic* really indicate, are indeed but symptoms of a very continuous and widely working influence." By the same token, the charm of the classic is ever "that of the well-known tale, to which we can, nevertheless, listen over and over again, because it is told so well. To the absolute beauty of its artistic form, is added the accidental, tranquil, charm of familiarity. . . . It is the addition of strangeness to beauty, that constitutes the romantic character in art;

Introduction

and the desire of beauty being a fixed element in every artistic organization, it is the addition of curiosity to this desire of beauty, that constitutes the romantic temper."

We retell, then, an ancient tale: partisans condemning the new as upstart, suspect, and threatening, the old as barren and spent. And no student of history will be surprised to learn that in the neoclassic wars of our own day "romantic" became an epithet hurled with malice, by organists especially, at whole schools and their gifted figures.

It is merely factual to say that in the period 1950–70 our profession fell victim to hysteria. How else explain the appearance in a prominent journal of such a passage as this: "'Sludge' is an apt word to describe Guilmant, Widor and the others. . . . Franck is probably the best of them, but even his music is overrated"? How else explain the pronouncement by a respected musicologist and a venerable university press of so astounding a generality as this: "There is no other branch of music, except the liturgical, in which all musicians would admit the inferiority of everything written in the last two hundred years, of organ music written after 1750, to that written before"? How else explain the animus of a reviewer who, in the guise of reasoned discourse, holds to the calumny that in Bach the French masters advocated "use of the swell pedal, coupling of manuals and reedy registrations in contrast to the German preference for exposed pipes, independent choruses and clear, brilliant mixtures"—and who begins a review: "Soupy, mushy and muffled! Oh, that organ!"?

Little wonder that by the 1970s, obscured by smoke from the battlefield, "romantic" had not only become a tag for styles and works judged corrupt, a catchall term few writers or speakers bothered to define, but also evoked connotations as caustic as its denotation was vague. No one who did not live through this revolt could imagine its strength and malevolence. It ravaged instruments, repertories, and careers.

Its unhappy memory, however, furnishes a moral. Though today "romantic" at least sometimes connotes the admired and sanctioned—for the tide has turned again, and we appraise Franck and the others more reasonably—a wiser connotation cannot alone make the word serviceable. What is needed is definition in common, and our vigilant resolve to be discriminating.

For the purposes of this book, at any rate, let us start by calling "romantic" the period 1789–1914 and the musical art created therein, bearing in mind that to assign as bounds the French Revolution and the First World War is a convenience, nothing more. History cannot without stretching be fitted to arbitrary form, the history of ideas least of all. But these bounds will be useful so long as we remember that distinctive changes had already begun to occur while Bach was alive, and to become manifest in the work of his sons; that some of Haydn's and Mozart's music continued this foreshadowing; that Beethoven was arguably the greatest of the nineteenth-century innovators though born and at work in the eighteenth century; that the new idioms arose on precedent meter, tonality, harmony, and rhythm; that organ art tends to evolve more slowly than the musics of other media; and that our designation of the period is unusually broad.

It is broad partly because the Romantic Movement as more customarily defined had begun to give way by 1840 to the clusters of idea and act later called Realism and Impressionism. As much was true, in any case, in literature and painting. The corresponding trends in music came later, and in organ music later still, the organ being confined, as we now find quite usual, to its own remote corner of the universe where news arrives late if at all. Thus the century produced no Realistic organ music warranting the name— *pace* the vogue of thunder pedals and battle pieces—nothing that approaches comparison to Courbet's art or Balzac's; and the entry of Impressionistic harmonies into the vocabulary of organist-composers took place later than in music at large.

Sentiment expressed in symbol has of course sprung up time out of mind. It did not come into being because of that overthrow of aristocracies, rise of the common people, exaltation of the individual, cult of the work of art, and love of nature which we associate with the birth of the Romantic Movement. Nor need "romantic" imply emotion told at the expense of form, nor "classic" necessarily mean the symmetrical and calm. The haven of eighteenth-century detachment is largely a pleasant myth.

For the art of centuries past is veiled from our eyes by a kind of scrim. Sometimes the backlighting, intensified by scholarship or by intuition or by happy chance, grows bright enough to make the scrim less opaque. But the viewer's perception remains perpetually beclouded, if only by ignorance of the thousand details of daily living that remain unrecorded because deemed obvious or trivial— the sounds, sights, fears, strivings that go to make up the feel of an age, hence go to shape a creator's attitudes and aims. Every generation is a secret society, as John Jay Chapman somewhere says, and for the most part its tastes, enthusiasms, and interests are incommunicable to posterity. So it is that interpreters, despite the most diligent study, can re-create only the echo, as it were, of past musics.

We may well ask if it is antiquity in itself that conjures stability and repose. Cannot stability and repose akin to what we think of as the eighteenth century's be found as readily in the work of romanticists and moderns? Is it not the passage of time—our cumulated experience—that gives to the music of the eighteenth century balance and clarity of form, objectivity and grace of expression? Do we not apply these qualities like a layer of varnish between old idioms and our perception? To Mozart's contemporaries, after all, the Symphony in G Minor doubtless seemed anything but graceful, the elegance sought by eighteenth-century minds being not necessarily the elegance we recognize.

Be that as it may, periods of exploration in the arts tend to be followed by periods of retrenchment, perhaps because this systole and diastole are innate in the race. And when we recall that other romanticisms arose in other centuries and were as stoutly ridiculed by successor movements, it becomes clear that neither nineteenth-century romanticism nor the neo-classic repudiation that followed was anything very new.

With respect to our French masters, in any event, the first fruits of romanticism may be dated to 1841, when at the Church of Saint Denis, as we shall see, Aristide Cavaillé-Coll unveiled the prototype organ. By then, after half a century of upheaval, the art of organist and of organ builder was in France at an ebb. Many of the organs that survived the Revolution and the Napoleonic campaigns, when churches had been closed and organ pipes melted down into tools of war, stood decrepit and unplayed. On the playable organs one heard gavottes, airs, and the mimicry of storms and shipwreck—this at the most solemn moments of the liturgy. "Organists are weak," lamented the scholar Fétis in 1830, "and what they produce is simply beneath criticism." And together with the increasing importance given to timbre as inherently expressive, and the concomitant perfecting of instruments and expansion of the Beethoven-Berlioz orchestra, came the belief that organs were too meager in tone to embody current intentions.

It is intention that most handily differentiates periods—"intention" here meaning the namable ideas and feelings governing the principal creators, the namable gestures animating their works. If Dupré, Langlais, and Messiaen are to be grouped under the same head as Saint-Saëns, Franck, Widor, and Vierne, we must seek an intention in common; and if it is to be called romantic, it must include certain prime romanticist motives that may be taken as givens because manifested by such archetypical creators as Weber, Beethoven, Mendelssohn, Schumann, and Berlioz: the need to build new structures to replace those decaying or dead; the view of human feeling as worth expressing in all its contrarieties; the conviction that art is serious, the profession of artist noble; and the concern with psychological and dramatic truth, with shadings and contrast, with tension and oppositions. These motives are prime because they underlie such secondary motives as the interests in the expressive qualities of timbre, in the supernatural, and in program music and other less patent inter-relations among the arts.

Various traits that embody these motives connect our seven masters. First, the works of each composer require for their suitable rendering the timbres perfected by Cavaillé-Coll. Messiaen conceives melodies or fragments in specific sonorities (for instance, the sonority of prestant and piccolo in "Le Banquet céleste") and insists that meaning changes if sonority changes. Langlais is influenced by Aeolian-Skinner, but so loves the organ at Saint Clotilde that he laughingly calls it his mistress; it inspires nearly all his works, and he is distressed when interpreters registrate them by whim. Widor and Vierne incorporate into their pieces the characteristic crescendo that starts by coupling to the foundations a full récit behind closed shutters. Saint-Saëns and Franck delight in Cavaillé-Coll's flutes and solo reeds no less than in his mutations, as witness the *Trois Rhapsodies* and "Grande Pièce symphonique." Even Dupré, who is better acquainted than any of the others with the sophistication of English and North American organs, conceives his music in the Cavaillé-Coll tone and mechanism—not excepting the "Variations sur un Noël," Symphony in G Minor, Suite Bretonne, and *Triptyque*.

Then too, these composers share a distinctive technique. Given impetus in midcentury by Cavaillé-Coll's mechanical innovations, technique became exigent and complex in ways undreamed of by Bach and his French contemporaries. It was to comprise arpeggios, chord progressions and repeated chords, double thirds and double sixths, stretches, leaps, runs, scales in all the keys and configurations, a meticulous legato made vibrantly alive by discriminating articulation, a counterpoint entailing substitutions of unexampled intricacy, and that singular lightening exemplified by such nimble works as the Vierne "Naïades" and the Dupré Prelude in G Minor. So it is that, without denying differences among these composers, we distinguish a keyboard technique common to all, and comprehensive enough to be called transcendental. The word is Liszt's, whose name reminds us that virtuoso technique at the organ took form and energy from the growth of virtuoso pianism, and that the primogenitors Lemmens, Saint-Saëns, and Franck were themselves splendid pianists.

In like fashion, Dupré's *Triptyque* reminds us that Dupré and the rest share the romanticist bent for extending old forms. Franck takes Beethoven as model and writes a work of startling length that is divided into movements, cyclical in its themes, rich in contrasts of timbre, and boldly labeled symphonic. Widor and Vierne follow suit, though instead of reworking sonata form, they conceive their symphonies as sets of pieces united by subtleties of mood. Dupré pays homage to Bach by writing ricercares, inventions, and chorale settings, Saint-Saëns by writing preludes and fugues. In fact all the French masters concur in their indebtedness to Bach, either by enlarging on his forms or by adopting his attitudes and techniques. Indeed, Bach, as we shall see, stands as cornerstone of their art.

They in addition regard their calling with an earnestness resembling Bach's. There is gravity in Reubke or Reger, to be sure, and great art, even comedy, cannot be fashioned other than soberly. But the French masters' sobriety is distinctive. It arises from qualities in the instrument and in churchly locale. By monumental physical aspect, by awesome sonority, by a setting typically vast and Gothic and magnificent, the organ seems to them to demand a music uniquely dignified and profound. This perception does not keep Dupré from devising music nimble and even frolicsome, as we saw, or Langlais from spinning gossamer textures in the "Arabesque sur les flûtes," or Messiaen from relishing the shepherds' lighthearted wonderment in "Les Bergers." But when Langlais writes a *De Profundis* or a hymn to the Virgin, or Dupré *Le Chemin de la Croix* or a symphony on the Passion, or Messiaen a suite on the Blessed Sacrament, each man feels that the instrument, no less than the subject, enjoins a unique solemnity.

This attitude has little to do with the biographical facts. Vierne's misfortunes, Langlais's early poverty, Franck's wretched familial relations, Dupré's discipline, Messiaen's piety, Widor's aristocratic connections, and Saint-Saëns's loneliness do not inescapably conduce to seriousness—compare Byron or Satie or Bernard Shaw—and it will probably never be shown conclusively how life goes to shape art. But a particular seriousness is here evident, the more austere for serving an ancient and eccentric craft.

Thus each master after his fashion endorses Widor's romanticist creed, put to Schweitzer one afternoon at the console of Notre Dame. "Organ playing," Widor said to that devoted pupil, as the rays of a setting sun streamed through the stained glass, "is the manifestation of a will filled with a vision of eternity. All organ instruction, both technical and artistic, has as its aim only to educate a man to this pure manifestation of the higher will." To Widor, it was Bach above all who bespoke "the emotion of the infinite and the exalted, for which words are always an inadequate expression, and which can find proper utterance only in art." Bach's music "tunes the soul to a state in which we can grasp the truth and oneness of things, and rise above everything that is paltry, everything that divides us."

That later generations would claim as much for the music of his own school Widor could not foresee. But his cultivated mind, in its vast acquaintance with history and biography, could have foretold the difficulties faced by those of us who try to defend that appraisal. Like us, he knew that genius can never be explained, and that all attempts to explain it are works of the imagination.

1

Aristide Cavaillé-Coll

THAT THE FRENCH ROMANTIC SCHOOL OF the organ owes its being to Cavaillé-Coll, a statement routinely heard, is true only in general. Unqualified, it misleads on three counts. First, two schools, not one, emerged in France in the nineteenth century: an earlier school, headed by Saint-Saëns and Franck, and a later, headed by Guilmant and Widor. The older is only indirectly influenced by Jacques-Nicolas Lemmens, a Belgian organist whom we shall meet in due course. To the younger, Lemmens's ideas are seminal.

Second, the Cavaillé-Coll organ so called is not one organ; it is many. Its tone and mechanism is standard in the aggregate but variable in particulars. Saint Ouen as much differs from the Madeleine as a late Bach fugue from an early, and in between come forty-five years of development, only aspects of which are represented at Saint Clotilde, Saint Sulpice, and Notre Dame.

Third, organs by other builders displayed innovative genius. The tones of the Ducroquet at Saint Eustache, which in 1854 Franck helped to inaugurate, could have stimulated many a composer. Its predecessor, a Daublaine-Callinet, whose inauguration Franck may have attended, was reputedly also first-rate. And the

Merklin firm built many an organ Cavaillé-Coll might have been proud to call his own. Yet by the length and eminence of his career, by the candor and charm of his personality, and by the sonority and facility of his organs, Aristide Cavaillé-Coll exerted an influence that became paramount. French masters from Saint-Saëns to Messiaen wrote their music for the instrument he devised.

During more than a century before his birth, the Cavaillés and the Colls prospered in southwestern France and in Spain as weavers, pharmacists, surgeons, and organ builders. Aristide's paternal grandfather, Jean-Pierre Cavaillé, built or enlarged the organs at the Benedictine abbey in Saint Maur, at the cathedral in Carcassonne, and at the Church of Saint Michel in Castelnaudary, among other sites in France, and in Spain at Santa Maria del Mar in Barcelona, and at the cathedral in Vich. Jean-Pierre's integrity and competence were praised by no less eminent an authority on organs than Bedos de Celles.

Aristide's father, Dominique Cavaillé-Coll—whose mother's name was adjoined, following Spanish custom, to her husband's—likewise became an organ builder. He was first the apprentice of Jean-Pierre, then partner, then successor.

Already in early youth, Dominique had mastered organ theory by reading and rereading Bedos's *Art of the Organ Builder*. By the time Jean-Pierre put him to work, the boy had resolved to master as well every skill required by the profession: that is to say, become an expert carpenter, plumber, metallurgist, acoustician, and engineer. In the pursuit of his goal he labored conscientiously six days a week, from five o'clock in the morning till eight o'clock at night. He rested on the seventh day only because his father scrupulously observed the Sabbath and made him do the same.

Indeed, father and son were throughout their lives esteemed as men of principle, and it was a conspicuous trait of each to deplore any hint of hypocrisy. Dominique was not merely known for his habit of looking straight into the eyes of anyone to whom he spoke (none but the deceitful, he would aver, did otherwise) but was to be remembered, not without humor, as having taken that virtue to a daunting extreme. At all events, the craftsmanship and probity that were to become hallmarks of Aristide Cavaillé-Coll's life and work were prefigured in father and grandfather.

Aristide Cavaillé-Coll was born on 4 February 1811 in Montpellier, the younger of two sons born to Dominique Cavaillé-Coll and Jeanne Autard. At about age five, after the family had moved temporarily back to Spain, the child began to learn Spanish by reading *On Prayer and Meditation* by Luis de Granada. He was to treasure the book, in later life keeping it on his bedside table together with the *Imitation of Christ* and, for secular reading, *Don Quixote* and Fénelon's account, written for the education of the duke of Burgundy, of the adventures of Telemachus. His esteem for these volumes was such that—as he told his own children—he could not see why one would bother to read anything else.

Apart from a few books, Aristide's early schooling was notably casual. The boy found grammar and Latin as tedious as literature. Only in mathematics did he excel.

It was plain by the time he was eleven that he loved to work with his hands, and his father spoke proudly of the lad who, at a workbench tailored to size, could manipulate wood and tools like an artisan. By 1825, at fourteen, Aristide had begun his apprenticeship, helping brother Vincent and their father to rebuild an organ in Gaillac, at the Church of Saint Michel. In 1827, the family moved to Toulouse.

In 1829, circumstances conspired to let the youth, though only eighteen, finish an organ unsupervised—and manifest the kind and scope of his faculties. Three projects were maturing at the same time. His father was needed in one town, brother Vincent in another. Aristide was therefore sent to Spain to complete a cathedral organ in Lérida.

Throughout the months he worked there, he characteristically sought perfection in the whole by first seeking perfection in the parts, and in so doing he not only finished an organ but also solved two hard and ancient puzzles. The first had to do with the fact that as reservoirs filled or emptied, their top did not remain level; nor were their movements free of haphazard friction. Wind pressure varied unpredictably as a result, in turn causing unsteady tone. To correct this fault, Aristide devised a parallel movement that kept reservoir top and bottom equidistant and which all but eliminated friction. Only later did he learn that he had reinvented a system of parallelograms that Watt himself had discovered and of which the inventor had been enormously proud.

Not content with one feat, the eighteen-year-old also contrived an answer to the question of how an organist might with least trouble change stops or couple keyboards. Theretofore, shifts of registration could as a rule be done only by hand; coupling required the organist to take hold of both sides of a keyboard and pull it forward *en bloc*. Such constraints were unimportant when one played the classical masters, whose pages demanded few changes of tone. But as classic styles gave way to romantic, organists began to wish for greater tractability—to be able to change tone color in the midst of movements and to be able to make crescendi and decrescendi. It now mattered much that one must either resort to an assistant, or else omit notes, or else halt, change registration, restart.

Taking as his point of departure a hand-operated mechanism his father had invented, and recognizing that players less often have a hand free than a foot, Aristide devised a pedal—his *pédale de combinaisons*—that allowed stops to be changed by a single motion while hands played on undisturbed. The device was superior to other mechanisms invented at about the same time (a pedal by the Englishman John Abbey, for example), because the affected stops could be varied by the organist to meet the needs of each piece, rather than being set once for all by the builder. Further, Aristide devised for the Lérida organ a pedal that opened or closed a box in which pipes of an echo division were placed: respectively a *pédale d'expression* and a *boîte expressive*.

We are told that at length, after the work was done and the

achievement weighed, organ committee and cathedral chapter expressed unbounded delight.

Returned to Toulouse, Aristide helped his father and brother perfect a free-reed keyboard instrument called the poïkilorgue—akin in tone and in degrees of loud and soft to the harmonium that supplanted it—and invented a circular saw that was to win a bronze medal from the Society for the Encouragement of Industry. Meantime, Aristide set to work to learn more of mathematics and physics.

It was in September of 1832 that Gioacchino Rossini, then at the height of his fame and one of the most influential musico-political personages in France, came to Toulouse and attended a performance of *Robert le Diable*. Meyerbeer's score calling for an organ, and the local opera house having none, a poïkilorgue had been supplied by the Cavaillé-Colls. Intrigued by the instrument and its expressive possibilities, and having asked to meet its maker, the great man and entourage arrived at the Cavaillé-Coll workshop on Saturday, 29 September 1832, and spent a full two hours conversing with the builders, examining the poïkilorgue, and admiring work in progress. Of the poïkilorgue, Rossini pronounced the tone lovely, and with all he was shown said he was satisfied indeed.

So much so that the next day, when Dominique and sons went to Rossini's hotel to pay a return call, Rossini asked bluntly why with such talent they remained in Toulouse. He urged Dominique to move the family business to Paris, where Rossini's connections could be of use. Dominique declined, but the idea obsessed his younger son. Hardly a year was to pass before Aristide set out for the capital.

· 2 ·

On 21 September 1833, shortly before dawn, after four wearisome days in a coach, the youth disembarked in Paris. He carried with him letters of introduction to such prominent artists and scientists as Cherubini, Lesueur, Berton, Lacroix, Prony, and Cagniard de

La Tour. Even so, as he wrote to his father that night before going to bed, Aristide spent the first day zestfully seeing the sights, his weariness forgotten. Not until the twenty-third did he settle down to business and call upon Lacroix.

The mathematician could not have been more deeply impressed by Aristide's bearing and acumen. Having a meeting to attend at the Institute of France, he took the young man along. There they first went in search of Félix Savart, a physicist who would earn renown for research pertaining to the frequency limits of human hearing. Not finding Savart, Lacroix contented himself with giving Aristide a letter of introduction, meanwhile presenting the youth to colleagues and demanding to know who among them was conducting research into acoustics. Present was Charles Cagniard de La Tour, who was famous in the field for having invented a device that counted the vibrations of a sound of any pitch. Like Lacroix, he soon came under the spell of Aristide's mind and manner, and, remarking that there was scant time for talk just then, asked Aristide to dine with him that very evening. Their meeting initiated a long friendship.

Having called as well on Prony and Lesueur, Aristide next went to see Henri-Montan Berton. The date is noteworthy, Friday, 27 September 1833, for it marks the very conception of those French schools of organ playing which are our subject. That day, because of a seemingly casual remark, was born not alone Aristide's illustrious Parisian career but also a musical repertory whose beauty directed the lives of many men of genius and enriched generations to come.

A pity Aristide and he had not met earlier, said Berton: the government was even then taking bids for an organ at the Church of Saint Denis, near Paris, the royal abbey of France. He himself, Berton went on, headed a committee named to recommend a builder, and no doubt the Cavaillé-Coll firm would have liked to compete. Alas, bidding was to close in a mere three days.

Ah yes, replied the youth, excited and dismayed. But what to do? He would barely have time to visit the site and take measurements, let alone devise a stoplist, calculate cost, make renderings, draft elevations, and, not least of all, consult his father.

Within three days nevertheless, foregoing meals and sleep, Aristide drew up the specification for a cathedral organ of eighty-four stops, together with detailed schemata of its construction. And despite the unrelenting intensity of his effort to draft a plan so persuasive it could not be refused, he somehow found time to write to Dominique.

On 30 September the proposal was submitted. On 2 October Berton's committee rendered judgment. The impression made by Aristide on the personages he had met swayed the vote. The committee chose the youngster from the provinces over such well-known competitors as Callinet, Dallery, Erard, and Abbey. A few weeks later the decision was ratified by the Academy of Fine Arts and accepted by the Ministry of Commerce and Public Works.

At least one Parisian journal condemned the choice as pure politics, deplored influence in high places, and predicted disaster. The contract ought to have gone to a builder whose work was at hand and examinable. Who in Paris knew anything of the provincial firm or had ever heard one of its organs?

Yet Aristide's proposal had been as impressive as his person. Competence, not to mention crystalline thought, was manifest in such passages as these:

> All vertical rollers shall be made from iron of the proper dimensions, their pivots lathe-turned, and their bearings of brass and carefully fitted; each part shall be carefully filed and polished. . . .
>
> All wooden pipes shall be thoroughly seasoned and in addition varnished inside and out, to improve their tone and their durability. . . .
>
> All metal pipes shall be made of tin, and the thickness of the metal in each pipe shall be gauged with the utmost care, using instruments that allow us to measure precisely and without guesswork. In this way, the metal in each pipe will have a thickness proportional to the length and diameter of the pipe, giving uniformity of tone throughout the keyboard. . . .

Wood is preferable to metal for trackers and traces, since metal expands and contracts with changes in temperature; the keyboards go out of adjustment when iron or brass wires are used. Since straight-grained wood does not change in length with changes in temperature, it is preferable, as experience has proved. . . .

The pedalboard shall be built in the German style, that is, throughout the compass the natural keys shall be long enough to accommodate the entire foot, and the sharp keys arranged for playing with the toes. This design allows the playing of legato scales with the same foot, chromatically or diatonically, which is impossible on conventional pedalboards. Furthermore, since the sides of the pedals are exposed and there is space between them, dirt or sand cannot cause them to stick. . . .

The biggest display pipes and any others of considerable weight shall have an iron hoop soldered around the top and an iron bar mounted on the diameter; from the middle of this bar— from, that is to say, the center of the pipe—an iron rod shall extend upwards through a wooden beam fastened to the case-work; a nut threaded on this rod will allow hanging the pipe or at a minimum steadying it in its original position. It often happens that when this precaution is neglected, these huge pipes collapse into their foot because of their own weight, deforming the mouths and preventing speech. Repairing these pipes is difficult and expensive. . . .

Aristide put the cost of the instrument at eighty thousand francs and the term of construction at three years.

Meantime, Dominique had received the amazing news. It remains unrecorded whether he at first felt the consternation we might expect. What is sure is that the memoirs he was to write disclose a father's pride: whereas the boy should by rights have been lost in that labyrinth of a city, Aristide had turned conqueror and brought off a coup.

Dominique hastened to Paris, and father and son decided how to proceed. They must complete the work in hand, which included six poïkilorgues, lease a headquarters, pack and ship tools and equipment, send trusted assistants, relocate the household, and amass needed capital. But first they revised the Saint Denis proposal, reducing to seventy-one the number of stops, improving the layout, and recalculating the cost, and saw the revisions accepted. In the event, they were to make other changes and encounter delays caused by repairs to the church, delays that gave Aristide time to experiment and refine. For the present, it merely added to the urgency that by the end of January 1834, when Dominique returned to Toulouse, yet another Parisian contract had been won, to build an organ of three manuals and forty-seven stops for the new Church of Notre Dame de Lorette.

· 3 ·

So began Cavaillé-Coll's career. The rest of the decade saw the firm relocated, the son supervising brother and helpers at the workshop in the rue Neuve-Saint-Georges (soon renamed the rue Notre-Dame-de-Lorette), the father at times traveling to Brittany or the Languedoc to secure more business and at times living and working on site at Saint Denis. Dominique, now well into his seventh decade, took charge of pipe-making and remained titular head of the company. Aristide, however, though still in his twenties, became head in all but name. By and large, he, not his father, gave estimates, negotiated contracts, and made decisions about assembly and design.

"My dear Father," he wrote in December 1836, "I have given Boulet the blocks for the first octave of the trompette and the basson. I would be obliged if you made these pipes without delay and in tin. I will be ready to mount them on the 15th if they are ready. I count on your forbearance and speed. Your devoted son, Aristide Cavaillé." A year later, father to absent son: "I'm not good for anything, so come back as quickly as possible. Maybe your being here will put me back on my feet." In 1839, son to father: "I have decided to build a small organ for the Exposition. I have drawn up the plans. . . . My wind supply has given good results."

Aristide it was who, before the decade was out, invented a way to supply steady wind at pressures that varied to accommodate the needs of different timbres and pitches. He it was who extended the system of ventil pedals to allow facile and instantaneous shifts of registration. He it was who saw in a device called the Barker lever, after the Englishman who invented it, a means by which key action could be rendered no weightier than that of a grand piano, regardless of the number of stops drawn or manuals coupled. Aristide it was who enlarged the echo division and so enclosed it as to make possible an unprecedented range of dynamics. And he it was who perfected tone colors of refinement likewise unprecedented—for instance the flûte traversière and flûte harmonique—that blended smoothly, for all their individuality, into an ensemble whose glory was its luminous mixtures and whose crown was its fiery reeds.

At a stroke, he granted to the organ expressive pliancy like that which for decades had absorbed such orchestrators as Gluck, Haydn, Beethoven, Stamitz, Weber, and Rossini. Their finds were even then being assimilated and elaborated by Berlioz, to whom may be credited the result for instrumentation and composition at large: that timbre, broadly defined to include tone color and degrees of loud and soft, became a constituent element of music rather than something added to music that stood complete without it.

Before the decade was out, half a dozen instruments had been constructed that benefited from Cavaillé-Coll's experimenting, and their workmanship and expressive innovations had been universally praised. At Saint Louis de Lorient the organ committee was grateful for changes made to the estimate, changes that benefited the organ but made the builders' work more arduous. At Notre Dame de Lorette the committee's report lauded both the outstanding talent of the builders and the selfless artistry with which they had fulfilled their covenants. At Saint Sauveur de Dinan the committee declared that in erecting the instrument the Cavaillé-Colls had cared less for gain than for perfection.

Accordingly, when at length the organ at Saint Denis was accepted by the government, on 21 September 1841, precisely eight years after Aristide's arrival in Paris, what had been con-

ceived as a big instrument in classic style had evolved into the prototype romantic organ, expressive and malleable—it would seem
to many—as a symphony orchestra.

Little wonder that here too a committee report, whose signa-
tories included eminent artistic and scientific names, was unstinted
in its compliments. It commended the care with which the work
had been done, the attention to detail, the fidelity with which every
promised new feature had been added. The obligation taken on by
the builders—the report concluded—had been amply met, in fact
surpassed; honor, not profit, had directed their work. As regards
tone, the sounds of the instrument astonished and delighted.

Scarcely a week would pass thereafter without someone asking to hear the new Saint Denis organ or to play it. Professionals
marveled at its sonorities and at the ease with which it could be
manipulated; amateurs thrilled to its thunders and its whispers,
unaware of its prodigies of engineering. And since the visitors included not just domestic and foreign musicians but also princes,
courtiers, and ministers, the Cavaillé-Coll reputation, now secure
in France, began to be spread abroad. Aristide had become an acknowledged master. He was thirty years old.

Pride of accomplishment was throughout his life to be out-
weighed by his compelling need to learn. So compelled, he planned
a journey to some of the ancient centers of organ building to meet
fellow builders and study their work.

He embarked on his survey in September 1844 and traveled for
six weeks. After examining Silbermann organs in Strasbourg and
visiting smaller towns in Alsace, where his inspections included an
organ being installed by Joseph Callinet, he went to Switzerland.
In Bern he met and liked the builder Haas. In Geneva, Zurich,
Freiburg, and Winterthur he observed that many an organ held
stops lovely in timbre but wind supplies which were poor in design,
that for this reason the overall sonority left much to be desired.
Such was his view also at Frankfurt and Cologne.

Except for the instruments of the builder Walcker, of Ludwigs-
burg, whose "genius and merit" impressed him, Cavaillé-Coll liked

Dutch organs better than German, and most liked those at Haarlem, Utrecht, and Rotterdam. "From what I have seen," he wrote to Dominique, "I believe that organ building in Holland, without having shared in the mechanical advances of modern building, has maintained and improved on the old traditions, in the solidity and simplicity which gave long years of life to the works of our predecessors. I am sorry that M. Schuhmacker [the inhospitable organist of Saint Bavo's] did not allow me to examine the Haarlem organ and so give you a description of the interior. But the Rotterdam organ, which seemed to be built on the same scale, makes me think that it has been rightly considered, till now, the greatest organ in the world, as much by its proportions architecturally as by the ensemble of its stops. The size of these giant organs is so well proportioned to the size of the churches, that in entering the church in Rotterdam I thought I was only looking at a sixteen-foot façade, about the size of our Paris organs. I put the question to the organist, who told me it was a façade of *thirty-two feet.* I did not want to believe it until, like Saint Thomas, I had touched it."

Letters to his father show with what bluff good humor Aristide talked shop with colleagues, and how attentively he examined their work. He learned from them, and he shared his own discoveries with extraordinary openness. Once, as he laughingly told Dominique, a builder was so ecstatic at the notion of how much could be gained by the new way of making reservoirs that Aristide feared the man would kiss him. Conviviality is also evidenced by the expense records of the journey, which from town to town cite not just shared food and wine but more than one bottle of champagne.

A visit to England brought his journey to a close. He was taken by the builder William Hill to see the principal London organs. These he found neither large nor lovely, though they made a better sound than the looks of their interiors led him to expect. He noted Hill's way of making the tongues of reeds, and examined with interest the separately mounted and winded tuba at Birmingham Town Hall.

The following two years saw him build the superb fifty-stop organ at the Church of the Madeleine. The inauguration took place on 29 October 1846 and drew so large an audience it had to be repeated two weeks later. Those years saw as well changes in family and firm. Vincent married and moved to Spain, though till 1864, when he established his own company in Nîmes, he would now and then return to help mount or voice an instrument. Dominique too was more often away, sometimes on business, sometimes visiting relatives, ever relinquishing duties to Aristide. When in Paris, Dominique had become a curmudgeon whose crustiness disturbed the harmony of home and shop. Although the documents suggest a familial affection that was lifelong and profound, apparently neither Vincent nor Dominique could tolerate, without occasional rebellion and periodic absence, the authority and single-mindedness of the younger son. By 1 January 1850, the company name reflected the actuality. The partnership of "Cavaillé-Coll, Père et Fils" was dissolved, and the firm began the transition to "A. Cavaillé-Coll et Cie."

Aristide himself, begrudging time for anything but work, and richer in fame than in means, had long put aside, it appears, any notion of marriage. But at last, on 4 February 1854, his forty-third birthday, he married Adèle Blanc, the youngest sister of an old friend and, Adèle's children tell us, the sister most notable for beauty, goodness, and artistic sensibility. She was a gifted portraitist, her style similar to that of Dominique Ingres, whom she much admired.

At about the same time, the building having been sold in which he leased his workshop, and the firm having grown in activity and personnel, Aristide secured at 94–96 rue de Vaugirard a new headquarters and a new home. That pleasant left-bank neighborhood then lay near the outskirts of Paris, and he enjoyed space and to spare, without and within. One immense hall, which was to serve as erecting room, would see many a program played by distinguished musician for distinguished audience. Liszt, Saint-Saëns,

Franck, Meyerbeer, Rossini, Thomas, Gounod, and the young Widor were only some of the players and guests.

· 4 ·

Now came in succession the masterworks of Cavaillé-Coll's maturity. The organ in Saint Brieuc was inaugurated in 1848; Saint Vincent de Paul, 1852; Saint Omer, 1855; Saint Clotilde, 1859; Saint Sulpice, 1862; Notre Dame, 1868; the Trocadéro, 1878; Fécamp Abbey, 1883; Saint Etienne de Caen, 1885; Saint Sernin de Toulouse, 1889; Saint Ouen de Rouen, 1890. The list is by no means exhaustive. Those decades saw in addition the building or rebuilding of scores of instruments great and small in Paris, the provinces, and abroad. One estimate holds that in periods of prosperity the equivalent of a seventeen-stop organ left the shop every month. In any event, by the late 1870s Cavaillé-Coll could boast of organs in Belgium, Holland, Italy, England, and South America as well as in Spain and France. Each instrument bore the maker's hallmark in craftsmanship. Each resembled the others as much and as little as offspring of the same father.

Certain timbres spoke with kindred voices in every instrument bearing the Cavaillé-Coll name, irrespective of size or date. The foundation stops at Saint Denis, for example, were close kin to those at Notre Dame, even though a quarter century of experiment and maturation interposed between the two designs. Nor was resemblance in foundation tone the less pronounced in organs much smaller—for instance Saint Clotilde. Nor did kinship arise merely because Cavaillé-Coll's eight-foot foundations comprised the same four or five stops: montre, bourdon, flûte harmonique, and gambe or salicional or both.

Yet the differences in foundation tone among these three organs—a dozen more comparisons would be as apt—were as striking as the similarities. Diversities were in fact so myriad that the five generic stop-names hardly begin to suggest the full range of nuance. The shades of difference, as Kurt Lueders has pointed out, are analogous to the gradations between colors in the visible spectrum, and as hard to pinpoint.

Some differences had to do with the personalities of voicers. Albert Dupré notes the impossibility of mistaking the "mellow and limpid voicing of Gabriel Reinburg [for] . . . the full and powerful voicing of Glock . . . the refined and delicate voicing of Garnier . . . the robust and dazzling voicing of Félix Reinburg." Some differences had to do with Cavaillé-Coll's ability to suit an instrument to its environment—his uncanny intuition of how the very stones of a building would act as sounding board to make instrument and edifice one. And some differences defy verbal definition altogether, having to do less with voicing, scales, wind pressure, and other tangibles than with the nature of beauty and perception. For artistic insights are unavoidably synesthetic. To stand and listen inside Notre Dame was to perceive such a visual grandeur and recall such a history and pageantry as must direct one's aural sense in a thousand subtle ways. There the foundations took on a majesty not evoked by any other locale, not even Saint Denis, not even Saint Ouen.

Although size determined the presence or absence of certain sonorities—thirty-two foot stops, say, or bombarde divisions—size alone affected some Cavaillé-Coll timbres no more than did placement. Whether speaking from rear gallery, transept, side wall, or chancel, the hautbois or flûte harmonique, for instance, was round in tone and adroitly balanced in relation to other timbres—and voiced of course with perfect evenness, pipe to pipe. Nor were Cavaillé-Coll's big organs as overwhelming in loudness as their size may suggest; it seems evident that to him *puissant* (strong) meant not loud but full. During the recent rededication of the superbly restored organ at Saint Sulpice, the thoughtless were disappointed by the seeming understatement of the tutti, for they failed to take into account the influence on modern ears of our noisy century.

Exigencies of architecture affected timbre only subtly, and kinship not at all. At Saint Vincent de Paul the organ had to be installed in a rear gallery in such a way as not to cover the rose window and cast the nave into gloom. Cavaillé-Coll therefore divided the instrument into two parts that framed the window, and placed the console to one side. At Saint Sulpice some ornate eighteenth-century casework, whose columns and statuary blocked the egress of sound, had to be used to house the pipes. This, and the acoustic peculiarities of a nave smaller than that of Notre Dame, necessitated an organ fourteen stops larger. At Notre Dame itself the nave was so long, and the organ loft so high, that reeds of uncommon strength were needed to help fill the great vessel with music.

Among the greatest of Cavaillé-Coll's skills, then, was his ability to judge how pipes must be scaled, in proportion to the cubic capacity of a building, so as to speak with neither too much nor too little force, the while embodying his ideals of tone. No doubt he could as easily assess the acoustical properties of a room by casting a glance at its shape. But he nevertheless tried by ceaseless study to put on solidly scientific footing the kinds of judgment that builders had for centuries made empirically. Indeed, he believed his experiments sufficiently remarkable that he published some of them and described others in papers read before the Academy of Sciences. In 1856 he wrote on acoustics and on the design of organ façades, in 1859 on standard pitch. In 1860 he spoke to the Academy on the tonal qualities of organ pipes, in 1863 on the regulating of wind pressure.

His findings touched on other fields than his own. "The many experiments to which I have devoted myself, on the wind supplies of organs and on the means of regulating air pressure in the various parts of this huge instrument," he stated in 1863, "have led me to hit upon a new system of regulators which is of great simplicity, and which can render useful services not only to the building of organs but also to every manufacturing activity that needs to obtain a constant flow of compressed air or of gas." In an age that venerated science, Cavaillé-Coll saw his reputation fortified by the esteem he won from scientists.

The respect and affection he won from musicians was in like

manner fervent, and he in turn valued their friendships and sought their opinions. By the early 1850s he had been convinced by Lemmens and others that the music of Bach deserved special regard and for its rendition needed manuals of fifty-four notes and pedalboards of thirty. His pedalboards would thereafter begin at C, and not at F or A, as in the past, or, as at Notre Dame de Lorette, at C for the foundations and A for the reeds. Widor tells us that Lemmens showed the builder that Bach's music needed a "proper dose" of mixtures. And we have it from Cavaillé-Coll himself that from about mid-century onward he strove to unite old with new, incorporating into his designs what he admired in the art of his predecessors.

Owing partly to the advice of musicians, his consoles became models of convenience. Most consoles faced the nave, to let a player without craning observe the proceedings at the altar. The drawknobs were within easy reach. The music desk facilitated reading and turning pages.

There was no crescendo pedal. Rather, the series of ventil pedals let the organist prepare certain stops before beginning to play, then at a desired moment activate those stops by depressing a pedal that let air into their pallet boxes. The gesture was deft and the result instantaneous; stops could be added or removed on a desired beat precisely, and without impeding the activity of the hands.

All was designed for simplicity and ease. Located above the pedalboard, which was straight and flat, were typically arranged, left to right, the manual-to-pedal couplers, the manual couplers, the octave couplers, the pedals controlling mixtures and reeds, and, in early instruments, the hitch-down pedal controlling the récit shades. The hitch-down pedal, which did not always have notches for intermediate positions, was supplanted in organs built after about 1870 by a balanced swell pedal placed above the middle of the pedalboard. The order of the manuals was typically grand-orgue, positif, récit, and solo or bombarde. The lowest manual at Notre Dame and Saint Sulpice was a coupling manual, the grand-choeur.

Invariably, the keys were comfortably fitted to the hand and foot, and, whether or not assisted by the Barker device, the tracker action was exquisite in evenness and weight. Invariably, the builder meant for his consoles to look as lovely to the eye as the sonorities they ruled would sound to the ear, and for the employment of his mechanisms to be effortless.

To present-day interpreters, Cavaillé-Coll's uniformity in matters mechanical and tonal offers helpful implications, having led, as it did, to uniformity of use by composers. For instance, his placement of the ventil pedals, which themselves betoken his conception of overall sonority as composite, gave rise to the characteristic crescendo already mentioned. Produced by adding to the coupled foundations a gradated succession of mixtures and reeds, it is to be found in the music of Vierne, Dupré, Langlais, and Messiaen in just the way it is to be found in the music of Saint-Saëns, Franck, and Widor, though decades elapse and manifold differences obtain in personality and style. By the same token, when any one of these composers calls for a passage to be played mezzo forte, the usual intent is that it be played on foundations 8 or on foundations 8 and 4. Similarly, fortissimo requires the coupled foundations, mixtures, and reeds, at 16, 8, and 4. Chorus reeds, incidentally, are almost never drawn without mixtures. From these givens, and with thought and inventiveness, the modern interpreter can devise for modern organs more or less closely analogous registrations.

· 5 ·

Cavaillé-Coll knew adversity as well as triumph. To begin with, his firm, like almost every organ-building firm in history, was chronically undercapitalized and more than once near bankruptcy. It had suffered early on from the delays in completing Saint Denis, later from the economic decline which preceded the revolution of 1848 and which closed his doors for six months. Yet even in good times money troubles were to plague him, because clients were slow to pay, creditors and silent partners quick to enforce shortsighted demands.

The difficulties were made the more urgent because he stead-fastly refused to set his prices as low as those of his competitors: to engage in bidding would have compelled him to use inferior mate-rials and let workers give less time to a task than perfection en-tailed. "Yes, the old Cavaillé," Albert Schweitzer recalls a builder saying, "when one of his men worked on something for three weeks and it did not please him entirely, he had him start again at the beginning; and if again it did not satisfy him, still another time. Who among us can do that? We should not last three months."

Instead, he sometimes bound himself to contracts offering slen-der profit, content to meet expenses if only he could build a fine instrument. He preferred to trust his clients to see in the excellence of a finished organ their duty to grant him a modest profit above the agreed price—a duty he naturally thought evident if, as fre-quently happened, he had installed features not called for in the estimate. Unfortunately, his trust was often misplaced. Time and again his letters show him asking churches, town councils, and gov-ernment ministries for payments long overdue, and show him wait-ing not months but years.

The obvious conclusion is that Cavaillé-Coll as businessman was inept. Yet it can be argued to the contrary that his business acu-men is demonstrated by the continued existence over half a century of a firm whose life was threatened a dozen times over. Actually, though steady profit eluded him and calamity threatened at every turn, a just verdict would convict the circumstances, not the man. As his letters show, he mastered the principles of accounting, long-term planning, estimates, contracts, cash flow, and the handling of em-ployees, clergy, government officials, and public opinion. He wisely tried to center his business on the manufacture of small organs and on contracts for maintenance and repair, recognizing that this would establish a base on which the firm could subsist while the monumen-tal—and monumentally less profitable—organs took form. It as plainly demonstrates good business sense that he would recommend as performers those players best able to show off the merit of his or-gans while pleasing the public: in the early days, Lefébure-Wély;

later, Widor and Guilmant. And he manifested in his relations with workers, family, and clients a downright common sense as rare among geniuses as in the race at large.

In yet other ways he knew adversity. In 1859, his two youngest children contracted whooping cough, at that time among the most dread of respiratory diseases, and died within days of each other. In 1862, Dominique also, though in apparent good health, died suddenly. He had long since left Paris, and the relationship had known as much storm and stress as affection, as we saw, but grief was as profound as exasperation had sometimes been. "I am sorry to see vanish the composure that you maintained for such a long time," Cavaillé-Coll had once written to his father, in words mixing love and vexation. "May God keep you in that serenity of spirit which you now need more than ever before. Do, please, stop complaining. We all have our crosses to bear, and I hope that you will have the courage to bear yours, just as we all must endure what falls to us."

He himself would endure more sadness and more grief. Soon after Dominique's death, Cavaillé-Coll's mother died. Soon after that, Vincent moved permanently to the south. Then, the city having appropriated part of the rue de Vaugirard property in order to extend a street, Cavaillé-Coll found himself forced to abandon a cherished home and workshop where he had enjoyed the rewards of toil and of family. He had managed to resign himself to the loss, and to the disruption and expense of establishing and tooling a new headquarters, when in October 1868, in the very days of his move to 13–15 Avenue du Maine, where private apartments had been beautifully decorated for her, his wife of fourteen years, Adèle, died in childbirth. Cavaillé-Coll was fifty-seven years old. Three sons and a daughter remained.

The last quarter century of Cavaillé-Coll's career likewise began with misfortune. In 1870–71, the Franco-Prussian War sent most of his workers to the lines to defend Paris. To protect his workshop and home from bombardment, Cavaillé-Coll reinforced window and wall with heavy timbers intended for thirty-two-foot pipes, and, together with the rest of the populace, faced the danger, the hunger, and the cold of four long months of siege.

With the armistice, however, came new activity and rewards. Not prudence alone impelled him to leave Paris during the horrifying days of the Commune, though there was perhaps scant risk that his royalist connections would have been noticed by the revolutionaries: thanks to an English admirer he was to be present as an honored guest at the inauguration of the Willis organ in Royal Albert Hall, the then largest organ in the world. That the gala was attended by the Queen and her court probably piqued his interest less than the organ itself and its sounding board, an auditorium seating more than five thousand. He noted acoustical deficiencies, and noted too that the instrument spoke less lustily than expected. The builders had discounted the cubic capacity of a vast dome, and the organ had eventually to be enlarged.

From his visit to England Cavaillé-Coll gained more than honor. To his great delight he was asked not simply to build an organ for a proposed new town hall in Sheffield, but also, in order that acoustics might be ideal, to help design the hall itself. He had long studied the acoustics of concert rooms, and from drawings of halls in Birmingham, Bradford, Leeds, and elsewhere, together with observations by friends who were performers, he had reached various conclusions.

Experience and research persuaded him, for example, that curved surfaces caused echoes that distorted a reflected sound in much the way curved mirrors distorted a reflected image; that a ceiling too tall compromised sonority; and that in general the oblong or the rectangular room conduced to clarity and resonance. Keeping these precepts in mind, Cavaillé-Coll helped the architects to design at Sheffield a hall in which three thousand persons could enjoy music of every kind, and not least the tones of his organ of four manuals and seventy-four stops, of which three were trompettes *en chamade*. The instrument was opened in December 1873, and the enthusiasm it engendered helped bring him more work in England and Scotland. Before the decade was out, he was to build organs for half a dozen abbeys and churches, in addition to a splendid organ at Manchester Town Hall.

He had furthermore constructed, before the decade was out, one of the finest of his Parisian masterworks: the organ of four manuals and sixty-six stops in the Palais du Trocadéro, the flamboyant assembly hall built for the World's Fair of 1878.

This time the architect designed the hall without benefit of the organ builder's advice, though Cavaillé-Coll did warn him that curved surfaces would bring disaster. And so they did. The acoustics turned out maddeningly defective: nearly any sound of short duration, whether a word spoken by a lecturer or a note struck by a pianist, returned a double echo. Even singers and orchestras found that a note need merely be quick or percussive to yield the diabolical effect. Only the tones of the organ were exempt, spared by their very nature. These, moreover, remained sublime, as we learn from the testimony of Franck, Saint-Saëns, Liszt, Guilmant, Widor, and Dupré. In recognition of his work, the Fair awarded Cavaillé-Coll a gold medal, and for the acclamation he brought his country, the government awarded him the rosette of the Legion of Honor.

Although the sixty-seven-year-old master was to continue working for a score of years, and to build the masterpieces at Saint Etienne de Caen, Saint Sernin, and Saint Ouen, it was a fitting climax to his career that his workers, to celebrate the new honors, inscribed in gold this encomium and presented it with due ceremony: "We are gathered to express to you the joy and happiness that each of us has felt in learning about your many triumphs and the distinctions that have been so deservedly granted to you by the jury of the great Universal Exposition of 1878. No one is in a better position than we are, your assistants and employees, to recognize how right and just it is that this twofold honor be granted you. May we also be allowed, on this solemn occasion, to express our gratitude for the fatherly good will which you have always shown us, and which bespeaks the sensitive kindliness you possess in so high a degree." Seventy-five signatures followed, among them those of five pairs of fathers and sons, and of many another worker who had joined him decades before.

Cavaillé-Coll directed his company until the mid-1890s, when failing health compelled him to retire. With his daughter, Cécile, he moved to the rue du Vieux-Colombier, not far from Saint Sulpice. On Friday, 13 October 1899, Cavaillé-Coll died. "I can never forget him," Schweitzer was to write. "I can still see him today with his little cap, and with the good, true eyes in which so much of art and intelligence lay, sitting every Sunday beside Widor on the organ bench. . . . Until some day Paris has become a heap of rubble like Babel, those who are susceptible to the magical beauty of his organs will leave Notre Dame and Saint Sulpice thinking with deep feeling of the man who dared in spite of the times to remain a pure artist."

ᛉ 2 ᛉ

Camille Saint-Saëns

TO TURN NEXT TO SAINT-SAËNS IS TO DEPART
from chronology, since Franck was his senior by more than a decade. Yet Saint-Saëns felt so passionate an attachment to what he
deemed the classic virtues that he looks back toward the eighteenth
century in a way that Franck, for all his love of Bach, Beethoven,
and Schubert, does not. Even if Saint-Saëns's earliest organ works
had not preceded Franck's—a first Fantasy and the "Bénédiction
Nuptiale" antedate the *Six Pièces* by a handful of years—his predilection would place the younger man at the beginning of our
survey.

This priority is not contradicted by the astonishing length of
his career. Although Saint-Saëns did not compose the two sets of
preludes and fugues until the 1890s or *Sept Improvisations* and the
fourth Fantasy until the First World War and after, his conception
of the classical never ceased to govern his thought. With every note
he put on paper, he may be seen to strive for that balance and
clarity of form, that objectivity and elegance of expression, and that
repose and stability of manner which he found in Gluck, Rameau,
and Mozart.

His art of course evolved. He would take advantage in his harmony of some of the freedoms won by Wagner and Debussy. He would echo in his melody folk tunes and Oriental scales. He would name as the greatest of organ solos Liszt's Fantasy on *Ad Nos, Ad Salutarem Undam*. And yet Saint-Saëns held fast to his ideal.

Comments made in his old age reflect attitudes and aims embraced early on: "He who does not get absolute pleasure from a simple series of well-constructed chords, beautiful only in their arrangement, is not really fond of music." Or again: "To me, art is form above all else. . . . The artist who does not feel thoroughly satisfied with elegant lines, harmonious colors, or a fine series of chords, does not understand art." And again: "When beautiful forms accompany powerful expression, we are filled with admiration, and rightly so. In such a case, what is it that happens? Our cravings after art and emotion are alike satisfied. All the same, we cannot therefore say that we have reached the summit of art, for art can exist apart from the slightest trace of emotion."

In thinking about composers (or painters, writers, sculptors) it is all too easy to confuse elements of biography with elements of style. To be sure, works of art are not created impersonally, and if good they inevitably express some deep part of an artist's self. They are shaped as well by place of birth and by the cultural preoccupations of an era. It follows that the materials of history are aids to comprehension—certain schools of criticism to the contrary notwithstanding—and of these aids biography is clearly the most useful. So much is true, at least, if we grant as a main purpose of criticism the discerning of intention and the measuring of its fulfillment.

But in using biography we sometimes forget that traits distinctive in a creator are not necessarily manifest in a work, and vice versa. Nor, when manifest, are they exclusive. Beethoven's person may well have been as stormy as some of his music, or Ravel's as suave, or Stravinsky's as cerebral, or Chopin's as delicate. But to say so is to risk depreciating coexistent traits of sometimes equal moment. Chopin's fragile health can serve to elucidate his music only by doing injustice to that solidity and strength which undergird, say, the Fourth Ballade or the "Revolutionary" Etude. Correspondingly, Beethoven, when called on by artistic exigency, knows how to be genteel: witness the slow movement of the Fifth Symphony; and Ravel boisterous: witness *Boléro;* and Stravinsky poignant: witness *The Firebird.* In short, we tend to affix to works or their makers labels that reflect one characteristic only, foregoing nuances of description, passing over inconvenient facts, classifying without discriminating.

If we keep that warning in mind, the generality that Saint-Saëns leaned more toward decorum than toward abandon, in both his temperament and his art, will not greatly distort the truth, so long as we place as counterweight to the one quality the rapturous close of the *Organ* Symphony, and to the other the cheery spectacle of a bearded Saint-Saëns attired as a ballerina, laughingly dancing Galatea to his friend Tchaikovsky's Pygmalion. These images will help us to maintain a balanced view when we recall that a certain fastidiousness marked Saint-Saëns from his childhood, together with innate gifts whose caliber and scope rivaled Mozart's.

· 2 ·

Camille Saint-Saëns was born in Paris on 9 October 1835. By age two he had begun to attend with the greatest delight to every kind of sound. He would plant himself in front of clocks to listen to them strike. He would make the doors creak. He would find ecstasy in the murmurs of the teakettle as it began to warm, and in its variegated crescendo that culminated in the appearance of a "microscopic oboe" as water came to the boil. Berlioz must also have heard that oboe, Saint-Saëns remarks, "for I rediscovered it in the Ride to Hell from *The Damnation of Faust*." Placed for the first time before a piano, the two-year-old did not condescend to drum at random like most infants, but in rapt deliberation struck the keys one at a time, not going on till each note had died away.

He learned the Le Carpentier primer in a month, then indignantly refused to bother with the usual children's pieces of simple melody and vapid accompaniment. "The bass doesn't sing," said the boy in disgust. Instead, he happily set to work on Mozart and Haydn, encouraged by the widowed mother and her aunt who reared him, the latter a pianist. The aunt "taught me how to hold my hands properly so as not to acquire those common faults that are so difficult to correct later on." By age five he was playing sonatinas "gracefully and very correctly," but he consented "to play them only before listeners capable of appreciating them. . . . I would not play for those who did not know."

He began to write music that his hands could not yet play. "I was already composing the music directly on paper without working it out at the keyboard. . . . I have looked over these little compositions lately. They are trifling, but it would be impossible to find a technical error."

At about this time "someone had the notion of letting me hear an orchestra. . . . So they took me to a symphony concert and my mother held me in her arms near the door. Until then I had only heard single violins, and their tone had not pleased me. But the impression of the orchestra was entirely different, and I was listening with delight to a passage played by the strings when all of a sudden came a blast from the trumpets, trombones, and cymbals. . . . I broke into loud cries. 'Make them stop. They keep the music from being heard.' They had to take me out."

At age seven he began to study the piano with Camille Stamaty, who had studied briefly with Mendelssohn and been one of the best pupils of Kalkbrenner's. Considering finger dexterity the *summum bonum* of technique, Stamaty centered his instruction on a device perfected by Kalkbrenner and named by him a *guide-mains:* an adjustable rod, installed parallel to the keys, on which the forearm was so placed as to curb all muscular action save that of the hand. In later years, despite the opinion of his friend Liszt, who called it a guide-jackass, Saint-Saëns was to reflect that such was the way "one ought to begin, in developing firmness of the finger and suppleness of the wrist, in order to add by stages the weight of the forearm and of the arm. . . . Firmness of the finger is not the only thing one will learn from Kalkbrenner's method, but also refinement in the quality of the sound made by the finger alone."

He had one reservation: because a musical phrase must breathe, he deplored as exaggerated to the point of suffocation the relentless legato advocated by Stamaty and Kalkbrenner. As to Liszt's pasquinade, it reflected a quite different pianism, whose power and masses of tone grew from a technique not strictly comparable with that of Saint-Saëns and his mentors—and reflected the truth that comparisons are deceptive and invidious.

The child made progress on a par with his talent. Declared Stamaty: "Nothing remained but to perfect." Accordingly, Saint-Saëns was only ten years old when he appeared in public for the first time. In the spring of 1846, at the Salle Pleyel, assisted by an orchestra and playing from memory, he performed a concerto by Mozart, a fugue and a theme with variations by Handel, a toccata by Kalkbrenner, a prelude and fugue by Bach, and a concerto by Beethoven. As if this were not enough, he offered to perform as an encore, likewise by heart, any one of Beethoven's thirty-two sonatas.

The audience was enchanted by the slender lad. Even the critic Henri Blanchard, sometimes the most astringent of reviewers, found his playing effortless, expressive, neat. Adamant, however, Saint-Saëns's mother refused to let Stamaty launch her son on a career as child prodigy. She entertained higher ambitions for the boy and feared for his health. Besides, the prodigy himself announced that he wanted to be, not a pianist, but a musician.

His mother's good sense was matched by her acuity. "One day someone reproached her for letting me play Beethoven's sonatas. 'What music will he play when he is twenty?' she was asked. 'He will play his own,' was her reply."

So it was that of all the debts he owed to Stamaty, Saint-Saëns recalls as supreme that of being introduced by him to the composition master Pierre Maleden. Belgian by birth, thin and longhaired, kindly, timid, honest to excess, Maleden was "incomparable" as a teacher. Not that Saint-Saëns swallowed his tuition whole. "From time to time questions came up on which I could not agree with him. He would then take me quietly by the ear, bend my head and, for a minute or two, hold my ear to the table. Then he would demand to know whether I had changed my mind. As I had not, he would think it over and sometimes admit I was right." And although we may note in these recollections from Saint-Saëns's old age his glee at having the last word, and wonder if he is to be trusted, it is a fact that under Maleden's guidance the impertinent youngster learned harmony, counterpoint, and a system of chordal analysis he never ceased to praise: it let one "penetrate to the depths of music" and illumine "the darkest corners." He began composing songs and attempting such forms as the overture, the chorus, and the cantata.

Meanwhile, he had begun to study the organ with Alexandre Boëly, a Parisian master uniquely qualified to introduce him to contrapuntal playing and to the technique of the German pedals.

Unlike the organs of northern Europe, French organs of the period 1600–1789 typically had few pedals. Independent pedal technique as exercised in Germany and Holland had no counterpart in France, the high accomplishment of French composers being of another order. Whether a similar technique might eventually have emerged in France is moot: the Revolution prevented that development of styles which in the normal course might have occurred. Of the myriad ways in which the Revolution diverted the progress of culture, moreover, one sequel made Italian opera by the 1830s the sovereign force in French musical life, all the while robbing the organ of what small importance it still had. Hence in the decades when French organ art had sunk to a nadir, when liturgy was accompanied by homophonic oompah, Boëly was one of few musicians to respect contrapuntal idioms and the dignity of instrument and setting. Indeed, he was eventually obliged to leave his post at Saint Germain l'Auxerrois, because clergy and flock found his style too austere.

An admirer of Haydn, Mozart, and Beethoven, Boëly revered Bach, and was for a time the only leading French organist to perform Bach's music or to urge the building of German pedalboards. Late in life, he set to work transcribing for organ Bach's *Art of Fugue*. He transcribed as well, and furnished registrations for, works by François Couperin, Clérambault, Daquin, and Dandrieu.

That Boëly and Saint-Saëns got on well is suggested by Boëly's later dedicating a work to Saint-Saëns, and by Saint-Saëns's declaring that Boëly was an "impeccable" composer, a "first-rate" theorist, and a "talented and conscientious" musician in whose music was to be found "not one error in taste, flaw in composition, or hint of popular style." We may note that Franck too found Boëly inspiring—as affirms Théodore Dubois, Franck's colleague at Saint Clotilde—and played Boëly's works often.

Trained by Maleden and Boëly, Saint-Saëns felt himself magnificently booted and spurred when, at age thirteen, he entered the Paris Conservatory, there to study composition with Jacques-François Halévy and the organ with François Benoist. The boy's dismay may be imagined when his debut in the organ class turned out anything but auspicious. "They sat me down at the keyboard, but I was badly frightened, and the sounds I made were so bizarre that the students all burst into laughter." He was relegated to the status of auditor, a very junior auditor at that.

· 3 ·

Before watching Saint-Saëns free himself from his chagrin, we must turn our attention to the Conservatory of his day—and beyond, since the policy and temper of the school changed little in the eighty years from his matriculation to Messiaen's.

Founded in 1784 by Louis XVI as his Ecole Royale de Chant et de Déclamation, superseded after the Revolution by an Institut National de Musique, reformed in 1795 and several times afterward, the Paris Conservatory was the first school in Europe to devise a systematic curriculum for the study of all branches of secular music. Its methods were to be imitated by the conservatories of Madrid, Rome, Brussels, and a host of lesser schools, and the textbooks written by its specialists were to be standard. Early on, its faculty numbered more than a hundred, and by Saint-Saëns's time teachers and students had come from every country. Its director in those days was no less eminent a figure than Luigi Cherubini — composer, master of counterpoint, disciplinarian, lover of system and order, and thoroughgoing conservative. To him Bach was a barbarian because he took liberties with harmony, and Berlioz a criminal undergraduate because he once entered the library by the girls' door instead of the boys'. Neither was Cherubini, himself a Florentine, willing to let the school any longer welcome foreigners. He denied entrance even to the young Liszt.

The Paris Conservatory was the sole graduate-level, state-supported music school in France. Admission requirements were correspondingly strict. As a rule, candidates auditioned before a jury, but sometimes a markedly able student would be admitted on the authority of a professor.

That authority was vast. Though the administration could impose endless petty regulations, it seldom interfered with a teacher's method of instruction or choice of repertory. Only if some glaring incompetence came to light might the director criticize a teacher. There were no supervisory deans and department heads like those in the English or American academy of today. The teacher could carry out his duties as suited his nature, and ignore the opinions of colleagues. Franck could make his organ class a course in composition, despite the resentment this aroused. Guilmant could take students to hear *Pelléas et Mélisande* and extol Debussy, despite the opposition to "these anarchists of music." Fauré could promote the career of his pupil Ravel, despite the wrangling of colleagues who had denied Ravel the Rome Prize. Widor could exact a disciplined style of organ playing to which he made improvisation subordinate, despite the ire of traditionalists at this violation of precedent. In sum, freedom prevailed in which genius could flourish and often did.

Independence aside, the teacher gained or lost prestige by virtue of his students' performances at the annual prize examinations.

To teachers no less than students, then, the drama of the competitions, which took place before a jury and the public, furnished the musical and emotional summit of the long school year, a culmination toward which all activity aimed. Instruction thus centered on performance—centered for organists on improvisation and the accompaniment of plainsong, since these were the practical needs of Catholic liturgies—and was given exclusively in classes.

A class would hold at most a dozen pupils, and would usually meet for two hours three times weekly. Except for occasional coaching by senior classmates, no one received private lessons. The student accustomed himself to performing before a critical audience of his peers, whose performances he in turn judged, profiting at the same time from the teacher's criticisms of all. The student could stay in any class a maximum of five years; if by then he had failed to win a first prize, he was constrained to leave the school with a minor award, either a *second prix* or an *accessit*. He was dismissed if he failed within two consecutive years to win any prize at all.

Given the intimate and inescapable alliance of Conservatory with government, and the exceedingly political nature of French cultural life then as now, the prizes shaped lives and careers. For an instrumentalist, the first prize typically led to employment in an orchestra or in private teaching. For a singer, the first prize opened the doors of the Opera. And for a composer, the Rome Prize brought much more than immediate celebrity. The newspapers full of him, his reputation assured, the *Prix de Rome* laureate would be given a generous stipend and sent to the Villa Medici. There he would spend years taking inspiration from the culture and countryside of Italy. He would need to think of nothing but art. Most of all, he could feel confident that his works would be heard. Such, at any rate, was the theory. In practice, even the most worthy laureates returned home to face an incurious public and an impregnable bureaucracy. Berlioz, Bizet, Gounod, and Debussy, not to mention their confreres in sculpture, painting, and architecture, lost and won a thousand skirmishes in trying to promote their works, apprehending to their sorrow that in the arts as in the workaday world, neither indifference nor benighted hostility is easily overcome.

It is thus ironic that Parisian cultural life, and the Conservatory in particular, should over so many decades have set standards for Europe and the world. Ironic too that so grand a school should have been housed in a former barracks. The Conservatory later moved to more seemly quarters, but for years its gloomy, ill-smelling corridors gave no visible hint of the glory of art and the life of the mind. Still: "I loved its decrepitude," Saint-Saëns would recall, "the utter absence of any modern note, and its atmosphere of other days. I loved that absurd court, filled with the wailing notes of sopranos and tenors, the rattling of pianos, the blasts of trumpets and trombones, the arpeggios of clarinets. . . . I loved it deeply as we love the things of our youth. . . . I loved the memories of my musical education which took shape in that ridiculous and venerable palace."

He soon put behind him the discomfiture in which that education had begun. Shortly after his entrance into the organ class, his master began to appreciate his gifts.

François Benoist had himself attained the Rome Prize, after having entered the Conservatory in 1811 and having won first prizes in harmony and piano. He did not win a first prize in organ, because the chair in organ had been vacant since the resignation of Nicolas Séjan, its first titular, in 1802. Appointed in 1819 on his return from Italy, Benoist was to remain professor of organ for fifty-three years and to number among his pupils Alkan, Dubois, Bizet, Fessy, Lefébure-Wély, Chauvet, and Franck.

Saint-Saëns describes Benoist as "charming" in manner, "admirable" as teacher, and a better improviser than executant. Adept in the contrapuntal forms, sharing something of Boëly's seriousness and classicism if not his technical proficiency, Benoist excelled at improvising fugues. He was a man of few words, Saint-Saëns adds, "but because his taste was refined and his judgment sure, nothing he said lacked weight."

Though merely an auditor, Saint-Saëns was "extremely hard-working" at home, and in class "never missed a note or one of the teacher's words." He soon became a participant, and thereafter progressed so rapidly that at the end of the year he won the second prize. "They would have given me the first, but for my youth and the disadvantage of having me leave a class where I needed to stay longer." When two years later he won the first prize, he so extravagantly outplayed his competitors that the jury declined to award a second prize.

Saint-Saëns's composition teacher, Jacques-François Halévy, showed less dedication than Benoist. Halévy was preoccupied with his career as composer of operas—*La Juive* the best known of his many successes—and failed more often than not to appear, leaving his students to fend for themselves. This they did to good effect, Saint-Saëns avers, since they examined each other's work with an eye less indulgent than that of the master, whose chief defect was an immoderate geniality. Saint-Saëns took advantage of Halévy's absences to go to the library, "and there I completed my education. The amount of music I devoured, ancient and modern, is beyond belief."

Extraordinary too was his zest for other kinds of knowledge. Besides sculpture, painting, and literature, Saint-Saëns was to delight in archaeology, anthropology, mathematics, and astronomy. As a boy, he used the proceeds from a set of harmonium pieces to buy a telescope, and he would take his geologist's hammer to the quarries southwest of Paris to dig up fossils for his collection. Later, he submitted to learned bodies papers on acoustics and on the instruments illustrated in the murals at Pompeii. He was to become fluent in Latin and would study the great historians and philosophers and discuss them with insight and wit, regretting until the end of his days not having mastered Greek. He would write poetry. And he would write crystalline prose as remarkable for its acerbity as for its charm.

· 4 ·

In the summer of 1852, at age sixteen, perhaps impelled by disappointment and pique at failing to win the Rome Prize, Saint-Saëns left the Conservatory. His failure was soon to be compensated, for in December the Saint Cecilia Society performed one of his works.

His debut as a composer filled him with pride, but the event proved less telling than the relationship it advanced with the founder of the society, the violinist and conductor François Seghers. Year after year, Seghers's chorus and orchestra introduced to Paris audiences whole repertories by such innovators as Mendelssohn and Schumann—innovators scorned by the diehard Société des Concerts du Conservatoire. And Seghers and his wife took an interest in Saint-Saëns. The next season Seghers performed the Symphony in E-flat, which gained for Saint-Saëns the respect of Berlioz and Gounod. What is more, the Seghers were friends of Liszt's, and at their home introduced Saint-Saëns to the man who was to become his idol.

Liszt had reappeared in Paris after a long absence, Saint-Saëns remembers, and had become something of a demigod. "I studied his works with all the youthful enthusiasm of my eighteen years. I already thought him a genius and almost superhuman as a pianist. . . . Amazingly, he surpassed the conception I had formed." No description of Liszt's playing "could possibly convey an idea of it to those who did not hear him in full possession of his talent." To the youth's adoration Liszt responded with the generosity for which he was famous, offering encouragement, counsel, and a friendship that was to be lifelong and unstinted. We learn that *Samson et Dalila* would never have been mounted without his aid, that Liszt, "not knowing a note of it, engaged me to finish it and put it on at Weimar." Nor, it may be, would Saint-Saëns have written for the organ and orchestra together, had not Liszt urged him on. Fittingly, Saint-Saëns was to inscribe the *Organ* Symphony, which he regarded as his finest work, to Liszt's memory.

Saint-Saëns also made friends with Hugo, Rossini, and Pauline Viardot, in whose drawing rooms gathered the great and near-great for often boisterous evenings. The youth's booming voice, distinctive walk and lisp, and relish for playing charades in costumes that absurdly set off his unhandsome features made him irresistibly amusing. He once enlivened a soirée by donning a blue and white bonnet and two thick plaits of blond hair and singing in falsetto one of Marguerite's arias from *Faust*. Another time he put on pink tights to play the female cadaver in an autopsy mimed by Turgenev.

But a bustling social life did not lessen the pace, or high spirits the earnestness, of his work. In his late teens and twenties, Saint-Saëns wrote two symphonies, concertos for piano and for violin, a quintet, a mass, an oratorio, and many pieces in smaller forms. To gain a foothold at the Opera, where prejudice decreed that no writer of chamber music or symphonies could write operas, he again tried for the Rome Prize—and again failed. He meantime accepted at the Ecole Niedermeyer the only teaching post he would ever hold. During his brief tenure he counted among his students Eugène Gigout and Fauré.

Saint-Saëns was in his late teens when he began his quarter century of work as a professional organist. He was named in 1853 to the Church of Saint Merry, a populous parish whose many weddings and funerals provided a welcome supplement to his salary. But during his five years there he more often than not played a harmonium, the seventeenth-century organ of Saint Merry being decrepit and capricious. It had been rebuilt by Clicquot before the Revolution, rebuilt afterward by Dallery, and overhauled at least twice more. A first task was to list needed repairs.

Saint-Saëns took this opportunity to urge changes that embodied progressive ideas. He wished to extend the compass of some of the stops and of the pedalboard; to add an enclosed division; to alter the instrument's pitch (musicians were then at odds over the merits of adopting an international standard); and to install four combination pedals. Whether he was required to do battle for his modernist views is not known. What is sure is that the work was entrusted to Cavaillé-Coll, then forty-four years old and already acclaimed for Saint Denis, Saint Brieuc, Saint Vincent de Paul, and the Madeleine.

The master builder and the young composer had presumably met before—in Pauline Viardot's drawing room, it may be, where in 1851 Cavaillé-Coll had placed one of his finest residence organs, or at Rossini's, or even at Mme. Saint-Saëns's during one of her Monday evenings, which Cavaillé-Coll was for years to attend faithfully. But the rebuild at Saint Merry brought the two men into collaboration as artists. As might be expected, Cavaillé-Coll endorsed Saint-Saëns's proposals and elaborated on them. He reduced the number of manuals from four to three and extended them to fifty-four notes, installed a pedalboard of twenty-seven notes beginning at C, converted the grand-orgue mutations to unison stops, added a bottom octave to the second trompette to make a sixteen-foot bombarde, combined and enclosed the récit and echo and placed in the new division the voix humaine previously part of the grand-orgue, and installed not just four combination pedals but eleven. The contract was signed in May 1855, the work completed in June two years later.

In the interval, Cavaillé-Coll gave evidence of esteem for Saint-Saëns by including him among the performers recommended to clients for the inaugurations of new organs and by inviting him to play at soirées in the rue de Vaugirard. There in that immense erecting room, in 1856, Saint-Saëns demonstrated before an audience of connoisseurs the organ built for the cathedral in Carcassonne, and saw his name linked, perhaps for the first time, with that of Franck, who also performed.

Saint-Saëns's proficiency as an organist is certified by the reviews that now began to appear in praise of his virtuosic pedaling, tasteful registrations, adroit improvising, and dignified handling of the sacred machine. His manner was lauded as "musical—even severe," "solemn," "magisterial," "ingenious," and as exemplifying "that style which best suits the organ: the fugal." Yet such testimony signifies little more than how sober his ways appeared in comparison with those of colleagues. It gives no practical help to present-day interpreters who hope to lay hold of those tempos, those timbres, and those articulations which best embody his aims. For this, other data may prove more revealing.

To begin with, Saint-Saëns's dexterity on the manuals can be inferred from his dexterity at the piano. More to the point, his express dislike of tones too closely linked, together with his training by Kalkbrenner's *guide-mains*, suggests that Saint-Saëns employed at both instruments a touch whose refinement was of a different order from that of, say, Guilmant's touch or Widor's. These masters, as we shall see, based their respective touches on a legato in which one note joined the next with no overlap or break, and in which the separations of repeated notes and of phrasings were meticulously measured.

Not so with Saint-Saëns. The reports of persons who heard him lead one to conclude that his piano arpeggios and scales, especially in rapid tempo, comprised with astonishing finesse the tiniest separation of note from note, remaining scintillating and graceful and even. Lacking evidence to the contrary, we may presume a like touch at the organ. On this premise, his legato would have been articulate in the way Schweitzer had in mind when he posited a similar transparency in Bach's. Well-executed passage work in Bach, says Schweitzer, resembles a good dish of rice in which all the grains are sufficiently cooked so as not to be brittle, but not overcooked so as to lose their form and consistency and become mush.

As to pedaling, Charles Tournemire asserts that Saint-Saëns used toes only, thereby achieving rare precision. But Tournemire's argument that the less one uses the heel the more unerringly one plays is specious. Experience shows that the proper use of the heel leads to accuracy and ease not otherwise attainable, hence to that ideal control which renders imperceptible all mechanical intermediaries between thought and tone. Nor is the notion less dubious that fidelity of style demands identity of technique—that if Saint-Saëns used toes only, the interpreter must do likewise or else fail to convey certain nuances. Dupré, for one, would argue to the contrary that nuance is more reliably conveyed by technique exactly regulated than by technique arbitrarily defective.

As to tempo, we learn from Eugène Gigout that Saint-Saëns at times played fast when improvising counterpoint, seemingly untroubled by the obscurant effect of reverberation. But this does not necessarily imply that Saint-Saëns advocated fast tempos for every fugal passage, let alone for every work. Still less can it mean that he considered clarity inessential: his classical leanings go to prove the reverse, that to him clarity was at one in importance with shapeliness of form. Little more can be said than that Saint-Saëns's works are sufficiently open in texture to allow quick tempo without loss of clarity, and that with every note, he—like Franck, Vierne, Dupré, and the rest—took resonance fully into account. All told, the interpreter must be left to recur to the scores, mindful that they furnish only a point of departure and that with Saint-Saëns, as with any composer or period, tempo must be determined by the mood and complexity of a work in accord with the tractability of an organ and the reverberation of a room.

As to registration, we are told by Jean Huré that Saint-Saëns liked colorful timbres in the styles of the old masters. This is corroborated by Joseph Bonnet and Alexandre Cellier, who point to Saint-Saëns's familiarity with classic Dutch organs and fondness for "the charm of a nasard combined with a gambe or bourdon, a cornet solo, a grosse quinte or a carillon in the pedal and a récit de tierce en taille or en dessus." Add Vierne's wonderment that Saint-Saëns would play a melody on the voix humaine *sans* tremulant, and we sense the composer's originality and his delight in finely drawn contrasts and shadings.

Although the scores offer little explicit help—neither set of preludes and fugues, for example, specifies tone color—they at times provide hints, the early works especially. In the first Fantasy, in the "Bénédiction Nuptiale," and in *Trois Rhapsodies sur des Cantiques Bretons,* Saint-Saëns calls in distinctive ways for the hautbois, trompette, and cromorne, for flutes 8 and 4 or 8, 4, and 2, for flutes and gambe, and for the couplers; from this we may begin to infer preferences and apply them to other works. Any work may be eloquently registrated in several ways; as the composer himself would advise, we may draw at a given organ the stops that sound best.

From such facts as these Rollin Smith concludes, in *Saint-Saëns and the Organ,* that "Saint-Saëns was a master of the art of registration—a fact little supported by the few stop indications in his music" and that a telling clue to his practices is given in the words of an old organ-blower: "We have had the very best organists here . . . but only Monsieur Saint-Saëns could make such beautiful effects with very little wind."

On the evening of 3 December 1857 Saint-Saëns inaugurated the Saint Merry Cavaillé-Coll. He opened with an improvisation that showed off individual stops, played his recent Fantasy in E-Flat and a movement from Mendelssohn, and closed with the Bach Fugue in D Major, his solos complemented by vocal motets. Although some listeners found the Mendelssohn heavy going, the audience was appreciative and the reviewers were friendly. But what was to have marked a beginning in fact marked an end. Only days later Saint-Saëns announced his departure for the Madeleine.

. 5 .

For the twenty-two-year-old composer to be named organist of the richest and most fashionable church in Paris, a church as renowned for the prominence of its parishioners as for the elegance of its ceremonies, seemed an almost fabulous advancement. No harm could come to his career—he must have reflected—should he there be appreciated by some luminary whose merest word could obtain the mounting of an opera. No harm, either, in taking charge of a four-manual Cavaillé-Coll that counted among the builder's most majestic creations. Nor would the ample salary and honoraria be without use.

His duties were ample as well. Rollin Smith points out that except in parts of Advent and Lent, Saint-Saëns played for no fewer than three services every Sunday of the year, not to speak of many and often lavish weddings and funerals: "The most elaborate of the week's masses was the eleven o'clock high mass when the choir was present and usually sang special settings of the Ordinary. At the one o'clock low mass or 'organ mass,' the organist played throughout, stopping only during the sermon." At vespers, "the organ alternated with the choir during the singing of numerous psalms and hymns." Masses on the Marian feasts and other high holy days were celebrated with ornate rites and music.

In general, however, the rubrics allowed time for hardly anything but interludes. Only at the Offertory and Communion might Saint-Saëns extemporize more than momentarily on the Gregorian melodies of the day. Otherwise, as Smith notes, he would briefly play during the intervals between the celebrant's entrance and the Introit, between the Alleluia and Sequence, between the Credo and Orate fratres, and between the Ite missa est and Deo gratias, perhaps alternating with the choir at the Kyrie, Gloria, Sanctus, or Agnus Dei. When at last the postlude arrived he was able to play at length, and for this he would generally improvise fugues, fugues reportedly so disciplined in style and balanced in form that they sounded written, composed at leisure. Musical design, but also a risibly practical notion, accounted for his preference. Fugues, he would quip, made exemplary postludes because "in measure as the voices enter, the public leaves; by the time every voice has come in, every parishioner has gone out."

As to what constituted good church music, instrumental or vocal, his convictions were serious indeed. Saint-Saëns contended that liturgical music should be grand in style, serene in spirit, and aloof from all that was worldly. He deplored the singing of operatic airs and the adapting of sacred texts to tunes composed for the drawing room. He denounced the mixing of diverse styles at a single service, the juxtaposing of one composer's Gloria, for instance, with another's Credo. And because he held that the purpose of church music was to assist meditation and prayer, not to entertain or distract, he adjudged even the works of Bach inapt: Bach's music was concert music, the Mass in B Minor a case in point. Nearly all Bach's preludes, toccatas, fugues, and variations were virtuosic in effect, he would explain, and even the chorale settings were unfitted for Catholic liturgy by their essentially Protestant intent. Yet Saint-Saëns was progressive enough to suggest that Gounod's and

Franck's music not be rejected in favor of an uncritical zeal for Palestrina or for the neumes of plainsong.

Actually, he writes, the question of suitability is "impossible to decide—and for the very simple reason that in reality there is no religious art, properly so called, to be distinguished absolutely from secular art. There is good music, and there is bad music; as to the rest it is a matter of fashion, of convention, and nothing else." Not alone in the uncultured can feelings of deepest reverence be evoked by the most insipid harmonies—whence the truism that artistic worth bears no necessary relation to intensity of devotion. Disavowing current fashion none the less, Saint-Saëns came to be known as a rigorous church musician of esoteric and uncompromising taste.

His strictness had an amusing side too. He was to relish the memory of a bride who begged him to play no fugues at her wedding, and of another bride who asked him to play funeral dirges, else she would not be able to weep. He relished an encounter—retelling it time and again—with a clergyman who reproached him for his austerity: "Monsieur l'Abbé," Saint-Saëns replied, "when I hear from the pulpit the language of the Opéra-Comique, I will play light music. Not before!"

As noted above, Saint-Saëns composed the first of his organ works, the Fantasy in E-flat, in 1857. He published soon after, as opus one, three short pieces for harmonium—"Méditation," "Barcarolle," and "Prière"—written half a dozen years earlier. His "Bénédiction Nuptiale" and "Elévation ou Communion" likewise date from the 1850s. And though displaying an earlier opus number, *Trois Rhapsodies sur des Cantiques Bretons* dates from 1866. Except for these, and notwithstanding his sometimes daily preoccupation with the organ, Saint-Saëns, during his twenty years at the Madeleine, composed exclusively for other media. The period 1858–77 saw the creation of three operas, four symphonic poems, four piano concertos, the first cello concerto, two violin concertos, the Introduction and Rondo Capriccio for violin, and the Piano Quartet in B-flat, among other major works, and dozens of songs, choruses, chamber pieces, and instrumental solos.

Of his two hundred works, some twenty are for the organ. In the 1890s, when no longer a professional organist but a frequent guest on Sundays in the loft at Saint Séverin, he composed two sets of preludes and fugues, the Fantasy, Op. 101, and "Marche Religieuse." In 1916–17 he wrote *Sept Improvisations,* and in 1919 the Fantasy, Op. 157. In addition, he transcribed for organ some vocal and instrumental works, and he wrote duos for harmonium and piano; a serenade for piano, organ, and strings; a romance for violin, piano, and harmonium; a barcarolle for violin, cello, harmonium, and piano; "Prière," for cello and organ; a fantasy for the Aeolian player-organ; *Cyprès et Lauriers,* for organ and orchestra (1919); and the *Organ* Symphony (1886). Not disesteem for the organ, but predilection and encyclopedic competence directed his activity—these, and the bias of an age that called successful the composer who wrote a successful opera.

His activity was not limited to composing. Saint-Saëns was constantly to be found either attending concerts or giving them. In the 1860s and 1870s he performed all Mozart's concertos, revived some of Bach's, and promoted the works of Mendelssohn and Schumann with such gusto that audiences came to admire the two previously spurned modernists. He played his own works. He played Liszt's. Once or twice he directed an orchestra, though conducting turned out to be one of few musical disciplines at which he remained inexpert. He participated in the inaugurations of organs, chiefly Cavaillé-Colls: in 1862, Saint Sulpice; in 1868, Notre Dame; in 1869, Trinity Church; in 1873, the chapel at Versailles; in 1878, the Trocadéro. He began to edit the works of Gluck, a task he would complete a quarter century later. He co-founded the Société Nationale de Musique to promote the music of his countrymen. Meantime, some of his own works were giving new impetus and shape to the concerto form, and by this exerting influence on the course of Western music. He began a series of tours abroad, and drew applause most warmly in England, where he was long to be regarded as the greatest of French musicians.

But he was sometimes less balanced in his judgment than in his art, and it was with a regrettable lack of deliberation that Saint-Saëns entered in February 1875 on the most calamitous of his endeavors: he married Marie-Laure Truffot, a charming girl twenty years his junior, the sister of a pupil, and brought her to live in his mother's house.

That the marriage was doomed from the start by the mother-in-law's antagonism, the couple's disparities of age and of temperament, and the husband's homosexual inclinations and egocentricity can only be conjectured; the evidence is scant and inferential. But any hope of a lasting relation seems to have been lost when in 1878, within barely more than a month, two infant children, both boys, died. The older son was killed in a fall from a window, and the younger succumbed to illness. The marriage had no other issue, and in 1881 Saint-Saëns abandoned his wife, never to see her again. Nor, to the end of her ninety-five years, would Marie-Laure publicly speak of her husband in any but veiled words.

Other sorrows and joys visited this steadily productive life: the repeated success of *Samson et Dalila* in Germany and *Henry VIII* in Paris, the appointment—thanks to his devoted pupil Albert Périlhou—as honorary organist at Saint Séverin, the literary works, the late chamber and symphonic music, the friendship with Fauré, on the one hand; on the other, the animosity of d'Indy and others who forced his departure from the Société Nationale de Musique, the death of his mother and his irremediable solitude, his unhappy flights from Paris to seek solace in Algiers, Cairo, and Las Palmas, his repudiation by a new avant-garde.

Disliked for his power and his irascibility as much as for his conservative views, Saint-Saëns came to be considered neither classicist nor innovator but merely old and out of date. Recognition at home and abroad, crowned by election to membership with the immortals in the Institute, did not keep him from tasting the bitterness of rejection, or from finding Debussy's ill will, like d'Indy's, particularly malign. So it happened that his career, begun early and exuberantly, grown rich in satisfaction, honor, and promise fulfilled, turned melancholy in the years leading up to his death, on 16 December 1921, at eighty-six.

Saint-Saëns spent his final years not only in revising earlier works, literary and musical, but also in composing music as remarkable for its energy as for its skill—among other works the sonatas for oboe, for clarinet, and for bassoon. His health declining, he embarked nevertheless on concert tours, giving in London his cycle of the Mozart piano concertos and traveling to North and South America. In Buenos Aires, in 1899, his String Quartet in E Minor received its première. In San Francisco, in 1915, he represented France at the Panama-Pacific Exposition and joined in three gala concerts devoted to his music. Everywhere, he continued to garner acclaim.

⅀ 3 ⅄

César Franck

THAT SAINT-SAËNS AND FRANCK WERE ANY-
thing but friends is readily understood. In origins and experience,
in habits of mind, in esthetic ideals, the two masters differed so
greatly that they regarded each other across a gulf which only the
warmest fellow feeling might possibly have spanned.

Even casual conversation must have been awkward. Saint-
Saëns was urbane, a Parisian sophisticate through and through;
Franck was embarrassingly artless. Saint-Saëns embraced conservative politics, Franck liberal. Saint-Saëns knew literature, science,
history; Franck's schooling had been unexceptional, and his musical training itself had been cut short. In attire and demeanor,
Saint-Saëns was fastidious. Franck, as Vincent d'Indy recalls, was
"perpetually in a hurry, perpetually absent-minded and making
grimaces, running rather than walking, dressed in a frock coat a
size too big and trousers a size too short." It was easy to think
him ridiculous.

More to the point, Saint-Saëns thought the highest art to be
form divorced from feeling, or at the least superior to it, whereas
Franck thought such divorce or superiority neither practicable
nor desirable. Still less did Franck care whether a score was pro-

grammatic. "It little matters," he told his pupil Guillaume Lekeu, "whether music sets out to awaken ideas about a given external subject, or limits its purpose to expressing a state of mind . . . ; what is indispensable is that a work should be *musical,* and emotional as well."

Common purpose did sometimes unite the two masters, as in the founding of the Société Nationale de Musique, and amity did sometimes break out, as in Franck's inscribing to Saint-Saëns the "Prelude, Fugue and Variation" and the Piano Quintet, and, for that matter, in Saint-Saëns's acting as pallbearer at Franck's funeral. But each mind found the other unsympathetic.

Even so, it was pupils of Franck's, not Franck himself, who detested Saint-Saëns and intrigued against him, while Saint-Saëns, who was abundantly capable of spite, perhaps harbored toward Franck less malice than puzzlement. We may give him the benefit of the doubt.

César-Auguste Franck was born, on 10 December 1822, in what was then part of the Netherlands. His father, Nicolas-Joseph Franck, was a Walloon of mixed French and German culture and had been a student in Germany when he met César's mother. In the summer of 1835—a few months before Saint-Saëns's birth—the father took his twelve-year-old son to Paris. Diligent as well as gifted, the boy had entered the conservatory in his native Liège at about the age of eight, had received unanimous praise from his teachers of counterpoint and harmony, and had already composed a half-dozen works. By age eleven he had in addition carried off the first prize in piano and undertaken a tour that culminated in a performance before King Leopold. From this came the notion that in Paris, by dint of cunning exploitation, the prodigy might so charm and amaze as to fill with gold the pockets of the father, whose most telling attribute was neither his cruelty nor his arrogance but, by all accounts, his greed.

To set his plan in motion, Nicolas-Joseph engaged two eminent teachers, Anton Reicha for composition and Pierre-Joseph

Zimmermann for piano, basing his hopes on their fame and connections. And indeed they were sufficiently taken with their pupil that not six months had passed before they stated their approval in print—thanks to Nicolas-Joseph as impresario and publicist. Zimmermann declared that "César-Auguste Franck has one of the best-balanced young brains I have ever come across; he combines the most brilliant aptitude with a capacity for assiduous study which gives every promise that he will become a highly distinguished artist." Reicha predicted that he would "develop into one of the most notable musicians, since already he shows powers far beyond his years." But César Franck's Parisian debut, at the Gymnase Musicale on 17 November 1835, caused no slightest stir. His father's expenditure in guile and money was proving fruitless.

More than a year elapsed, filled for the boy with study and composing and for his father with scheming, whereupon Nicolas-Joseph resolved to enroll César and a younger son, Joseph, at the Paris Conservatory. His plan was only briefly hindered by the rule denying admission to foreigners; Nicolas-Joseph learned that obtaining French citizenship for himself would obtain it also for his children and hastened to apply. Both boys entered the school in October 1837: César, now nearly fifteen, to begin with counterpoint and the piano; Joseph, twelve, with the violin and solfège.

The change of citizenship seems not to have extended to Franck's German mother, even though the entire family eventually moved to Paris. Of Marie-Catherine-Barbe Frings little is known, and nothing of her feelings at being transplanted to France. The daughter of a cloth merchant at Aachen, she had already been uprooted at least once. All indications are that her wishes counted for nothing.

To call her elder son Belgian rather than French, as some do, is to overlook the technicality that the Kingdom of Belgium did not come into being till nearly a decade after his birth. Marie-Catherine, moreover, exerted an influence not even a despotic husband could annul, as we may infer from the touching detail that César to the end of his life said his prayers in German. The question of nationality is best answered, it would seem, by the patriotic odes he composed in the revolutionary years 1848 and 1870–71: they eloquently argue his loyalty to France and his pride in being a Parisian.

Franck's academic career lasted until 1842, and it afforded a peculiar mix of recognition and discouragement. To begin with, his first year had hardly passed before the youth won a dazzling award in piano. At the examination, after having performed the set piece beautifully, he took it into his head to transpose the sight-reading test down a minor third. Astonished, the jury deemed a first prize inadequate and devised for him a *Grand Prix d'honneur*, the only such award in Conservatory history. Teachers and classmates cheered him on, and, to Nicolas-Joseph's delight, so did the public prints.

Success also came, though more slowly, in counterpoint and fugue: in 1838 a third prize; in 1839 a second ("Good . . . he is making progress," records the director, Cherubini); and finally in 1840 a unanimous first prize.

But the last of his victories tasted bitter. In the autumn of 1840, at seventeen, Franck entered François Benoist's class in organ— the class Saint-Saëns was to enter eight years later—no doubt driven to learn improvisation and plainsong accompaniment so as to qualify for employment in the Church. Though he won the second prize after only ten months, in July 1841, he held this to be defeat rather than triumph. He was convinced he deserved a first.

Two themes had been assigned him on which to improvise, and between them he sensed an affinity. Having therefore decided to treat them simultaneously, he improvised at uncommon length and with uncommon intricacy, infringing the prize rules and bewildering the jury. Cherubini, the master contrapuntist who might well have commended the stroke and ignored the infraction, was ill and absent, and the jury only consented to award a prize after Benoist's intercession.

And yet to portray that jury as hostile or ignorant, as some of Franck's biographers have done, is almost certainly unjust. The greater likelihood is that Franck was more polished in his mental skills than in his executive—even as a master he would at times let ideas outrun technique—and that the jury rightly foresaw him benefiting from additional study. Such was to be the case when Saint-Saëns competed for the organ prize, we know, and in fact a first prize was seldom achieved after a first year. What is sure is that a few months later Franck neither tried again for an award in organ nor made the anticipated next move of trying for the Rome Prize. Instead, to everybody's consternation, he resigned in mid-term.

He did so at his father's command. Apparently "César-Auguste Franck, senior," as a reviewer caustically named him, had decided on another stratagem: to seek once again the patronage of King Leopold. For this it would have been imperative that the nineteen-year-old be thought Belgian, yet to enroll him for the Rome Prize would have irrevocably labeled him French. Or so we may surmise. At any rate, the King played his part by accepting the dedication of Franck's first published work, the Trios, Op. 1, and father and sons, armed with this endorsement, toured Belgium in the months following the resignation. Leopold's patronage turned out to be ephemeral, however, and Father Franck's sole reward was a gold medal César received in token of royal thanks.

Returned to Paris in the autumn of 1842, Franck entered on the career of a virtuoso-composer whose livelihood came chiefly from teaching. Handicapped by the forced abbreviation of his training, he would labor ever afterward to gain knowledge and proficiency, musical and other, that he ought to have gained as a student. He was later to begin setting aside at least a few minutes each day for reading—Kant and Tolstoy among his chosen authors—and to acquire a practice pedalboard to improve his organ technique.

Franck's hasty departure from the Conservatory doubtless stood among the most painful events of his life. Even his student work-books attest the fulfillment and solace his study had given him: their every symbol is drawn with loving care, their every class or date or teacher's name decorated with flourishes. Nor could he any longer go regularly to hear Beethoven and Haydn played by the Société des Concerts du Conservatoire, whose rehearsals the students freely attended. Of that delightful instruction too he had been deprived.

· 2 ·

Young as he was, Franck had long since established a studio and had been supporting the family. As early as 1838 the announcement appeared that "César-Auguste Franck will inaugurate on October 1 two classes in piano, one for ladies and one for gentlemen. The course will extend over nine months and consist of three lessons a week of two hours each. Every class will be limited to five pupils. One day a week will be devoted entirely to sight-reading, analysis, and transposition, on an elementary method devised by M. Franck." The course had continued in subsequent years, and he had also begun what was to be his lifelong and arduous routine of scurrying from one side of Paris to the other to give lessons in homes and at schools. He took on in addition odd jobs as an accompanist, and he and Joseph sometimes performed with instrumentalists and singers—the solo recital à la Liszt being as yet a rarity.

It was at the family's parish church, Notre Dame de Lorette, where in 1838 Cavaillé-Coll had built his first Parisian organ, that Franck began his career as an organist. There, as deputy to Alphonse Gilbert, he accompanied the choir and in Gilbert's absence would preside at the organ, taking delight, needless to say, in its three manuals and forty-three stops. Furthermore, thanks to the elevated taste of a music-loving pastor, the parish boasted not only a good organ and organist but good choral music too; at services were heard motets and masses by Haydn, Mozart, Cherubini, Lesueur.

As to composition, Franck was turning out the serious and able Trios as well as the showy fantasias and variations with which his father still hoped to enrapture a paying public.

And here we note the ultimate riddle of César Franck's personality. Few things are more obvious than the human mind's ability to accommodate mutually exclusive ideas. But it is odd that in such a genius as Franck the extremes of vulgarity and sublimity could so happily coexist. The great originator, after all, typically achieves greatness with the aid of a cultivated critical sense. Franck was at times the most astute of self-critics, but he was at other times the least: he savored whole repertories that some would call trifling— the symphonies of Méhul, for example, and the operas of Grétry and of Dalayrac—and allowed them to affect his language. Nor did this alliance of the commonplace and the noble end with his apprenticeship. As late as his final months, at the very time he was achieving transcendence in passage after passage of the *Trois Chorals,* he was thoughtfully penning in *L'Organiste* mawkish harmonies and melodies.

Be that as it may, he now began to be regularly noticed. In 1838 the *Ménestrel* had praised his playing and some of his works. In 1839 the *Revue et Gazette musicale* noted the "young virtuoso's abilities, the brilliance, vigor, precision of his execution"—the words those of no less discerning a critic than Berlioz. In 1842 the Trios appeared in print by means of a subscription that included such shining names as Meyerbeer, Chopin, Donizetti, Halévy, and Liszt. As might be expected, Liszt encouraged his young colleague and took pains to get his music performed. "I do not know three in France who are his equals," Liszt wrote, but "he will have a harder time than most. . . . It seems to me he lacks that convenient tact which opens all doors. . . . This is perhaps why . . . men of good will should come to his assistance." Thanks to Liszt, Franck's oratorio *Ruth*, which had received its première, in 1845, without chorus and with only piano accompaniment, was granted a fully scored performance at the Conservatory the next January.

Not all notice was good-natured. In 1842–45 the *Revue et Gazette musicale* published a series of damning reviews in which Henri Blanchard—who was in 1846 to praise Saint-Saëns's debut so warmly—reckoned Franck's talent mediocre, his given names absurdly pretentious, his father intolerably meddlesome.

But even Blanchard might have found it shocking that César-

Auguste was forced to practice and to teach until exhausted, that his out-of-pocket expenses were scrutinized, that an exactly calculated time was allotted him for travel between lessons, that he was not permitted friends to sustain him, that he was not allowed evenings of repose but to save candles was sent to bed at nightfall, and that in his mind and heart his father's warning ever re-echoed: "If you disobey, you know it is your *mother* who suffers for it. . . ."

Enrolled at one of the schools where Franck taught was a girl, Félicité Saillot, whom he found particularly fetching. Two years younger than he, gifted enough to study with him not just the piano but also harmony and composition, Félicité sprang from a celebrated line of actors. Her maternal grandparents and great-grandparents had been widely known as the Baptistes, and her mother and father, billed as the Desmousseaux, were for decades on the boards at the Comédie-Française. Félicité had broken with family custom, perhaps by her mother's desire, and was being given the strict upbringing of a proper middle-class young woman and kept far distant from what some condemned as the disreputable glories of the stage.

Her schooling completed, she continued studying with Franck at her home. There he began to spend more time than needed for tutoring, resorting to one ruse or another to quell his father's suspicion, encouraged in this show of independence by the increasing affection of Félicité's parents. There, in tranquility, he would read, compose, reflect, and talk to Félicité—with, to be sure, her mother knitting quietly nearby.

As for Félicité, a companion recalls that she "doted" on her suitor. "Wanting nothing so much as to satisfy Monsieur Franck, she would be seized with desperation at the smallest finger-slip in her lessons, or when he tapped his foot impatiently, which was frequent with him." Rarely did a lesson pass without tears.

When Nicolas-Joseph eventually learned the secret, he was doubly enraged by the disobedience and the probable loss of his son's income. One angry scene followed another till at last, when during an outburst he ripped to shreds the manuscript of a song Franck had inscribed to Félicité, he rent as well the filial bond: Franck left home for good. Franck was then about twenty-four, a year short of his majority; not till December 1847 could he and Félicité post the banns. They were married on 22 February 1848 at Notre Dame de Lorette. In the end, Nicolas-Joseph attended the wedding and allowed Franck's mother to attend. We may presume he relented when the son agreed to repay the father's debts—the huge sum of eleven thousand francs incurred, it was claimed, in promoting the stillborn career.

Small wonder Franck thereupon disappeared almost completely from public view, and that for years the demands of earning a living left him almost no time to compose. He would begin his days at 5:30 and work until spent. But the fees he earned playing the organ, accompanying at the piano instrumentalists and singers, and, when political upheaval did not rob him of his pupils, teaching— all this barely sufficed. He was not merely discharging the burdensome debt, he was soon partly supporting both Félicité's widowed mother, who came to live with the couple, and a brother-in-law. In due course, between 1848 and 1856, four children were born. In due course—for the nineteenth century—Franck suffered the deaths in infancy of two of them. "The sorrow one feels on losing these little ones, whom one loves the better for their frailty," he wrote, "is so great that it nearly becomes injustice toward those who are left. . . . It seemed as if those who remained to me were less good by nature, less bright in mind, than the one I had just lost."

Brother Joseph too made demands. He had crowned his own career at the Conservatory by likewise becoming an organist and composer. Author eventually of some two hundred published works, he was long to be better known than César (reviewers for years felt obliged to designate César as Franck "the elder") and was always to lack self-control. In temperament and moral fiber the brothers greatly differed, and after their father's death, in 1871, Joseph's extravagant conduct and continual lack of money drove them apart.

So irreparable was the break, we are told, that their children knew almost nothing of one another.

· 3 ·

In about 1853, when Franck was writing his opera *Le Valet de Ferme*, trying, as Saint-Saëns was to do a bit later, to succeed in the only medium by which Paris measured success, the pastor of Saint Jean—Saint François, formerly a priest at Notre Dame de Lorette, invited him to become the organist. Franck at once accepted, the more enthusiastically because Cavaillé-Coll had installed there an organ which, though smaller than that of Notre Dame de Lorette, surpassed it in loveliness—or so Franck ardently believed. The tonal palette represented by its two manuals and eighteen stops offered him, he exclaimed, a veritable orchestra. And with this appointment, which happened to take place at about the same time as Saint-Saëns's first appointment, at Saint Merry a few blocks away, the royal instrument began moving toward that central place in Franck's activity which it would ever afterward occupy.

Not that Franck considered himself an organist above all. In his day, specialism, musical or other, was neither so obsessive nor so exclusive as it has since become. Had the question crossed his mind, he would presumably have called himself a musician, as we heard Saint-Saëns do. At all events, his output includes a mere dozen large-scale organ works: *Six Pièces,* composed in 1859–64, *Trois Pièces,* composed in 1878, and *Trois Chorals,* composed in 1890. Like Saint-Saëns, Franck more often wrote for the voice, orchestra, piano, or chamber ensembles. Yet the organ became the main agency in his artistic development, and to the organ, week after week for forty years, he confided some of his deepest thought and feeling.

His outward motives seem clear enough. If it is axiomatic that musicians feel compelled to hear and make music, nothing could be more natural than that Franck, for whom going to hear an orchestra was an infrequent luxury, would turn for incentive and refreshment to an instrument he thought an orchestra in itself. He would turn to the organ with redoubled zest when it was such a Cavaillé-Coll as many might envy. And when in time Félicité's youth and wish to please gave way to middle age and shrewishness, and she took to berating him, as his father had done, for not writing music the public would pay for, he more than once escaped her tongue by fleeing to his organ loft.

There, with a discipline and order belied by the connotations of the word "improvise," he cultivated the art of improvisation. Like such predecessors in the *extempore* as Mozart and Bach, and such contemporaries as Chopin and Liszt, each of whom seems to have viewed improvisation as an essentially cerebral phenomenon, Franck impromptu *composed*. This is not to say that his improvising, or theirs, was cerebral in the sense of abstract or dry, still less to claim for it the polish of work written and revised, but to suggest that feeling was the stronger for being constrained by form. His improvising was distinct from the meandering in search of pleasant harmonies which "improvisation" has lately come to mean, and which is sometimes unthinkingly ascribed to him. He attended to structure as well as to sonority, distinguishing less sharply than we do composition from improvisation, deeming them if not a unity, nevertheless something more than kindred operations of the mind.

As with his grammar, so with his diction. Unlike Saint-Saëns, who held to classical precedents, Franck felt as little interest in the French classicists as he later admitted to feeling in Palestrina. Rather, he expanded on the scholastic style learned at the Conservatory by transliterating into the organ's idiom a vocabulary mainly confected from his knowledge of the great classic-romanticist Germans.

Anton Reicha, we saw, had figured among his first teachers— the Reicha who had drilled him in harmony and counterpoint, himself an innovator in teaching the two disciplines as one, a composer and theoretician of no mean attainment, Czech by birth and German by training, friend to Beethoven and Haydn, teacher of Liszt and Berlioz. Though Franck spent barely a year with Reicha, the pairing was decisive if only because Reicha showed him how to use the tools of counterpoint and brought him firmly under the sway of Beethoven. Franck esteemed almost as warmly Schubert, and to various degrees at various times Gluck, Weber, Mendelssohn, Schumann, Liszt, and Bach.

These forebears led him to conceive out of his introspection a language contrapuntally and harmonically luxuriant, whose salient qualities Léon Vallas enumerates as a "disciplined intensity of spirit," "prolific melodic invention," "captivating lyrical outpouring," and "deep dramatic feeling" of a kind previously unknown in French music, the art of Berlioz excepted. Even Saint-Saëns, serious-minded though he was, did not reach this acme. Such qualities warred with Franck's liking for the second-best, and they took so many decades for their perfecting that Franck remains of all the great composers the slowest to mature. But not alone of his final improvisations was it true that, as Vierne said in awe to Dupré, "No one who did not hear Franck could imagine . . . their harmonic wealth, which never ceased to move you, the flow and vitality of his counterpoints, the balance of his forms."

For already in the 1850s, when he first performed as an organist in *audition* or *séance musicale,* his playing and improvising differed from what the public was used to. The critic Joseph d'Ortigue, who together with Montalembert, Fétis, Danjou, Morelot, and Dietsch stood among the earliest to call for reform, hailed Franck's work as scholarly, a term then favored for any church music not histrionic or mindless. When in 1854 Franck helped to inaugurate the Ducroquet at Saint Eustache, in company with Lemmens and others, the *Revue et Gazette musicale* praised his "fantasy composed with care [and] energetically performed." When in 1856 Franck demonstrated at Cavaillé-Coll's workshop the organ built for the cathedral in Carcassonne—in company with Saint-Saëns, as noted above—the same journal endorsed Cavaillé-Coll's own tribute: Franck was an "excellent" organist who showed off all the instrument's tonal resources "at first by playing some austere music of his own, skillfully written, and afterward by brilliant improvisations."

But though Cavaillé-Coll praised Franck's powers, he recommended others to inaugurate organs. Such performers as Cavallo, Simon, Durand, and, above all, Lefébure-Wély were second to none at conjuring up thunderstorm, battle, or shipwreck in cascades of sound like fountains of toilet water; their improvisations, which exploited every resource of a new organ, could be counted on to charm the public and gratify the client. For this, Cavaillé-Coll rightly judged Franck too austere, and doubtless too unassuming. Even when a "learned" performer was required, for demonstrations if not for inaugurations, Cavaillé-Coll in those days turned to Lemmens, who was not only as serious as Franck, but also had a more accomplished technique and a more lordly, not to say arrogant, personality. So far as we know, Franck felt no ill will at being passed over, and his friendship with Cavaillé-Coll appears to have remained steadfast and rich in mutual esteem.

Lefébure-Wély's art, incidentally, struck most of his contemporaries as anything but frivolous, and though it was far from sublime, we are wrong to dismiss it with that easy contempt which later ages tend to feel for earlier. Bernard Shaw reminds us of a principle when he says that Donizetti's *Lucrezia* was once really tragic, and the "Inflammatus" in Rossini's *Stabat Mater* really grand—that what came to be known only as the spavined battle horse of obsolete Italian prima donnas and upstart Italian tenors was formerly a true Pegasus which carried fine artists aloft. Dispute as we may Shaw's citations, we would do well to apply his principle to Lefébure-Wély and others of the second rank.

When and how Franck met Cavaillé-Coll it is difficult to say. The opportunities were many if only because mutual acquaintances were many; nearly everybody in Parisian musical circles, then as now, knew everybody else. Perhaps Pauline Viardot, whom Franck had met when a boy, introduced them, or Benoist or Berlioz or Liszt. Perhaps they became acquainted in the loft at Notre Dame de Lorette, while Franck was deputy at that organ and Cavaillé-Coll its caretaker. They were definitely in touch by about mid-1848, when Franck is known to have visited Cavaillé-Coll's workshop, and by February 1854 the friendship was warm enough that César and Félicité figured among the dinner guests at the Cavaillé-Colls' wedding.

By then, plans had long since been drawn up for the new church and organ with which Franck's name would ever be linked: the Church (later Basilica) of Saint Clotilde. And we may suppose that by then Cavaillé-Coll, who sometimes advised the clergy in the hiring of organists, had already thought of Franck as candidate.

We may also suppose that he asked for Franck's suggestions when planning the new organ, for which the contract was signed in June 1854. Some argue that Franck cannot have had a hand in the design, since the proposed stoplist duplicated that of an organ dating from 1849, long before his appointment; and it is true that no document has come to light to prove collaboration. But other readings of the evidence are tenable. Cavaillé-Coll freely sought organists' advice and was anything but close-minded, as we saw: it may be that he consulted Franck informally, in the way of instrument makers and musicians time out of mind.

Certainly he seems to have done so late in the project, when after Franck's appointment to Saint Clotilde, and without emending the contract, he added to the stoplist a voix céleste and clairon in the récit; a bourdon 16, flûte octaviante, unda maris, and clairon in the positif; and a soubasse 32 and basson 16 in the pedal—some of which voices Franck had greatly liked at Saint Jean–Saint François. True, Cavaillé-Coll may have added the clairons and pedal stops after discovering that acoustical deficiencies of the newly completed nave required added strength of the ensemble. But no motive other than that of pleasing Franck can account for Cavaillé-Coll's adding the voix céleste, flutes, and unda maris after installation had begun.

We know that the additions were made at the last minute; that they demanded the reworking of chests and console; that the price of the organ accordingly exceeded the estimate; that the overrun was nothing less than forty percent, an inordinate margin even for Cavaillé-Coll; and that the final invoice offered as justification only the vague phrases "obliged by unusual circumstances . . . more labor and expense than anticipated . . . the abnormal height of the loft." All things considered, the odds are that the genial builder once again wished to accommodate an artist and serve the cause of music.

The Saint Clotilde organ stood completed in August 1859. It comprised forty-six stops, three manuals of fifty-four notes each, a pedalboard of twenty-seven notes starting at C, and fourteen combination pedals. It bore Cavaillé-Coll's hallmark in craftsmanship and sonority. But among all his works, and notwithstanding family resemblance, its loveliness was unique. To the end of his life, the builder would call it one of his finest achievements.

Vierne, Dupré, Bonnet, Duruflé, and Marchal knew the organ in its original state, and they recall its sound as rich and full yet notably unaggressive. The récit in particular was at once Herculean and delicate. Its position at the rear of the case let the récit draw a singular resonance from nearby walls and arches. The shades' extreme sensitivity made the récit minutely expressive; and when coupled the récit lent this quality to the instrument as a whole. The récit had no sixteen-foot stop. More significantly, the récit had no montre; its eight-foot foundations consisted of only a gambe and two flutes—from which may have come Franck's habit of strengthening the foundations by adding the hautbois or trompette, and the presence of these reeds in the registrations he specifies in his scores. The trompette spoke gently but incisively, the hautbois more gently still, and the hautbois and trompette blended into the foundations to form an ensemble of seamless refinement.

By the same token, the positif cromorne was well-spoken whether used solo or in chorus. Also of note were the parity of grand-orgue and positif, whose respective stops so closely resembled each other as to be virtually interchangeable, and the absence of a récit-to-grand-orgue coupler: récit and grand-orgue could only be joined by coupling récit to positif, positif to grand-orgue.

It is remarkable that the character of this organ corresponded so intimately to the character of its master, that its restrained power echoed, as it were, Franck's kindliness and self-effacement. Franck was very likely often present day to day while the instrument was being voiced; and the notion, though fanciful, is compelling that by the subtlest and gentlest of means he induced the voicer, the incomparable Gabriel Reinburg, to embody in tone that spirit.

We may pause to note that Tournemire revised Franck's organ in 1933. He relocated stops, revoiced others, and added ten wholly new. Among the changes, the positif cromorne became a récit clarinette; some flutes were transformed into octaves, some octaves into flutes; and the unda maris became a salicional. Langlais in turn, in 1962–65, added four stops and an electrified console, replacing the Barker lever with electro-pneumatic action, the ventils with combination pistons; and he suppressed the suboctave couplers.

When in January 1858 Franck entered on his duties, the church had been consecrated but not finished; services were held in a chapel. A month later, the Pleyel firm delivered to him the practice pedalboard mentioned above; he meant his technique to be worthy of his new organ, and was not too proud to go back to the rudiments. And when in December 1859 he played for the inauguration, sharing the program with Lefébure-Wély, he included among his selections no less weighty a piece than the Prelude and Fugue in E Minor by Bach.

· 4 ·

The dozen-odd years between Franck's appointment as organist at Saint Clotilde and his appointment as professor of organ at the Conservatory saw his compositions grow more proficient and more thoughtful. Popular taste continued to move him, but Franck now began fashioning a music whose gravity countered the occasional lapse. This maturation may be found in his motets, masses, and organ or harmonium sundries from the period. But no music reveals it more plainly than the *Six Pièces*. They were his earliest masterpieces for the organ, in fact his earliest of any kind.

Among them, the "Final," though numbered last, may have

been composed first: Franck performed in the inaugural program at Saint Clotilde a "Final" that drew critical praise, and inscribed the printed work to Lefébure-Wély, who also performed on that occasion. Or it may be that the Fantasy in C came first; it could have figured in that program as the work "large in scale . . . whose forceful style impressed the whole audience." Then too, a certain ascendancy lets us surmise that he wrote the "Grande Pièce symphonique" after the "Prelude, Fugue and Variation," "Pastorale," and "Prière." But the facts have yet to be unearthed.

What is indubitable is Franck's sovereignty over elements which, though neither the sole nor the loftiest components of great music, are none the less praiseworthy and rare. The *Six Pièces* manifest a shapeliness of melody, freshness of timbre, economy of means, balance of form, fecundity of invention, and depth of feeling that go to make them great. They are, to paraphrase Jacques Barzun on greatness, intelligible work of a certain magnitude that other artists could not make even if they would. But they are more: a new creation of which century on century of organ art gave no foreshadowing.

Take the shapeliness of the fugue subject Franck invents for the "Prelude, Fugue and Variation"—a living, plastic melody he was proud of—and the eloquence of its working-out. Or take, at the beginning of the "Pastorale," the play of a few passing notes on tonic and dominant triads above a pedal point: simple means, startling inventiveness; and at the close of the "Pastorale," A-B-A form embellished by a descending melody admirably orchestrated—Cavaillé-Coll's flutes always sang out with a living voice—and as admirably contrapuntal. Given this counterpoint alone, only the heedless could think Franck's idiom pianistic or chordal. Listen to the timbres in the "Grande Pièce symphonique": the piquant mix of reeds and flutes in the second allegro, or in the andante the solo cromorne backed by reedy foundations; the newly perfected timbres evoke from Franck graceful thematic complements. Reflect on the solemnity of the "Prière," a work Dupré and Vierne each judged the most profound of all Franck's organ pieces, its passion the more intense for its restraint. And consider the ebullience of the pedal solos in the "Final," their difficulty, and their function in stating the theme.

In a word, Franck fashioned in the *Six Pièces* a music which for technical skill, seriousness of intent, and depth of feeling was unprecedented. That he did so despite the obstacles which his father's vindictive egotism had raised up in his path, and while constrained by family duties and burdened with unremitting daily tasks, makes his achievement the more laudable, the homage owed him by all who play his music the more richly deserved.

The allegiant interpreter, then, not only of the *Six Pièces* but also of the *Trois Pièces* and *Trois Chorals*, will grant as first principle Franck's seriousness. There may well have been levity in his behavior, despite hardship or because of it. But there is none in his twelve masterworks for organ. Not even the "Final" is lighthearted. It is only magnificent and spirited.

This being so, what is chiefly required is a judicious choice of tempo. Very often nowadays, even in unresonant rooms where clarity is not at hazard, is Franck's music played too fast—and not Franck's or organ music only. The press and pace of modern life imparts to music-making of all sorts rapidity bordering on frenzy. But given the organ's tones and surroundings, its music can least afford to be hurried. The student should therefore take to heart some points made by Robert Donington about early music, for they apply universally: that a fast movement taken steadily may gain breadth and dignity, even brilliance, which mere speed cannot compensate; that a slow movement may be more poignant when kept moving than when dragged; that no slow movement should call attention to its slowness, and no fast movement to its dash, but that a certain pulse should keep the slow movement vital, a certain ampleness keep the fast from sounding rushed; and that, these conditions met, slow tempos can be made the richer in feeling, fast tempos given breathtaking poise.

The faithful interpreter of Franck will grant as requisite the composer's timbres. After about 1830, it will be recalled, sound was no longer regarded chiefly as a conveyor of meaning but as inherently expressive. Timbre had interested previous composers, to be sure, but their interest was of an order different from that of Berlioz and others to whom timbre became a constituent of structure. And whereas Saint-Saëns's organ music, like its bygone models, allows divers registrations without much change of meaning, Franck's music requires for apt rendition the timbres in which it was conceived.

To learn to identify the timbres Franck knew, the performer can confidently study recordings, which thanks to the digital computer have achieved unexampled fidelity. But a twofold caution must be borne in mind. First, one will be deceived if one takes as authentic such organs as those at Saint Clotilde, Notre Dame, and the Madeleine, in which revision has left scarcely more than a vestige of Cavaillé-Coll's sonorities. More trustworthy, at present, are Saint Ouen, Saint Sulpice, and Saint Sernin, which have either been faithfully restored or left in essence unchanged. Daniel Roth, to name but one master, has made superlative recordings at Saint Sulpice, before and after the faithful restoration he oversaw with loving care. Second, one should bear in mind while pondering the aural documents that in the thirty years between Saint Clotilde and Saint Ouen the art of Cavaillé-Coll, as mentioned, was by no means static; that Saint Clotilde, which was not an enormous organ, differed from other Cavaillé-Colls in the ways we noted; and that although Franck took inspiration from Saint Clotilde he knew other organs well—the Trocadéro organ, for example, which he helped to inaugurate and for which he wrote the *Trois Pièces*. Indeed, Franck suits his registrations, in the scores of his twelve masterworks, to the generic Cavaillé-Coll of fifty or sixty stops rather than to the resources of Saint Clotilde. For example, when in the "Final" he calls for récit chorus reeds that include a 16-foot pitch, he calls for a timbre that the récit at Saint Clotilde did not possess. All that said, family likeness can serve as guide.

The question of timbre need not be perplexing even when one plays Franck on neo-romantic or eclectic organs. The rule still applies that his tone colors must be reproduced as faithfully as possible, but observance only requires ingenuity, common sense, and taste. If on a modern organ the reeds or mixtures are too bright, the player can draw a low mixture rather than a high, or no mixture, or a trumpet rather than both trumpet and clarion. If a solo trumpet blares, one can instead draw the oboe. If foundations sound too thick, one can thin them by replacing the principal with a gamba and flute. If reeds fail to blend, reeds can be omitted. It is the spirit of the law that counts. To begin the Chorale in E Major or the "Prière" on foundations dominated by a strident reed, merely because a reed is called for in the score, is to spoil Franck's intended effect. It need hardly be added that to play Franck on a neo-baroque organ is to distort meaning as flagrantly as playing Chopin on a harpsichord.

Two disparate traditions purport to embody Franck's attitudes and aims overall. One comes from Tournemire, among others, via Langlais; the other from Guilmant via Dupré. Tournemire's is free as to rhythm, phrasing, and legato, and keeps to Franck's registrations; a reed is usually added to the foundations. Guilmant's is strict as to rhythm, phrasing, and legato, and modifies registrations; the reed is usually absent from the foundations. Each tradition claims legitimacy by virtue of its proponent's having studied the works with Franck and been given Franck's mandate.

To ask which tradition deserves our assent, then, is to face a dilemma. For testimony is unanimous that the expressiveness of Franck's playing grew from his singularly pliant rubato; that his custom was to add a reed to the foundations; and that his legato was much less precisely calculated than Guilmant's. In these essentials the Saint Clotilde tradition, as exemplified in its several forms by Tournemire, Langlais, Marchal, Mahaut, Marty, Duruflé, and others, cannot be gainsaid. But neither can we lightly dismiss Dupré's account of Guilmant's stewardship:

> Guilmant, named organist of Trinity Church in 1872, knew Franck through Aristide Cavaillé-Coll and admired him with all his artist's soul. Franck played his *Six Pièces* one evening, at

Cavaillé-Coll's workshop at 15 Avenue du Maine, for Saint-Saëns, Widor, and Guilmant together. This was reported to me first by Guilmant, later by Widor, and last by Saint-Saëns. . . . All three agreed on the year of their meeting, 1875.

After the appearance of the *Trois Pièces,* in 1878, it was Guilmant who played, before Franck alone, likewise at Cavaillé-Coll's, the nine pieces then in print. . . . Franck was moved to tears, never having heard his works performed in that way. Guilmant took advantage of the opportunity to ask him for all possible details regarding their interpretation. Franck gave them to him willingly, and Guilmant scrupulously noted down all his indications. . . . Franck also showed Guilmant the sketches of his *Trois Chorals,* thanks to which Guilmant knew them before their posthumous publication.

We can well imagine Franck touched by Guilmant's stately tempos, articulate legato, and pellucid phrasing—and surprised too. So might Rachmaninoff have been touched and surprised by Rubinstein's performance of the Concerto in C Minor, *mutatis mutandis,* or Beethoven by Toscanini's Third Symphony, or Bach by Schweitzer's chorales—each composer entranced by his child's looks in an unthought-of garb. And knowing Guilmant's passion for nuance in registration, and his punctilious concern for detail, we can well imagine Guilmant not failing to ask Franck whether, from the foundations on most organs, the reeds should not ordinarily be absent.

So if we inquire which of the two Franck traditions merits our trust, the answer must be: neither and each. On the one hand, the question wrongly assumes that a work of art can have an ideal interpretation compared to which all others fall short, that the essence of greatness is not manifold. On the other hand, players wishing to grasp Franck's intent will respect both traditions as its partial embodiments, recognizing the while that no tradition can reasonably profess indefectibility.

Handed down by thinking and feeling custodians who each bring to bear unique perceptions and preferences, any tradition tends to become obscure in proportion as it is animate. The law is rooted in human nature and exempts not even the Franck traditions, well defined though they seem. Yet elements of truth do survive intact, in Franck's as in other traditions, even when error is perpetuated too. We are left to draw conclusions by applying mind and heart as best we can, remembering—again with Shaw—that no manipulation of the dead hand on the keys can ever reproduce the living touch.

· 5 ·

In February 1872, on Benoist's retirement from the Conservatory, Franck was named professor of organ. The appointment struck many as unsuitable. Franck lacked the necessary stature.

Over the previous decade, it is true, he had now and again been heard publicly and been favorably reviewed. He had helped to open new instruments, including the Cavaillé-Colls at Saint Sulpice, Notre Dame, and Trinity Church. He had performed the *Six Pièces* at Saint Clotilde. There he had moved Liszt himself, who publicly compared him to Bach. Together with Saint-Saëns and others, he had founded a fraternity of composers, the Société Nationale de Musique, to promote the works of Frenchmen, earnest works orchestral and chamber. At its first concert, he had seen one of his Trios acclaimed. A few months later, he had conducted parts of his revised oratorio *Ruth* and been as warmly applauded. Still, opponents pointed out that he had never won a *premier prix* in organ. His brother Joseph, who had, remained the better known. Joseph campaigned against him.

Franck was backed by Saint-Saëns, who had been offered the post but declined, and by Théodore Dubois, who had been a loyal colleague at Saint Clotilde, and by Cavaillé-Coll. "Franck had great ability," remarked Saint-Saëns twenty-five years after Franck's death, "and it was I who took steps to find room for it to grow, and gave him the chance to stop wasting his time in mere teaching and devote himself to writing. Genius needs more than just ability to develop." Nothing disproves Saint-Saëns's claim, though we know that his memories are at times self-serving and his feelings for Franck were mixed. We may take it that Saint-Saëns, like Dubois and Cavaillé-Coll, argued Franck's cause before the director of the school, Ambroise Thomas, and that Thomas, who may well have thought the matter unimportant, made the choice.

In any case, Franck's appointment bred strife. By custom, as we saw, the organ course trained musicians for the choir lofts; it centered on improvisation and plainsong, not on composition properly so called. Franck, however, led by his conception of the improvisatory art, *de facto* taught his pupils to compose. This, together with the popularity of the composition lessons he gave privately, encroached on the domain of the composition professors, some of whom found his offense insufferable because he expounded a style adverse to their own.

They found in his origins a handy excuse on which to peg their dislike. In the early years of his tenure, when French pride had recently been shattered by Prussian arms, some of such colleagues denounced his art and his person as Germanic, therefore odious. It did not help matters that he confessed to liking Wagner—with reservations—at a time when conservative musicians looked on the idiom of *Tristan* as a virulent intellectual poison. And when eventually Franck's pupils began to excel as composers, and leapt to defend the master by insolent words that mixed art with religion, class, and politics, dislike grew to hatred. This Franck's kindliness did nothing to assuage. His modesty itself offended some, because they could feel behind it the cast-iron will of the great creator who brooks no interference, knowing he is right.

Enmity did not turn Franck from his path. To the end of his life he would be found three times a week—typically on Tuesday, Thursday, and Saturday mornings from eight o'clock to ten o'clock—confronting the dilapidated organ that had served Benoist for half a century. Equipped with but twenty pedals, half of its dozen stops free reeds, it stood between two rooms and spoke into both—a recital hall on one side, classroom on the other. Nobody cared to recollect who had built the lackluster thing. Yet Franck could draw from the students who played it music aspiring to the sublime.

He would enter by the back door, a spring in his step, in aspect always the same: frock coat, gray trousers, tall hat, an umbrella hooked over his left arm or dragged behind him. He would invariably arrive early. While waiting, he would sit down at the wretched organ and improvise. If eight o'clock struck and no one appeared, he would go in search of his delinquents, some of whom he might find in a nearby room listening to a lecture of Massenet's. Franck would open the door (he and Massenet were on cordial terms) and ask in his heavy voice, which was loud but not unpleasant: "Isn't there anyone for me?" or: "Won't one of you gentlemen come to my room a moment, just to keep me company?"

As a rule, he spent little time on technique or repertory, though he did introduce his pupils to the works of Bach, Handel, Boëly, Schumann, and Mendelssohn. Rather, he would devote five of the six weekly hours to improvisation, in large part to the sonata-allegro form known as *thème libre*.

The *thème libre* had been introduced into the organ course in 1842–43, and was more freely structured at first than it became by the end of the century. But it was freer only by comparison. As Ann Labounsky Steele explains, it came to be codified as a hybrid ternary form treated very strictly indeed. It "contained elements of both a sonata allegro and an andante. Based on a single theme, the exposition included four phrases in the main key, two of which were slightly modified and heard in the relative and subdominant. A bridge based on a motive from the theme led to two statements in the dominant. The development used two additional contrasting motives from the theme entitled rhythmic and lyrical which were eventually combined. The recapitulation in the main key was shorter than the exposition and reintroduced the bridge motive."

In order that the pupil improvising a *thème libre* could wholly attend to style and content, Franck himself would pull the stops, work the ventils, and manage the swell box. Never would he halt a pupil working out a theme. Instead, he would hurl advice. *Modulate!* he would cry. *Now some flat keys . . . Now some sharp keys . . . Now back to the tonic . . . I don't like that at all! . . . Ah, that was good . . . I like that!* His "I like it!" was coveted praise. Its recipient would beam with pride.

Franck was the soul of patience, but on occasion, as we saw, even he grew exasperated. He would tap his foot with increasing violence, and if goaded beyond forbearance shout *No! No!* and fling a book across the room. He would at once relent, apologizing abjectly for his loss of control.

More typically, he would put his hand over the pupil's and take hold of one note and then another till by degrees he came to be sitting in the pupil's place, teaching by example the deftness in counterpoint that was his special delight. His deftness was of mind rather than of hands and feet, since he was no virtuoso; the persuasiveness of his playing grew from the beauty of his thought.

In this way he raised up a group of composers noteworthy for seriousness and competence, among them Lekeu, Castillon, Ropartz, Bréville, Chausson, Bordes, d'Indy, Duparc, Pierné, Tournemire, and Vierne. And though each man stood unique in aptitude and intent, each has come to be linked with the others in the group posterity calls the Franckists.

Some were pupils in the organ class, though only a few became professional organists. Some worked with Franck privately. Some studied for years. Some took but one or two lessons. Others were not his pupils, but felt his influence nevertheless: Bizet, for instance, who audited Franck's class when already a master himself. And some of the pupils, of whom Debussy was one, mixed respect with irritation. Yet nothing could undo Franck's influence.

Overall, that influence grew so strong that Franck and Berlioz are sometimes said to be the two determinative figures in French music of the nineteenth century. As to the organ, the *Six Pièces* were in the strict sense epoch-making: they set precedents on which others would build.

⚜ 4 ⚜

Charles-Marie Widor

AS NOTED ABOVE, THE YOUNG CAVAILLÉ-COLL
traveled abroad in the autumn of 1844 to examine organs and meet
their builders. During his stay in Alsace, where he shared with
Joseph Callinet a particularly amiable bottle of champagne and
some pleasant hours of shoptalk, he met, perhaps not for the first
time, Jean Widor, Charles-Marie's grandfather, who had long been
Callinet's employee and confidant. Jean Widor took him on a tour
of the Callinet workrooms and warehouses, and escorted him, at
five o'clock in the morning, to his train. Friendship was to link
Cavaillé-Coll's art with three generations of the Widor family.

Jean Widor was apparently of Hungarian descent, but it was
from Switzerland that he had emigrated, near the turn of the century, to Alsace. At Rouffach he first worked for François Callinet,
then for Callinet's son and successor. In 1806 Jean Widor married
Anne-Marie-Eve Frey, of Rouffach. Their third child, François-
Charles, the composer's father, was born in 1811, the same year as
Cavaillé-Coll.

By about 1834, when the Cavaillé-Coll firm moved to Paris,
François-Charles too had gone to work for Callinet. Greatly gifted
at music, he learned not only to build organs but also to play them.

And when in 1838 son and father traveled to Lyon to erect an organ at the Church of Saint François de Sales, an organ whose compass of four manuals and forty-eight stops betokens the importance of the parish, the Lyonnais were so taken with the youth that they offered him the post of organist. He was a good musician and devout too, they declared, and he understood what church music ought to be. François-Charles long remained in the post, and won prominence as a teacher and performer. He played for the first time in Paris—the *Revue et Gazette musicale* praised him warmly—in the year Cavaillé-Coll visited Alsace.

That year is memorable in other respects. In 1844 the Peters firm began to publish the organ works of Bach, few of which had theretofore appeared in print. It issued an Urtext edition, by Friedrich Konrad Griepenkerl, whose prefaces acquainted contemporary musicians with Bach's neglected ways. The volumes' distinctive green covers were to adorn many a French console, and over the decades to mark the rise in France, not solely among organists, of a veritable Bach cult.

In Paris, the year 1844 saw Bach's advent as well in Adolph Friedrich Hesse's performances. The most celebrated of these took place on 18 June before a huge crowd at Saint Eustache. Invited to inaugurate an organ of four manuals and seventy-eight ranks, in company with Benoist, Fessy, Boëly, and Lefébure-Wély, Hesse carried to France a style he had learned from Rinck, who had been trained by Kittel, who had been trained by Bach himself. Taut, polyphonic, its *sine qua non* the independent pedal, Bach's style as exemplified by Hesse comprised steady rhythm, moderate tempo, period registration, and a legato touch. Notable for its clarity and dignity and for the practitioner's calm deportment, such playing, classical in more than one sense, had largely vanished from Germany. It had never, as we saw, prevailed in France.

By that June evening Cavaillé-Coll had doubtless caught a glimpse of his future path, reform having been talked of for years. But most listeners, lacking his perspicacity, and still accustomed to organists who played airs and depicted battles, relished Fessy's or Lefébure-Wély's art and found Hesse's intolerably boring.

A few who found it significant, however, endeavored to sway opinion. "Of note was the appearance that the German organ school made in the person of M. Hesse," wrote Stephen Morelot in the *Revue et Gazette musical*. "This heir to the traditions of the school of Bach, whose famous Toccata in F he played with so much verve, dazzles, as a player, by the dexterity with which he treats the *pedal* part, which we in France have long viewed as an unimportant accessory. . . . The German school, so little known among us, and which sends us so worthy an interpreter, seems to have attained a perfection to be hardly surpassed." Again: "He is a giant," wrote Berlioz in the *Journal des Débats*. "He plays with the feet as many another would be hard put to it to play with the hands."

Spurred on by such publicists, reform had so far advanced by half a dozen years later, when Hesse's pupil Lemmens first played in Paris, that the style Hesse propounded had begun to be lauded by some as the "Pure Tradition of Bach." The phrase itself was coined later still, and it of course greatly oversimplified; reason suggests that Bach's playing must have been not single in intention and manner but manifold, and we saw above that no tradition endures without change, however subtle and unintended. But the phrase named ideas that came to serve as the base for a new construction.

And this being so, the year 1844 is memorable for the birth, in Lyon, on 21 February, of the composer and teacher who, more than anyone, saw to it that new structures rose from that foundation. For not just in his own playing and composing did Charles-Marie Widor take Bach as a standard. With single-mindedness second to none he caused Bach to be revered by a line of young musicians, masters in their turn.

Charles-Marie Widor was born to François-Charles Widor and Françoise-Elisabeth Peiron. Mme. Widor was related to the famous Montgolfier family of manufacturers—granted a peerage by Louis XVI—among whose scions were Joseph-Michel and Jacques-Etienne, the inventors of the hot air balloon. The motto "Soar Above," which Widor was to print in English at the head of his scores, may recall something more than merely his philosophy of art.

He studied the piano and the organ with his father. By age eleven, Charles-Marie had become an assistant at Saint François de Sales and the organist for his school. There he played a two-manual Callinet built by Joseph's younger brother, Claude-Ignace.

A visit by the family's now eminent friend set the course of Widor's life, and with it the course of French organ music. "It was always a festive occasion," Widor was to tell Dupré, "whenever M. Cavaillé-Coll, passing through Lyon, was the guest of my parents. I was fourteen years old when at table one day he said something like this: 'After Charles-Marie finishes school, he must go and study in Brussels with the great organist Lemmens. I shall introduce him. I have already sent him young Guilmant, from Boulogne-sur-Mer, who is so gifted he can sight-read a piece of Bach's, playing hands and feet at once!'"

· 2 ·

Jacques-Nicolas Lemmens had come to know the old ways early on. At the Brussels Conservatory he studied the organ with Christian Friedrich Johann Girschner, formerly of Berlin, and counterpoint and fugue with the director of the school, François-Joseph Fétis, himself an organist, historian, and reformer. Lemmens won a first prize in piano (1842), second prize in composition (1844), and first prizes in composition and in organ (1845), and became Fétis's protégé.

Deeming the cultivation of "good" organists as great a want in Belgium as in France, and deeming Lemmens a sapling ideal for nurture, Fétis obtained a government grant that enabled Lemmens to spend several months (1846–47) with Hesse. Fétis's putative plans were nearly foiled, however, when Hesse conceived an implacable dislike for Lemmens—who was not, it must be admitted, the most likable of men. But Lemmens stayed in Germany long enough to master Hesse's principles and to be heard once or twice in public, and these credentials, together with his own ambition and Fétis's indomitable will, sufficed to see him appointed (1849) professor of organ at the Brussels Conservatory.

It remains one of history's pleasantries that a pupil whom Hesse disliked became of all his pupils the most influential. Lemmens helped to train a succession of organists—Widor and Guilmant were only two—who spread Hesse's doctrines afar. And with the result we noted, Lemmens convinced Cavaillé-Coll that Bach's music deserved special regard and for its performance needed special kinds of tone, special kinds of manual and pedal. The reform that culminated in the music of the French masters in a sense owed everything to Lemmens.

It accordingly owed a debt to his patron. François-Joseph Fétis had by the late 1840s taught counterpoint at the Paris Conservatory, taken charge of its library, become a leading critic, tasted success as a composer, and published many books and treatises besides the massive *Biographie universelle des musiciens* that gained him his chief fame. Before moving to Brussels to head the conservatory and become court musician to King Leopold, Fétis had in addition founded and edited the *Revue musicale* (after 1835 the *Revue et Gazette musicale*) and, driven by a passion for old musics, used its pages to urge reform. Thanks to his forcefulness, erudition, and connections, he wielded about as much power in France as in Belgium, and when, soon after Lemmens's conservatory appointment, he asked Cavaillé-Coll to help him introduce Lemmens to Paris, the builder obliged out of business acumen as much as out of good will. He wrote to Fétis on 21 May 1850:

> I hastened, sir, to do what I could to further your plans, not only by placing at M. Lemmens's disposal the organs at Saint Denis, the Madeleine, and the Panthémont that we built, and the one at Saint Roch that we restored, but also by making it possible for him to inspect the works of our colleagues. . . . Though brief,

M. Lemmens's visit to Paris did not go unremarked. Our finest organists . . . hastened to offer him their instruments. . . .

Allow me also to thank you for the interest you kindly accord us in your report to the Academy of Fine Arts, about which M. Lemmens informed me, and in which you bring our name to the notice of the government. . . .

Though I should like to have been able to arrange a public *audition* by M. Lemmens, the same obstacle that prevents this sort of *audition* in Belgium is met with similarly in Paris. . . . I must add that we were nevertheless permitted to hear him four times at the organ of the Madeleine (at three weddings and at the high mass on Pentecost) and . . . in several other *auditions* at the Protestant church of the Panthémont. Finally, at a small party given by M. Lefébure at his home, Ambroise Thomas, Adolphe Adam, Stamaty, L. Lacombe, d'Ortigue, H. Prévost, and Danjou, who happened to be in Paris, heard this learned artist and were not less happy than we were to compliment M. Lemmens on his clear and marvelous playing of the great masters, no less than on the scientific originality of his admirable compositions.

When two years later Cavaillé-Coll arranged for Lemmens to perform at Saint Vincent de Paul, the progressives among the invited guests saw Lemmens as symbol and embodiment of the classical art. His Bach, as Widor would later assert, was nothing less than a revelation to all the artists and amateurs of Paris. What is more, they agreed that Lemmens *qua* composer raised the classical art to perfection by infusing its dry forms with emotion. Rossini himself concurred in this, proclaiming Lemmens's compositions to possess both head and heart. So did Joseph d'Ortigue, alert and discriminating as ever: "Do you want to know why Lemmens's appearance among us was an important historical fact . . . ? It is because Lemmens knew how, without relinquishing anything of what constitutes classical style, to wrap modern genius in ancient garb, as it were, wonderfully uniting severity and grace, seriousness and charm, work and imagination, the constraints of formula and the free play of idea."

Retrospect, it is true, would apply these words more justly to the compositions of Lemmens's successors; his skill and originality seem at best mediocre when compared to Vierne's, say, or Widor's or Dupré's. But such was the breadth of his reputation that his admirers were to be counted, in d'Ortigue's view, "among the austere and somewhat opinionated defenders of the old scholastic traditions, and among the avowed partisans of the modern school. He is the link between two august schools that make up, when all is said and done, but one school." As to Lemmens the interpreter, we recognize the superficiality of his penetration when we learn that he held most of Bach's music to be devoid of religious sentiment. Indeed, he not only shared Saint-Saëns's belief that Bach's Protestant spirit was out of place in Catholic liturgies, but in general found Bach satisfying only cerebrally and digitally. To Lemmens, and for long to Widor, Bach's counterpoints appeared untouched by the poetic, the descriptive, the impassioned.

But as technician and teacher, Lemmens was second to none.

· 3 ·

Charles-Marie Widor was in his late teens when in 1863 he studied for several months with Lemmens privately. He recalls taking an organ lesson each evening and, with Fétis, a counterpoint lesson each morning. Widor spent his days working at his keyboards or his writing table, his routine so strenuous that he saw nothing of Brussels but the park he crossed going to his lessons.

The effect on him of Lemmens's personality and ideas we have in Widor's own words, penned years later. To begin with: "Not a person who heard Lemmens will forget the lucidity, the strength, the grandeur of his playing: the smallest details given weight, but always in proportion with the piece as a whole. . . . Lemmens played with nobility, clarity, and ease." His agility looked the more astonishing for his height and powerful build. "One thought of an animal tamer confronting the beast . . . : classic posture, knees and ankles together, player motionless, hands and feet near as possible to the keys . . . the minimum of movement." To Widor, Lemmens seemed the apotheosis of sovereign control.

Not alone in the physical was control absolute, but also in the interpretive; and as Lemmens played, so he taught. Widor continues: "The ideal of foolish youth is speed. Just when I believed my playing attained that ideal perfectly, profound disappointment. 'Worthless,' he said. 'Mechanical. Lacks will.' What did he mean by 'will'? I dared not ask him. But I came to see. It is the art of the orator, his authority that makes itself felt through the serenity, order, and proportioning of the discourse. With us musicians it is by means of rhythm that the will chiefly manifests itself: a player piano holds our interest no longer than the ticking of a clock; we do not listen to it; whereas the mastery of a Liszt or a Rubinstein, *who did not play fast* [emphasis Widor's], moved everyone. Such was Lemmens's authority at the organ."

His registrations were as discreet as his tempos. Be on guard, Lemmens was to write, "against the constant changing of stops that is a singular abuse nowadays. Modern building has enriched the organ with myriad devices for changing timbres, and . . . many organists sacrifice thought and feeling to material effects." And as regards church music broadly speaking: "The organist mistakes his function if he neglects to observe the specific mood of each service. Catholic ceremonies have each their own essential character; the good organist will not fail to make his effects accord with the feelings the Church means to evoke by her liturgy."

But it was in execution above all that Lemmens brought Widor to see, as he himself had been brought by Girschner, Fétis, and Hesse to see, that certain precepts must be scrupulously obeyed. This was so because in one essential the organ's nature remained constant down the centuries: to wit, a key once pressed, tone did not vary. From this self-evident fact everything derived.

The agogic principle necessarily ruled supreme. And because subtleties of accent and phrasing could be conveyed only by the adjustment of durations, it followed that every adjustment must be precise, that in precision alone lay any hope of nuance. "To detach a note from its neighbor," Lemmens therefore maintained, one should "create between them a rest equal to half the first note's value." He insisted as strongly that the release of a note or chord be no less precise than the attack. And he enjoined such quasi-mathematical exactitude for the sake not just of nuance but also of rhythm and clarity, both of which it enhanced a thousandfold.

Such exactitude could not be perceived, let alone convey meaning, except against a background of legato touch—the release of a key at the moment the next key was pressed. Because one tone was exchanged for another with neither overlap nor break, planned breaks stood out in high relief, hence accents could be "placed" and nuance tell.

Lemmens's convictions became Widor's, the more firmly held with experience and reflection. Lemmens's legato especially, to which a characteristic control of mechanicals and durations was inseparably allied, Widor found systematic, exact, and the fruit not of intuition but of reason. It thus concurred with the homage Widor came to pay, in common with many others of his day and class, to anything even remotely scientific—"science" then connoting clarity, simplicity, rigor, skepticism, hypothesis and tested truth, and a dozen other things considered estimable. In a word, Lemmens's convictions gratified Widor's taste for the neatly methodical, and their audible results complemented, by the objectivity that was their natural concomitant, Widor's aversion from feelings indecorously displayed. Naturally, then, it was on these convictions that Widor grounded his playing, improvising, composing, teaching, his very conception of the organ. He deemed these convictions the self-evident basis of rational technique.

This being the case, Widor naturally took Lemmens's legato for Bach's own. Did not rational thought decree legato touch to be ideally suited to the organ? And was not Bach the peerless rationalist?

Actually, Widor's inference may have come closer to the truth than one might suspect. History tells us that fidelity to Bach's legato set Bach's pupils apart from their contemporaries. What history does not unequivocally show is whether Bach's legato joined tones together with neither break nor overlap, and whether it varied from work to work, though we may confidently presume its being articulate in every sense of the word. But true or false, the belief that Lemmens's legato and Bach's were identical shaped Widor's understanding, hence his teachings and compositions, hence the thought, the teachings, the compositions of his pupils. So it was that Dupré, the most influential pupil of all, honored the "Pure Tradition of Bach" as dogma incontestable.

But this culmination lay in the future, when on his return to France in the early 1860s young Widor began to draw notice.

· 4 ·

"Your excellent pupil," Cavaillé-Coll wrote to Lemmens on 3 August 1863, "spent a few days with me and reminded me of the pleasant times we had together during your first visit to Paris. He told me a good deal about the interest you have taken in him and the fine instruction he received. . . . I arranged for him to be heard . . . in a session at Saint Sulpice." There Widor played an andante of his own, together with works by Lemmens, Handel, Bach, and Hesse, perhaps dreaming the while that that magnificent new organ might someday be his. Two years later (8 March 1865) Cavaillé-Coll wrote to Lemmens: "I spent a week in Lyon with your pupil Widor, who works prodigies at his organ and his piano. He will be coming to spend April with us in Paris."

It was thanks to Cavaillé-Coll that by the end of the decade young Widor had performed in Portugal and England and widely in France, had garnered praise from important journals, and had been presented to celebrated artists. Liszt, Benoist, Lefébure-Wély, Gounod, and Thomas received him kindly. Saint-Saëns and Rossini took a special liking to him. All seem to have thought his abilities transcendent, his manners and family connections admirable, his looks magnetic. Widor irresistibly charmed the fair sex, one may add, and was irresistibly charmed in return. He more than once spent an evening at the opera oblivious of the stage because distracted by bare shoulders in the audience.

He attended chic salons, sometimes playing the piano, sometimes conversing, always made welcome by his gift for repartee. "Madam," he was later to entreat an ill-tempered viscountess, the daughter of an industrialist, "dare I ask you to mingle in your conversation a trace of that sugar which your father manufactures so well?" He made friends with painters, writers, sculptors, philosophers, politicians, scientists. He conceived a passion for history and architecture, the greater for his love of Paris, the city as rich in antiquity and monument as it was in artistic and intellectual debate.

At the hands of Baron Haussmann, Paris had recently been undergoing the renovation and expansion that turned her into the jewel later ages would treasure, and it was in keeping with the panache of the new *grands boulevards* that Widor lived and breathed—and dressed. Not for him the conservative black of the church musician, still less the shabby-genteel look of Franck. Widor sported an elegant blue suit, dappled tie, soft hat, and walking stick.

Like Saint-Saëns, to whom Widor's classical bent was as commendable as his aristocratic manners, Widor came to regard Franck with mixed admiration and puzzlement. The occasional meeting was genial, in any case, at Cavaillé-Coll's workshop and elsewhere. In 1866, Franck included young Widor among the invited guests at a private *audition* given at Saint Clotilde before Liszt. In 1868, Franck and Widor, together with Saint-Saëns and others, opened the organ at Notre Dame, the cathedral lately restored, the occasion the most glittering of galas. In 1869, Franck and Widor, together with Saint-Saëns and others, opened the organ at Trinity Church, where Franck's improvising moved Widor unforgettably; it surpassed in theme, form, and development, he said years later, anything Franck wrote down.

Widor had meantime been writing music of his own. By the end of the decade he had composed chamber works, duos for harmonium and piano, and pieces for piano solo. Some works he had seen into print, some he had heard performed. His career as virtuoso and composer was thus already well launched when in Christmas week of 1869, while substituting at the Madeleine for Saint-Saëns, he learned of the death of Lefébure-Wély, the organist at Saint Sulpice. Cavaillé-Coll, in Dupré's version of events, happened to be present when the news came. He nudged Widor and murmured: "I'm thinking."

Accounts vary, but it is clear that Cavaillé-Coll resolved to see Widor succeed to the post, stayed firm in this resolve even after Franck decided to apply, and prevailed against odds when a group of organists—of the second rank, he pointed out—denounced his meddling and Widor's inexperience. Among the likely cavils: Widor was a mere boy from the provinces; he had never matriculated at the Paris Conservatory; the eminent post, once occupied by such figures as Clérambault and the Séjans, ought to be filled by competition rather than by arbitrary choice else a bad precedent would be set; and so on. In the end, the outcries were sufficiently loud, and the vestry sufficiently divided, that the curé of Saint Sulpice could do no more than name Widor temporary organist and grant a year's trial. Even the public prints, which might have been expected to trumpet the appointment, maintained a discreet reserve. They published scarcely more than the bare fact when, in January 1870, he took up his duties.

Came a stroke of good fortune for Widor, though calamity for his homeland. By the time his trial year was up, France and Germany were at war; the Second Empire had fallen; besieged Paris lay victim to famine and cold, Saint Sulpice to bombardment. Widor himself had taken up arms as an officer in the artillery, though granted leave to ride back from the lines on Sundays. In the tumult of invasion and of subsequent civil war, the authorities quite forgot the terms of his employment. Its anniversary came and went, unnoticed by anyone but him.

For his part, he was only too glad to keep silent. And he did not venture to complain of the oversight when the post was never made permanent. Widor, who in his old age loved nothing so much as telling a good story, would cheerfully remark that he had been temporary organist for more than sixty-three years.

· 5 ·

To preside over that amphitheater of a console (as he called it) and command the hundred stops, unique in finesse, of Cavaillé-Coll's largest masterwork, to be required to supply week after week music befitting the size and fame of Saint Sulpice, the opulence of her liturgy, and the eminence of predecessors, to take on such an office at age twenty-five, doubtful of tenure and amid the ill will of colleagues—all this must have daunted anyone of less intrepid self-confidence than Widor. That he felt immediately at home bears witness to the strength of his character and the scope of his talent.

No doubt the Saint Sulpice organ became his inspiration and bulwark. It inspired uniquely, because of its design and setting, and more peremptorily than he might have expected. Like Franck and Saint-Saëns, Widor did not think of himself as an organist first of all. The ballet and the opera, besides the chamber, orchestral, and solo idioms, fired his imagination in themselves and, since he was ambitious, by their worldly prospects too. This being so, Cavaillé-Coll's royal instrument directed him into unforeseen paths: "Had I not felt the allure of these timbres, the mystical spell cast by these waves of sound, I would not have composed for the organ."

He wasted no time. Although certain movements predate his appointment, Widor, by about the end of 1871, had dispatched to the publisher no fewer than four of his eventual ten organ symphonies. The four appeared in 1872 as opus 13, and revealed a proficiency that was startling in a young composer at grips with a new form.

For in truth the organ symphony was invented by Widor, not by Franck. Its type is indeed Franck's "Grande Pièce symphonique," which Widor heard played in 1866 or earlier, and Franck's work and Widor's works resemble each other in being multipartite and secular. The works resemble each other as well in their essential gravity: their solemn moments evoke in receptive listeners images of kingly rite in vast and ancient rooms; even the introspective and the effervescent passages impart a feeling of dignity and occasion. But the two masters greatly differ.

To begin with, though Franck and Widor each devised music deeply spiritual and intensely felt, Widor's embodies an intellectual discipline unlike anything Franck might have achieved or have wished to achieve. In a way, Widor is to music as the Realists are to prose: the observer who with stunning intensity gives voice to human strivings, but who remains all the while—tries to remain—detached and unobtrusive. This objectivity leaves Widor's symphonies at once ardent and stern, passionate and disinterested. Franck, by comparison, is as lyrical as Hugo and as warmly intimate as Chopin.

In design, Franck's "Grande Pièce symphonique" is cyclical, the appearance of themes in more than one movement giving rise to a characteristic unity and coherence, and Franck takes as model a sonata form, which he alters and abbreviates. The Widor symphony, on the contrary, is a set of pieces that are more or less freely structured and more or less closely interconnected, a set whose unity and coherence come from studied contrasts among the parts.

This is tantamount to calling them suites. But as we learn from John R. Near, Widor's editor and biographer, only the first four symphonies so qualify. Their unity springs from variety: Widor places beside such old patterns as the fugue, prelude, and toccata such character pieces as the pastorale, march, and scherzo, inflecting around a well-defined key center the rhythms, tone colors, and moods of the component movements. The remaining symphonies, *per contra,* display unity more nearly like that of the symphony for orchestra; their linking is more refined, their plan more spacious. In addition, their virtuosity is at the same time precise in the manner of Bach, transcendental in the manner of Liszt; sweeping gesture is at one with minute articulation.

Franck and Widor differ in other ways. Franck does not so much develop his themes as transform and juxtapose them; Widor's are developed with subtlety and complexity that grow with the passage of years. Both men ply a virtuoso technique. But Widor's technique elaborates Lemmens's agility, precision, and articulateness, whereas Franck's technique is less refined. And Franck's pedaling, for all his practice, never matched Widor's in unconstraint. Lastly, both men employ Cavaillé-Coll's timbres. But Franck orchestrates in broad strokes, Widor in more delicate hues.

"Orchestrate" is apposite, since Cavaillé-Coll's organs provided a range of timbre that each composer expressly likened to the orchestra's. But "orchestral" and "symphonic" and their cognates did not offer to Franck's or Widor's mind the same cluster of ideas they offer to ours. For example, both men took "symphonic" to imply seriousness of purpose as well as resemblance of media. Indeed, the former connotation, which largely vanished before the century was out, seems to have been by far the stronger.

"Orchestral" and "symphonic" were as yet innocent, moreover, of troublesome connotations they acquired after electricity changed the course of organ building. Not till the 1920s did these words begin to connote the gigantic organ that was voiced on explosive wind-pressure, that purposely imitated orchestral timbres only, and that debased the "authentic" organ's nature and traditions by emitting from cramped chambers and ill-chosen locales nothing but tone deplorably opaque.

Such an organ more frequently existed in imagination than actuality—Robert Hope-Jones's instruments perhaps came nearest its realization—and little resembled the good organs with which it came to be confounded. But reaction against it, the more vehement for being linked with the neo-classical revolt described above, became as widespread as the revolt itself, and bred consequences as irrational. Misconception, made doubly harmful by polemic, led players to assume greater likeness of media than Franck or Widor had had in mind. "Orchestral" and "symphonic" lost all hope of clear meaning, and their use as pejoratives added to the confusion. As often as not, by the latter twentieth century, the masters' music was performed in timbres appropriate to Karg-Elert or to Böhm.

The fact is Franck and Widor well knew that the organ and the orchestra require dissimilar treatments. In the preface to later editions of his symphonies, Widor was at pains to say why. He begins by remarking that before 1839 the organ's tones were black and white: foundations and mixtures. The former were mainly used for slow movements, the latter for fast. There were few reeds and no swell boxes. Then, thanks primarily to Cavaillé-Coll, came "the feasibility of detaining a whole division in an acoustic prison opened or closed at will, the freedom to mix timbres, the means of gradually intensifying or reducing them, the independence of rhythms, sureness of attacks, balance of contrasts—in sum, a whole blossoming of wondrous colors, a rich palette of the most diverse tones: harmonic flutes, gambes, bassons, English horns, trompettes, voix célestes, foundations and reeds of a quality and variety unknown till then. Such is the modern organ, essentially symphonic."

A new instrument, he continues, demands a new language, a language befitting a mechanism whose limitations require that expression be achieved indirectly. "Whereas orchestral strings or winds, the piano, and the voices hold sway by virtue of accent and suddenness of attack, the organ, clothed in its primordial majesty, speaks like a philosopher. It alone can indefinitely maintain the same volume of sound, and in this way express the idea of the sacred and the infinite. Quick attacks and accents are not native to it. They are lent to it. They are accents by adoption. All of which suffices to indicate the tact and discrimination their use entails, and indicate also to what extent the symphony for organ differs from the symphony for orchestra. No confusion need be feared. One will never write for the orchestra in the same way as for the organ. But from now on, one will have to be as careful managing tone color in an organ work as in an orchestral."

By the mid-1880s when he wrote those lines, Widor was well

qualified to make the comparison, having long studied the history, fabrication, and use of the orchestral instruments. He was to become so learned in the subject, that when the publishers of Berlioz's epoch-making treatise decided a new edition with supplement was in order, they entrusted it to him. Nor was his knowledge just theoretical. Quick in writing music, endlessly self-critical in revising it, Widor had by the mid-1880s put his knowledge of the orchestra to use in a tone-poem, two symphonies, two operas, a ballet, and concertos for violin, piano, and cello.

· 6 ·

Widor delighted in other tasks than composing. He founded and directed a chorus, the Concordia Society, perhaps urged on by hearing the choir of men and boys at Saint Sulpice. It shows the breadth of his outlook that at a time when fanatical patriotism possessed many colleagues, the Concordia performed not only music by Frenchmen but also such works as Haydn's *Seasons*, Mendelssohn's *Athalia*, and Bach's *Saint Matthew Passion*. Widor directed his chorus for nearly ten years, and to accompany it founded an orchestra. His zest for conducting was unconquerable. When critics pointed out shortcomings—like Saint-Saëns he evinced less skill on the podium than at the console—he happily paid no heed. He conducted German, Swiss, and English orchestras as well as French, enjoying himself hugely the while.

He began to write criticism, in this too resembling Saint-Saëns, though less prone to mix acid with ink. A determined reformer who held fast to his convictions, Widor was an able and a persuasive writer. His many articles, books, and letters reveal more plainly the professional than the inward man, as one would expect; it is fortunate that the memoirs he began to dictate in his old age, which were viewed with disfavor by his wife and abandoned, have been retrieved by John R. Near's devoted scholarship and are to figure in a forthcoming biography.

In the latter years of the century, however, composing remained his chief pursuit. Experienced, mature, and in full command of his powers, Widor now composed some of his finest works. Incidental music for half a dozen stage productions, pieces for solo piano, and songs appear in company with the Fantasy for Piano and Orchestra, Piano Quartet, Piano Quintet, Symphony for Organ and Orchestra, Introduction and Rondo for Clarinet and Piano, Chorale and Variations for Harp and Orchestra, and the most accomplished of his works for organ.

In 1887 Widor published as opus 42 his fifth and sixth organ symphonies, written in 1878–79, and his seventh and eighth, written in 1885–87. He meant the long and intricate Eighth Symphony to be his last in the form, but his synesthetic view of music and architecture, together with journeys to open two superb organs, helped spur him to write the "Gothique" and "Romane" symphonies issued respectively in 1895 and 1900. The "Gothique" took inspiration from Saint Ouen de Rouen, which boasted a Cavaillé-Coll that Widor specially admired and a structure that Ruskin hails as the finest example of Gothic style. The "Romane" took as glowing inspiration from the Cavaillé-Coll organ and the Romanesque lines at Saint Sernin de Toulouse.

The melody and rhythm of plainsong inform the last two symphonies, Widor having become convinced, as he remarked at the time to Schweitzer, that except for some of Bach's preludes and fugues no organ art was holy which was not consecrated to the Church by its themes, whether plainsong or chorale. Till then, Widor seems only casually to have distinguished secular music from sacred: he had assigned as titles to the movements of the earlier symphonies designations of tempo, mood, or form, rather than such epithets as "Meditation," "Communion," or "Offertory"; had given the première of the Sixth Symphony at the Trocadéro, a secular hall some accounted the more unchristian for its stars, crescents, and turrets; and had echoed in his harmony Wagner's earthy progressions. (Widor admired *Tristan,* attended at Bayreuth the world première of the "Ring," and early became the Wagnerite he remained.)

Yet Widor often played the movements of his symphonies as voluntaries at Saint Sulpice, and so the designation of sacred or secular is moot. In the end he may well have believed, with his spiritual son Dupré, who emulated him in all things, that the "contemplation of beauty is a form of contemplation of God. Beauty, art, is an approach to God, a path to Him." This ancient idea would have been congenial to Widor's cultivated mind, which would have held as well that even the most worldly artist enlists, if only inadvertently, in the service of the divine.

It is noteworthy that in getting his music performed Widor seems not to have met such consistent opposition as hindered Saint-Saëns and Franck. More likable than the former, more worldly-wise than the latter, he had a knack for diplomacy and a positive genius for friendship, gifts that sometimes helped him overcome the rebuffs of impresarios and the jealousies of colleagues. Further, though pretentiousness annoyed him beyond bearing ("Pity a composer as intelligent as d'Indy isn't musical!"), and though, as we shall see, inapt comment gained him Fauré's displeasure and others', Widor customarily treated fellow artists with uncommon sensitivity. He more than once remained friends with both sides of wrangling factions—a feat, as we saw, in the politicized cultural life of Paris. Partly for these reasons, his works received capable performance and favorable review, and his reputation continued to grow. Probably no one was surprised when at the Opera his ballet *La Korrigane* achieved a triumph, or that the work eventually ran to some hundred and forty performances.

If we credit Flaubert's sardonic view that the public is eternally half-witted, cosmopolitan acclaim mattered much less than a compliment Widor received from Franck. Self-effacing as ever, but still badgered by his family to seek wealth in the theater, Franck too had been writing a ballet. He admired *La Korrigane* enough to bring his own work to Widor's apartment, play it on the piano, and modestly ask the advice of a colleague younger than he by twenty-two years.

⚔ 5 ⚔

Louis Vierne

IN THE EIGHTEEN YEARS REMAINING TO HIM after his appointment to the Paris Conservatory, César Franck composed the masterworks that brought him posterity's acclaim. But the Violin Sonata, *Variations symphoniques*, Piano Quintet, String Quartet, and Symphony in D Minor drew by and large only perfunctory notice from contemporaries. He was so lightly regarded that a full seventy years could pass and Schweitzer "still remember what a stir the *Trois Chorals* made. . . . Franck was a wonderful improviser, but no one expected from him so great a work."

But the *Trois Chorals* were published posthumously. Such repute as Franck knew in his lifetime came chiefly from his friends' proselytizing and from the traditive honors of his posts. It was not the composer whom the state decorated with the cross of the Legion of Honor, but the civil servant. It was not tribute to his art that impelled the Société National de Musique to make him president, but machinations designed to eject Saint-Saëns. And from cradle to grave Franck repeatedly fell victim to a sort of melancholy bungling. This was typified when in 1887 former pupils arranged a concert of his works. They had intended it to be a festival. But inept conducting and want of rehearsal yielded renditions that mortified everyone. Everyone, that is, but Franck. "No, children," d'Indy reports him saying, with a gentle smile, "you are too hard to please. I, for one, was very happy."

In the end, six months before he died, a work of his did gain apt recognition: the String Quartet received at its première long and insistent applause. Only when he was pushed reluctant to the stage, and found the cheering aimed unmistakably at himself, did Franck realize it was not meant for the performers.

The next day he doubtless resumed a routine whose pace neither recognition nor its lack could slow. He would spend an early hour reading or composing, as we saw, then hasten, usually on foot, to teach in homes or schools, attend meetings or concerts, or play in church. On Sundays his rounds took him by Saint Sulpice, where he would linger to relish Widor's performance on the organ he had hoped to call his own. It is not recorded that he ever showed bitterness at having been rejected for the post Widor won. He would wait at the foot of the gallery steps to shake Widor's hand and murmur compliments.

Sometimes in early summer he would head the juries at one or another prize competition. So it happened that in 1886, at the National Institute for Blind Children, he listened to a boy of fifteen play the piano and the violin so beautifully that a *premier prix* was awarded in each. He had already heard of young Louis Vierne, whose uncle Charles Colin—winner of the Rome Prize, distinguished organist, professor of oboe at the Conservatory—was one of few colleagues to be Franck's outspoken admirer. Mme. Colin was also an admirer and a colleague; she taught with Franck at the Ecole Monceau. Aunt and uncle had kept him abreast of their nephew's remarkable progress, and had so warmly extolled Franck to Vierne that the boy could not recall a time when he had not longed to become Franck's pupil. Now, the prize-giving done, Franck summoned the lad, his words to be etched on Vierne's memory.

"How pale you are, my dear child. Do I frighten you so very much?"—"Oh, yes, Monsieur Franck."—"Why?"—"Because you are a genius."—"Genius? Who told you that?"—"My

Uncle Charles and everybody here. I heard you at Saint Clotilde when I was ten, and I nearly died from happiness."—"Why?"—"Because it was too beautiful. I wanted it never to end."—"As beautiful as that? And why did you think it beautiful?"—"Because it sang. It took hold of my heart. It hurt me and made me feel good at the same time. It transported me to a place filled with such music."—"In that place, my dear child, the music is better. Here, we learn. There, we shall know how. . . . Next year you will begin studying the organ. Apply yourself with all your might, and when the time is ripe I shall take you into my class at the Conservatory."

Not even his uncle's encomiums had prepared Vierne for the pain and rapture he felt at Saint Clotilde. Franck's prelude overwhelmed him by its mystery, the offertory by a captivating theme. The postlude contained lyrical flights that boyish fantasy turned to visions of paradise, of processions of angels chanting hosannas. "Certain melodic turns, certain harmonies made me feel a kind of nervous malaise that was at the same time voluptuous pleasure. I could not keep back the tears." There arose in him "a vague presentiment of the true purpose of music." The ten-year-old could not put it into words. "It is beautiful because it is beautiful," he told Uncle Charles, "I do not know why. It is so beautiful that I would like to do as much and then die just after."

Spurred on by Franck's promise, Vierne studied zealously. Thanks to an exceptional organ teacher, Louis Lebel, and to Lemmens's *Ecole d'Orgue* used as text, thanks also to his own capacious memory—for facts, persons, and events as well as for poetry, prose, and music—he so quickly advanced that within months he was practicing Bach's Fugue in G Major. In 1888, while yet resident at the National Institute for Blind Children, he began to audit Franck's Conservatory class, visit Franck's organ loft on Sundays, and, at Franck's home, take weekly lessons in counterpoint. At the first lesson his heart was hammering, but the master was so affable, so fatherly, so warmly encouraging that terror soon melted away. "Franck drew me to him, kissed me on the forehead, and said,

'Don't be afraid, child. I have followed your progress. I know how conscientiously you work.'" Indeed, to polish counterpoint assignments Vierne regularly stole hours from sleep.

Franck gently but inexorably sought perfection. He made Vierne rewrite even pages free of faults, urging him to strive for elegance with limited means, to breathe life into dry exercise: to make music. From time to time he would examine the boy's attempts at free composition, giving penetrating counsel that carefully avoided casting him in a mold. Small wonder Vierne's love for the master grew to adoration, or that zeal and talent sped him to finish the course in a mere ten months. Meantime, week after week at the Conservatory, Vierne heard Franck demonstrate techniques of improvisation with fecundity so great the students' "mouths fell open in amazement." Thereupon even the ablest and best prepared, told to try their wings, "would often remain completely nonplused and flounder piteously about." In a year or two his own turn would come, said the young auditor to himself in dismay.

In October 1890 Vierne enrolled at the Conservatory at last. His fervent longings only just attained, he counted it the bitterest of sorrows that, hardly a month later, Franck died.

· 2 ·

Louis Vierne was the son of Henri Vierne and Marie-Joséphine Gervaz. Henri was a political activist and an intellectual who worked as a journalist and editor for newspapers in Paris and the provinces. Marie-Joséphine, practical, affectionate, painfully shy, looked after husband and children with signal devotion. Louis was the second child, his birth preceding that of two brothers and a sister. An older sister had died at the age of thirteen months, and to that loss and his disability Louis attributed the rare tenderness his parents showed him, a tenderness he believed made his innate sensitivity the more extraordinarily acute.

He was born in Poitiers on 8 October 1870, and born with cataracts that left his sight obscured by thick fog. When he was seven, surgery made the fog give way to a twilight, dazzling by comparison, that let him make out nearby objects and walk around unaided. Later he would be able to read large print held close, and draft his compositions on staff paper rather than in braille, but not to read a score placed on the music desk of a console.

His parents took notice of his musical bent, arranged for piano lessons, and delighted in his progress. Uncle Charles, on the boy's frequent visits, would set him down beside the piano and play for him works by Mozart, Beethoven, and Schumann, muttering "What a genius!" at every favorite passage; Vierne soon revered these composers especially. Reasonably enough, he came to link "genius" with the heroes and saints who peopled his bedtime stories. His lamp extinguished, his prayers recited, he could be overheard talking to Mozart.

When Vierne was ten his father's work took the family to Paris, where from age eleven to age twenty he studied at the National Institute for Blind Children. He followed in general the curriculum set down in 1784 by the founder, Valentin Haüy, a pioneer in the movement to educate the blind. Absent were Greek, Latin, and adequate courses in history—omissions Vierne later regretted—and all too present were the disagreeables of refectory and dormitory. But Vierne thought his school in most ways first-rate, not least for its devoted teachers, many as unsighted as he.

From its founding, the Institute had been not only an academy and vocational school but also a conservatory of music. As early as 1788 its choir performed at Saint Eustache. Louis Braille, a student at the Institute when, in 1824, he devised his system of dots, would later become organist at Saint Vincent de Paul and, still later, Saint Nicolas des Champs. An organ class was founded in 1826, and with the decades would supply incumbents to dozens of parishes in the capital and elsewhere. From early times, Paganini and other celebrities gave lessons, and visiting emperors and presidents offered approbation.

The regimen was harsh. The students rose at daybreak to face an unremitting agenda of classes, chapel, meals, and recreation. Ten to twelve hours a day they studied grammar, rhetoric, history, geography, arithmetic, chemistry, physics, philosophy, and the catechism. They practiced a craft—woodworking, for instance, piano repair and tuning, or caning chairs—in order to cultivate dexterity of hand as well as of mind; Vierne learned how to weave nets. And everybody studied music. Students gifted enough to specialize were required in addition to master solfège, harmony, and the rudiments of composition; to learn the piano and an orchestral instrument; and to sing in a chorus or play in the orchestra. They were regularly taken to concerts by the Colonne, Lamoureux, or Conservatory orchestras, to the Opera, and to the Erard or Pleyel. A typical day would include mass or vespers, grace before meals, prayers before classes, and a walk.

Vierne matured young, not just from regimentation or disability, but in a crescendo of affliction. He was seven when his younger sister died of a seemingly mild infection. He was eleven when his beloved Uncle Charles died of pneumonia. He was sixteen when his father, having suffered agonies the boy witnessed, died of cancer. Hence the death of Franck, on 10 November 1890, from pleurisy, dealt Vierne yet another and devastating blow.

He at first thought he could not go on, that he could not face entering Franck's classroom, that he must withdraw from the Conservatory. But some words of the master's re-echoed in his mind. To serve—Franck had once said, after an especially happy lesson—to serve always, in spite of everything, no matter what might happen, to love God, and next the love of God to love one's art, mindful of the good it could achieve, this Franck announced as his creed, which Vierne was to hand down in turn. "These thoughts gave me courage. I was filled with elation at the idea of joining battle with routine, officialdom, the powers that be, of avenging the lack of appreciation, the jeers of which he had been the object." To do less was cowardly betrayal.

Within three weeks, an interval Franck's grieving students

considered indecorously brief, Charles-Marie Widor was made Franck's successor. He soon put Vierne's courage, and theirs, to the test.

· 3 ·

On 11 December 1890, at the appointed hour precisely, Widor entered Franck's classroom and took charge. The students saw a moderately tall man, well built, dressed simply but elegantly, who looked younger than his forty-six years. His manner was a cavalry officer's: distant, self-contained, cold. About Franck he made a brief and well-turned speech that said no more than the proper things. It commended the master improviser. It commended the composer. It passed in silence over the executant. Then, Vierne writes, Widor made a declaration of principle that went something like this:

> In France we too greatly favor improvisation over execution. This is more than a mistake. It is nonsense. To improvise in the artistic meaning of the word, one must assuredly have ideas. But that does not suffice. In order not to betray one's thought, in order to express it faithfully in all the variety, complexity, and suppleness its development requires, the organist must command a technique that lets him play any pattern at any speed.
>
> Improvisation is spontaneous composition. It can only be achieved by means of a thorough knowledge and painstaking exercise of all the resources offered by the keyboards and pedals of the organ. What is more, I fail to see why the organist should be the only artist exempt from the need to know the entire literature of the instrument he plays. . . . I confine myself to citing that incomparable miracle, the organ music of Bach, the greatest musician of all time. Well then! To interpret Bach's works with integrity demands the technique I refer to. It must be scientific: rational, not empirical.

His declaration made, Widor set to work. "We shall proceed in order. I draw at random from my list. Monsieur Burgat, play me something." And Vierne never forgot how "the poor wretch, more dead than alive, was kept on that dunce's stool nearly an hour and a half. He played the allegro from Vivaldi's Concerto in G Major, transcribed by Bach, a piece supposedly not difficult, but which became extremely so when it had to undergo all the master's demands. Widor made him start each bar over again dozens of times, explaining everything with merciless logic, only passing to the next after obtaining execution perfect 'to a hair' as they say nowadays: strict legato in all the parts, precisely articulated repeated notes, tied common tones, punctuation, breathing, phrasing, nuances according to a plan. Everything was dissected, criticized, justified with marvelous clarity. We were dumfounded, flabbergasted—and discouraged, since we realized we knew nothing whatever of all these technical details."

To end the session, Widor sat down at the decrepit old organ and himself performed the piece superbly. "Willpower cannot make a bad instrument good," he said, rising to leave, "but it can make the best of available resources and give an illusion of something artistic. Don't you agree?" Vierne, Libert, Tournemire, and the others took Widor's words and actions as a slap in the face.

For weeks the class took on the atmosphere of a barracks, Widor the aloof officer, the students hostile but correct recruits. Franck had been paternal, Widor was austere. Franck had been kindly, Widor was rigid. Franck had taken pains to nurture each student's individuality. Widor, says Vierne, "seemed to want to compel us to think just like him, and made us submit to a training whose implications we could not as yet see."

As the January midterm drew near, Widor, unhappy with their progress, scheduled evening sessions at Cavaillé-Coll's workshop. The cavernous erecting room was unheated, the winter glacial, and the students played in overcoats and mufflers, hands and feet like ice. That Widor seemed impervious to the cold, disdaining even a topcoat, did not increase their affection.

And yet they began to perceive that he was not quite the ogre they thought. From time to time he would arrange for them to work at good organs, itself an anodyne. Or he would send to the library for scores by C. P. E. Bach, Haydn, Mozart, Beethoven, Schubert, Mendelssohn, and Schumann, and by word and example open up a universe they had scarcely dreamed existed. "What! You have played Beethoven's sonatas and never wondered how they were put together? Why, that is the mentality of a parrot, not an artist." Or he would draw from his encyclopedic culture apt story or allusion or incident, making clearer his unavoidably complicated instruction by comparisons with painting, architecture, literature. All this Vierne would recollect.

Widor in fact concealed a warm heart beneath a cold exterior, as we shall see; he was nothing if not sensitive, nothing if not young in spirit, and he well understood their resentment. As winter gave way to spring, having bided his time, he picked a favorable moment to declare: "Come now, gentlemen. I should like you to know that I am much more your friend than your teacher, and that everything I ask of you, arduous as you find it, is uniquely for your future good." With that he began to win them over. By degrees they began to outdo each other trying to please him.

And by degrees they came to see his precepts as the essence of discernment. What greater aid to accuracy, after all, than to sit squarely in the middle of the bench, comfortably balanced, fingers lightly curved and near the keys and feet near the pedals, or to depress each key with no more and no less force than required, or to avoid needless gesture?

"All random movement is harmful," Widor told them, "because it is a loss of time and strength. Before you decide a movement is necessary, the need for it should be verified during a period of slow practice. This period should be long. If you are resolute and conscientious enough to persist, it will be considerable time gained. Afterward, you will easily play every virtuosic passage in its proper tempo." What could be plainer?

Or what greater aid to clarity than precise legato and durations? For that matter, if clarity were not the sole aim of technique, what was? Thus when Widor made them relearn every exercise in the Lemmens text, and practice till every flaw was eliminated, they grumbled no more than students typically would when faced with a wearisome assignment.

Then came a staccato technique not prescribed in Lemmens. "Keep the fingers in touch with the keys as much as possible," coached Widor, "tighten the wrist slightly, and articulate from the forearm. When you have managed to do this slowly, speed will come of itself." He assigned as drill the toccata from his Fifth Symphony, the scherzo from his Fourth, and the intermezzo from his Sixth. "Not too short!" he cautioned. The key must be fully depressed. To be avoided at all costs was the "exasperating nervousness" of treating the keys as if red hot.

Widor imposed like rules on pedaling. The feet were to be kept in contact with the pedals, the knees together, the keys attacked not perpendicularly but by sliding the foot forward a centimeter or two; this aided accuracy and eliminated clatter. He assigned scales in all the keys—to be played up and down two octaves; the G major scale, for instance, began on bottom C—plus the chromatic scale, arpeggios, trills, leaps, and double notes. As with fingering, that pedaling was best which wasted motion least.

In improvisation Widor similarly imposed discipline, but of a kind that admitted flights of fancy. Far from objecting when the students ventured on the daring, he would show them how to turn boldness to grace. In this he resembled Franck, though in counterpoint Franck had been more exacting. And Franck had dwelt mainly on melodic invention, subtle modulation, the lucky find in harmony, and elegance of pattern, Vierne tells us, whereas Widor dwelt on organization, logical development, form. Not that Widor could not eloquently improvise. On the contrary, Vierne thought Widor's improvising "magnificent"; noble in craftsmanship, richly imaginative, it differed in manner, not competence.

But Widor stressed execution. Every week he had the class scrutinize a new piece: now a prelude by Bach, now its companion fugue; now something of Franck's or Mendelssohn's, now something of his own. And always he stressed the cardinal precept that technique must be not an end but a means. Flawless technique must be tirelessly sought in order to be forgotten.

The mechanics once mastered, Widor brought his students to ponder the subtleties of style. First, he would say, the organ is usually played too fast, though nothing more completely vitiates its dignity and grandeur. And he would tell them of Lemmens's reprimand.

As to Bach, the organs of his day did not speak as quickly and easily as the modern organ, he would explain, their action not permitting great speed; only with this fact in view could one begin to fathom Bach's thought. And that thought was so rich that "each time one plays a piece of Bach's, one finds some new detail. One tries to convey the composer's intentions . . . and plays less quickly so as to hear oneself better." Or again: "Polyphony cannot tolerate rapid execution, which only confuses it and makes it a breathless caricature of itself. Excepting the fugues in D major, D minor, C major and G major, which can be played briskly, I think all the fugues call for very moderate and even fairly slow tempos. Played fast, the big fugues in G minor, A minor, B minor, E minor become stupidly mechanical; likewise the first and last movements of the sonatas and concertos." So Vierne records him saying. It seems to have been distinctive with Widor, when he himself played a Bach fugue, to slow down almost imperceptibly before each entrance of the subject.

Widor taught that Bach generally employed two tempos: one not very fast, corresponding to a modern andante, one rather slow, corresponding to a modern adagio. Alla breve was slower than a modern allegro, something like an allegro molto moderato. Vivace did not mean "quickly"; it meant "lively." Prestissimo was a modern presto. Adagissimo doubled the values of the adagio.

As to registration, Widor warned against changing stops too often: "Please, no magic lantern!" Simplicity was best, in Bach and elsewhere. In Bach's sonata movements, for example, he held the ideal registration to consist throughout of a flute or a principal and a gambe, uncoupled, the pedal at eight-foot pitch. In the large Bach works, he noted the muddling effect on polyphony of powerful modern reeds, and suggested they be reserved for the Toccata in D Minor and the "Cathedral" Prelude in E Minor.

Bach's sonatas he accounted chamber music without peer. He made the class learn all six, and he used them to demonstrate phrasing. On the whole, he said, the organist should phrase more often than the pianist, and, for the sake of clarity, more decidedly.

Vierne recalls the master's dismay when phrasing was clumsily done. "Alas!" Widor would exclaim: "Organists never listen to themselves. . . . To hear some organists, you would think their instrument exempt from the duty of making scores intelligible." Other instrumentalists punctuated, articulated, breathed, and shaded to convey a composer's intentions. "Should the organ be content with an insufferable rumble having no artistic meaning? But why? Music is a special language, I grant you, but it has its requirements of expression just like a language spoken. . . . As to the devices of punctuating and breathing, one may proceed by analogy with the bowed or wind instruments, never forgetting that the organ can make use of these devices only by mechanical intermediaries, and that one should therefore punctuate with moderation, breathe less often, phrase more broadly."

Accordingly, the most difficult of all Widor's rules held that one must differentiate letter from spirit. By the letter of the law, to be sure, "repeated notes must be articulated quite exactly. If values are short, or the tempo is fast or moderately so, shorten the first note by half. If values are long or the tempos slower, cut off a quarter or an eighth. It is reasonable in slow tempos, with some exceptions, to take the smallest value, in a given piece, as the fraction to cut from the first of two repeated notes." True, and the more punctiliously heeded the better. And yet . . .

And yet one must know when to bend. Rhythm was the keystone, or more precisely the indispensable foundation: rhythm alone could convey that "will" which made the structure, in both senses of the word, sound. But to be rhythmic is not to be metronomic. "Losing a bit of time on certain notes, catching it up on others," Widor would say, "that is the secret. . . . Only, it must be done in such a way that the beat is respected. The listener must have no notion of the means employed to draw his attention to what you wish to emphasize. It is a very delicate thing, because the least exaggeration makes for a detestable mannerism."

All in all: "It is a matter of judgment. When one possesses a rational organ technique, one soon comes to recognize the possibilities and the incompatibilities. A new instinct evolves in us that makes us reject the unsuitable and adopt what is in the true style. . . . Leave nothing to chance. . . . Submit everything to the test of reason and, once accepted, express it with *will*."

· 4 ·

More readily even than the ingenious Tournemire, who won a first prize in 1891, Vierne grasped Widor's ideas and excelled in putting them to use. Widor, for his part, was quick to see in Vierne the makings of a consummate artist.

At the start of the fall trimester, Widor admitted five auditors. To save time that the full class might spend on style, he asked Vierne to take the newcomers aside and coach them in technique and plainsong accompaniment. Vierne agreed, flattered but apprehensive: at twenty-one, he was younger than some of his charges, and he feared he would lack authority. To his relief, the weekly sessions, which took place at Erard's or Cavaillé-Coll's, showed his "pupil-comrades" to be deferential, trusting, and eager to learn. They, in turn, found him a dedicated teacher whose enthusiasm made them feel that every goal could be attained, every obstacle overcome. He was warmhearted, protective, and sympathetic (as a later pupil, André Fleury, would remember) and called each pupil "*mon cheri*." His only fault was leniency: Vierne so disliked to wound that at times he was "too indulgent about wrong notes, or even in improvisation. He used to say, 'That's very good, *mon cheri*,' affectionately, stretching the truth out of the goodness of his heart."

Widor soon made another proposal, more unconventional than

the first. Obviously, he said, Vierne's career as performer would be outstanding; high accomplishment would simply be "a matter of will." Nevertheless, he felt sure Vierne would not be content to be performer only, possessing as he did creative faculties that cried out for development. Widor offered to give him lessons in composition. He would tutor him, he said, in vocal, chamber, and symphonic techniques that Vierne might not otherwise acquire. He would teach him instrumentation. He would teach him to orchestrate. All this he would do while continuing to train him in the fine points of execution. In a word, he would help him become the "complete" musician his faculties called him to be.

Vierne, whose hopes had died with Franck, felt a joy we may easily imagine. But there was the question of loyalty to his old master, and there was the question of fees.

The latter Widor dismissed out of hand. "Save your money to buy scores," he said in a tone that would brook no rejoinder. "I am not rich, but I may spend my time on whom I choose." As to the fear of apostasy, added Widor, he knew of Vierne's close ties to Franck, and would respect the artistic turn of mind Franck had instilled.

For the next half-dozen years, often two or three evenings a week, Widor devotedly tutored Vierne—and not in music alone. The lesson done, he would read to him from history and biography, or talk of painting or architecture, or of the leading figures in politics and science. For Widor's generous mind discovered in Vierne, as had others, qualities that joined with the pupil's rare gifts to evoke affectionate concern. The youth was too thin. His pallor was frightful. He worked incessantly. He was appallingly sensitive. He was terrified of straining his eyes and losing what delicate vision remained. But there was nothing fragile about his genius. Nurtured by Widor it quickly grew manifest, and his name began to be known. Even so, some resented the break with precedent when, in 1892, before Vierne had yet won an organ prize, Widor appointed him deputy at Saint Sulpice.

This office too Vierne received with mixed delight and fear.

With his disability, how manipulate the colossal machine? "I revealed my feelings to the master, who confined himself to teasing me, saying with a smile, 'I won't throw you in the ocean till after you learn to swim. You will know the drill sooner than you think. A question of memory and presence of mind. . . . The best training is for you to come as often as possible to my organ loft.'"

There Vierne soon learned the intricacies of Cavaillé-Coll's mammoth console. There, more important, he learned once for all "the special style to adopt when playing huge organs in vast spaces." And there he met beauty so breathtaking it stayed vivid in his memory a half-century later:

> Widor was without doubt the greatest organist I ever heard. Others have as good a technique, of course. But none has his authority, his sense of grandeur, his imperious mastery. And never, whether he was playing or improvising, did his tremendous virtuosity cease to be anything but a means of expression.
>
> And what accents! What breadth of phrasing! What superb legato! What sovereign taste in the placing of lights and shadows! One felt in him a will constantly alert, unshakable, determined to capture the listener's attention by purely musical means.
>
> He knew how to be majestic without grandiloquence, elegant without affectation, austere without dryness, fiery while remaining absolute master of his rhythm. His playing was alive without being hurried. His staccato was precise but never too short. He attacked chords and released them precisely, but took care to avoid that deplorable *détaché* which reduces the organ to a sorry imitation of orchestra or piano. Even in rapid chords he always had "tone" . . . .
>
> He played the pedals marvelously, without ever looking at his feet. Nor did he look at them to hitch or unhitch his combination pedals. He put into practice at his big console the principles of deportment he taught us by example on our little squawk of an organ at the Conservatory. Motionless in the center of his bench, body leaning slightly forward, he drew stops with mathematically regulated gestures causing him the minimum loss of time . . . visual harmony in accord with aural.

In 1894 Vierne won the *premier prix* with a nobly beautiful performance. Two days later, he was officially named Widor's assistant at the Conservatory. He would from now on take charge of the class whenever Widor was absent, and would alone decide which auditors to admit.

With the beginnings of recognition came private pupils too, among the earliest Charles-Marie Michel (grandson of the builder Merklin), Alphonse Schmitt, and Gabriel Dupont. Came also, thanks to Cavaillé-Coll as well as Widor, invitations to give the first of eventual hundreds of recitals. From the start of his career, Vierne toured not only in France, but also in Belgium, Austria, and the Netherlands, often proudly mailing his reviews back to Widor. Returned home from one such tour, he was touched to find waiting a note addressed in Widor's hand to "M. Vierne, the famous organist." Except for stage fright so intense it nearly made him ill, he enjoyed every element of performing, including the travel, the organs, the compliments.

Cavaillé-Coll, whom he often encountered on Sundays at Saint Sulpice, he had met in 1889, when with Adolphe Marty he played an organ on exhibit at the Paris World's Fair. He next saw the builder when Widor's class met in the workshop. A year later, Cavaillé-Coll began inviting Vierne "to come and see him in his office after finishing the lessons I gave in his erecting room." The old man "introduced me to organ building, about which I knew nothing, had me observe some experiments in acoustics, . . . directed my notice to details of pipe-making and of linking keyboards to windchests—in brief: roused my interest in a new domain." Cavaillé-Coll liked to reminisce, and from his "enormous stock of anecdotes about the artists who had frequented his workshop" Vierne "gleaned much that was beneficial."

He met Saint-Saëns at about the same time, introduced by the master's friend and pupil Albert Périlhou, the organist at Saint Séverin. Occasionally needing an assistant, Périlhou had consulted Widor, who agreed to lend Vierne. Saint-Saëns, now retired from the Madeleine, frequented Périlhou's organ loft, as we saw, usually to listen, sometimes consenting to play a voluntary, and so greatly liked Vierne that he exempted him from his wonted crustiness. Even when nettled by the "frightful harmonic indiscretions" in Vierne's improvising—or amused by them: more than once he burst into laughter—Saint-Saëns remained kindly and found much to commend. "It rubs me the wrong way," he would grumble, "but it is full of music. . . . You will go far, young man, with a little more experience and maturity. Meantime, sow your wild oats!" To friends he noted that the apprentice composer "unquestionably has something to say."

By 1898, Vierne had composed quantities of student essays, but had judged only a few pieces sufficiently polished to include in his catalogue of works; he gave opus numbers to an "Allegretto," a "Prélude funèbre," and a "Communion" for organ, to a string quartet, and to some piano music, songs, and motets. It was out of this modest background that his First Symphony sprang into being, the earliest of his masterworks. Indeed, its six movements, published separately in 1898–99, recall in finesse another pinnacle of organ writing, Julius Reubke's Sonata in C Minor (*on the 94th Psalm*), penned by its composer when he too was only in his twenties.

With unfailing self-possession Vierne takes a form inherited from Widor and pours into it deft counterpoints, irrepressible rhythms, supple lyricism, and colorful harmonic "indiscretions." At once luxuriant and transparent, his idiom is as deeply rooted in Franck's warmth as in Widor's objectivity, but achieves much more than a union of opposites, striking though that union may be. Ends and ideals are suggested by some words Vierne writes in praise of a colleague: "This music compels attention by an absolute freedom of language, a total indifference to all display for its own sake, a depth of thought and a solidity of construction that does nothing to impede emotional expansiveness or picturesque detail."

We may abandon chronology to note that Widor's multipartite symphonic form will remain the form Vierne prefers. Except for adapting to the organ the Schumannesque character piece, he innovates not at all. Franck's constructional influence is evident as well when in a second, fourth, fifth, and sixth symphony Vierne uses themes cyclically (he will plan, but never draft, a seventh symphony whose themes were exclusively cyclical), when in divers movements he uses a sonata form or its near relations, and when he recurs, as he often does, to characteristic syncopations. And Vierne resembles both men in writing works that for the most part are secular: notably, in addition to symphonies, his *Pièces de fantaisie* and *Vingt-quatre Pièces en style libre*.

Furthermore, though distinctive, Vierne's harmonies and rhythms grow naturally from Franck's and Widor's; Vierne lived well into the twentieth century, but he speaks a language of the late nineteenth. He feels the sway of Wagner, though he rejected the cult of Wagnerism, and feels Debussy's liberating power too; but he ignores the harmonic and rhythmic finds of Webern and Stravinsky, and remained aloof from the ensuing upheavals. This is not to say that Vierne's invention is anything but abundant; genius wells up in his chromaticism, his syncopation, and his melody, not to mention his flair for contriving delectable turns of harmony by (as he once put it to his pupil Alexander Schreiner) "entering through the back door." It is no reproach to point out that invention is not the same thing as innovation.

Timbre likewise Vierne inherits; he uses Cavaillé-Coll's tone colors much as Widor and Franck had done. Vierne's timbres consist in the main of foundations, foundations and mixtures, or foundations, mixtures, and reeds; of the solo cromorne, clarinette, trompette, hautbois, and flûte harmonique; and of the voix céleste and gambe. Vierne in trenchant ways lightens his scherzos with nasards or two-foot stops, perhaps emulating Saint-Saëns's piquant effects, heard at first hand at Saint Séverin, or perhaps emulating Guilmant, who, as we shall see, was a colorist unsurpassed; and after becoming acquainted with English and American organs, Vierne even calls for the French horn, ophicleide, and vox angelica.

But essentially he charts no new territory. Nor does he design his works for the Notre Dame organ exclusively: his registrations are confined to three manuals.

Nor is he original of manner. His is that "special style to adopt when playing huge organs in vast spaces" which he learned at Saint Sulpice, and at the heart of which stand the Widorian precepts he mastered at the Conservatory: precise legato and articulation, discreet registration, moderate tempo, stalwart rhythm, subtle accent, vital phrasing—all regulated by the rational will.

Vierne's touch was lighter than Widor's, according to Fleury, though the keys were always fully depressed; in strongly rhythmic works, his own or Bach's or others', Vierne's touch was "slightly detached," "incisive," and had "bite." As to tempo, Fleury notes that Vierne's metronome marks are consistently too fast; Vierne misread the device, from bottom rather than top. In performance, "Vierne set his tempo at the beginning of a work and maintained it all the way to the end. That doesn't mean that one should play mechanically. But one should keep the same basic tempo all the way through [a] work . . . and not change tempo unless indicated in the score. Vierne was insistent on this point. . . . One should play Vierne's music rigorously, that is, strictly, but from time to time adding a little inflection on a culminating note in a melodic line . . . [or] 'rounding off' a bit, such as at the end of a phrase or a section."

Hence in style, *mutatis mutandis*, Vierne is at one with his masters, and we must look elsewhere to account for his beguiling originality. We touch the surface of the mystery when we hear Vierne remark that a single aim, to move the listener, governs his every page, though as much may be said of any number of creators spurred on by that romanticist motive. But it begs the question to conclude that he, like them, adjusts the tension between form and content in unique ways because impelled by incommensurables of experience and personality. Nor will it help our understanding to trace the influence of venerated models. Certainly Vierne owes debts to Bach, Mozart, Beethoven, Schubert, Schumann, Wagner, and Fauré, debts he expressly acknowledges. Fauré's art in particular he admires, with its graceful forms and affective nuance, and Berlioz too he loves, though less the works than the man. But a creator is more than the sum of his influences.

Perhaps the question of originality cannot be answered satisfactorily, because answers lie hidden in depths of mind that psychology has yet to sound. But since Vierne pondered the creative enigmas, and was astute and a capable writer, we detect a clue of sorts in his reflections.

To him, there are two kinds of music: "pure music, the purpose of which is to give voice to the movements of the soul, and music descriptive or pictorial. Partisans of the first tendency ask musical art to express what words cannot. Adherents of pictorial music ask it to evoke sensations. . . . Since in artistic matters one is compelled to take sides and cannot remain indifferent, I do not hesitate to affirm my preference . . . for elucidating the interior life. . . . The pure musician sings of his joy, grief, hate, anger, hope, assurance. His creative field is without bounds, because he expresses all the feelings that pervade his personality."

We may go a bit farther than Vierne does, and reflect that those feelings are beyond number, comprising as they do limitless shadings. "Joy," for instance, is merely a convenient tag for a very large class of feelings. Within that class joys differ from one another more or less perceptibly. For the names we give to feelings—joy, grief, anger, and the rest—fool us into thinking each is one thing. "Each is a hundred different things," as Jacques Barzun writes, "with no names to tell them apart. That's where music comes in: it distinguishes—and we respond." Music is adjective, so to say, and adjective razor-edged: our feelings are not too vague for words, but, on the contrary, too precise. Then too, as William James said long ago, feelings differ because no object of thought can twice be perceived identically; the stream of consciousness flows onward without pause, and we do not twice dabble in the same waters.

As to method, Vierne continues: "The primal element in all deeply felt music is the theme. Its conception occurs just like that of infants, the only difference being that it does not spring forth from an initial rapture but from its recollection, which is a good deal more productive. Recollection provides the mental stimulus from which, soon or late, the theme will emerge. Once conceived, a theme can be reworked, transformed—think of Beethoven and Franck—but what counts is the first flash. Reason comes in afterward, to select, verify, and put in order. Its role is quite important, but most important, in everything touching on artistic creation, is the role played by sensibility. In a gifted and cultivated musician, sensibility is so acute that ordinary mortals who consider themselves normal may call it unhealthy." Vierne takes pains to perfect his themes because to him the theme contains in germ the feelings that seek utterance, contains in germ everything a work should express.

Finally, as to form: "Reason and taste determine the form best suited to expressing a feeling. Too often people mistake form's function, as if any framework by itself were able to generate ideas. Imagination alone can give birth to art. In essence dionysiac, music borrows form from Apollo only in order to be perceptible. Apollo remains an intermediary. Life is in Dionysus."

Such is Vierne's esthetics, writes his biographer Bernard Gavoty, who suggests that Vierne was extravagantly emotional, in art and also in life. Still, as Fleury recalls, Vierne could be dispassionate, "depending on his mood and the people he was with at the moment. A most curious thing about Vierne was that on the surface he appeared to have a strong personality, forceful and determined, but in reality he was rather weak. . . . He was a very good man— a very open-minded individual [who was] weak precisely because he was very good. . . . His music is virile, that is, energetic, heroic. Take, for example, the first theme of the opening allegro of his Second Symphony. I believe that he put into his music what he would have liked to have been in life."

· 5 ·

The pace of Vierne's life began to quicken in 1896, when Widor resigned the organ class to accept a chair in composition. He did so, according to Dupré, on condition that Guilmant succeed him. Guilmant kept Vierne on as assistant, and gave the twenty-six-year-old increased responsibility; during Guilmant's frequent absences on recital tour, Vierne would take charge for weeks on end, be professor in all but name. Vierne served, moreover, as liaison between the new regime and the former. At weekly luncheons with Widor, he "kept my dear master apprised of everything happening in his old course." With Guilmant he meantime collaborated in maintaining the "Francko-Widorian" traditions.

Logically enough, Vierne thought of himself as member of a triumvirate: transmitter, with Guilmant and Widor, of a "solidly based doctrine that was to form the most brilliant generation of artists our country had produced since the end of the eighteenth century."

Alexandre Guilmant, who had been trained by Lemmens, as we saw, held views congruent with Widor's on the broad questions of style and technique. Though his legato was more articulate than Widor's, and subject to adjustment in resonant rooms, Guilmant as professor, reports Vierne, changed almost nothing pertaining to execution: "Some additional articulations in various preludes and fugues by Bach, certain tempos a bit faster—these were his contributions." It tells something of the inner man that Guilmant was as punctilious in folding a newspaper as in fingering a fugue. And as to the outer man, Vierne writes: "This man fifty-nine years of age, having behind him a superb career as virtuoso and enjoying a deserved renown, . . . did me the honor of treating me as an equal, I who had only just entered the ranks." Vierne would assist him for fifteen years, "not a day of which, not an hour, did the least shadow disturb the ties of close friendship established between us."

Guilmant had indeed gained an eminent reputation in France and overseas. One of the first of modern touring organists, he played in Russia, Spain, Holland, Belgium, Italy, England, Canada, and the United States. One of the first of modern musicologists, he unearthed, edited, and performed works by old masters from many

countries: Bruhns, Buxtehude, Walther, Krebs, Scheidt, Byrd, Frescobaldi, Andrea Gabrieli, and Marcello, for example, in addition to
Bach and the French classicists. With Bordes and d'Indy he co-
founded the Schola Cantorum. At Trinity Church he served as organist for thirty years. He composed prolifically, improvised with
originality and brilliance.

In the classroom, Guilmant espoused views both liberal and
conservative. Though he changed little of Widor's procedure, he
did do away with the artless note-against-note accompaniment of
plainsong that had for decades been the inviolable rule; and as to
improvisation, Vierne remarks, Guilmant "went back to teaching
only the forms required by the competitions." In improvisation, his
"examples showed his solid compositional expertise, but his imagination was far less fertile than Widor's. A stricter, narrower heir of
the esthetics of his master, he seemed reactionary to students whom
we had been acquainting with a modernism much bolder than his
own." Yet without compromising his principles, he tolerated ideas
he found unsympathetic. He sometimes pronounced Vierne's harmonies, and those Vierne drew from the students, daring to a fault;
but more often than not he would just shake his head, mutter:
"That hits rather hard," and let audacity pass.

He was fascinated by subtleties of timbre. "Many times after
class," Vierne writes, "I accompanied him on foot to Montparnasse
Station where he would catch his train for Meudon. During these
walks he would speak at great length of the coloristic questions that
excited his interest. His vast experience, acquired during a singular
career as recitalist, let him share a host of observations I used to my
profit." In his love of teaching and of scholarship, in his fatherly
warmth toward his pupils, in his knowledge of organ building and of
repertories ancient and modern—in all this Guilmant was second to
none. "I never knew a man who carried to greater heights his passion
for his art. He devoted his life to it, exercised it like a priesthood."

The closing months of the century saw Vierne the protégé of two
famous masters, and saw him a published composer and a well-

known recitalist and teacher. He had attained his goals against heavy odds of disability and bad luck, attained them by dint of untiring discipline, and attained them before he was thirty. Then, in the spring of 1900, his career took another definitive turn. The post at Notre Dame fell vacant, and he, albeit reluctantly, decided to apply.

He hesitated because the post paid badly, and he had a family to support. About a year earlier, he had married Arlette Taskin, whose father was a singer at the Opéra-Comique; a first son had just been born. The cathedral parish was poor, and in respect of its four thousand souls, as Vierne would later comment drily, he could count on few weddings and funerals from among the charity hospital, the barracks of the Garde Républicaine, the police headquarters, and the morgue. In contrast he had just been offered a post at twice the salary, in the prosperous district of Neuilly, where numerous weddings and funerals and a good new organ awaited. And not least, he feared for his hard-earned reputation if he auditioned at the cathedral and lost.

He knew the contest would be formidable. Nearly a hundred competitors had applied, a few of them able indeed. The finalists, auditioning anonymously before a discriminating jury, must each accompany and elaborate a plainchant, improvise a fugue, improvise a sonata movement, and play by heart a set piece to be picked by the jury from among no fewer than five. The chant, the fugue subject, and the sonata themes would be assigned, and the set piece chosen, only minutes in advance. Could such a risk be justified, even to win the organ Cavaillé-Coll himself loved best?

Widor urged Vierne on, arguing that to be organist of Notre Dame, in succession to a long line of eminent musicians, would assure his place in history, and asserting that Vierne had a mission to restore the cathedral's once preeminent traditions. "If I had only myself to think of," Widor said, "I would not suggest such a thing." He would keep him at Saint Sulpice. "But we must think of the future."

Vierne takes up the story:

The day of the competition finally arrived. We were shut up in the little rooms above the sacristy. A quarter of an hour before competing, each candidate was taken to a small room, in the charge of a young priest, Father Renault, who gave him the themes and the chant. By lot I was selected first, and . . . by lot the jury chose Bach's Toccata and Fugue in D Minor. I was happy at this choice, since this work admirably suits the Notre Dame organ. The chant was the "Salve Regina." The fugue subject was by Guilmant, the *thème libre* by Deslandres. The jury, headed by Widor, included Guilmant, Gigout, Périlhou, Dallier, Deslandres, and Father Geispitz. On it the chapter was represented by Canon Pisani. . . .

After finishing, I went down into the church to listen to my rivals. Two were excellent, and this only added to my fear of failure. The trials over, I went back up to the organ loft, where the jury was coming in. Widor announced the result. I was unanimously, and with felicitations, awarded first place.

A few minutes later the clergy assembled to congratulate and welcome Vierne. "As of this date," he was told with a touch of ceremony, "you are organist of the Chapter of the Metropolitan Basilica of Notre Dame de Paris."

He took up his duties on the Feast of the Ascension, 24 May 1900.

⊁ 6 ⊀

Marcel Dupré

THE SPRING THAT WITNESSED FRANCK'S EN-
counter with the fifteen-year-old Vierne ("Do I frighten you so
very much?"—"Oh, yes, Monsieur Franck") witnessed the birth
of Marcel Dupré, their successor, heir, and consummation. And not
just Vierne's and Franck's, but also Widor's and Guilmant's. "This
will be an organist!" prophesied Guilmant, as he leaned over the
cradle and examined the baby's fingers. Indeed, this was to be such
an organist as the world had never seen.

Marcel Dupré was born in Rouen on 3 May 1886 into a family
of musicians. One grandfather was an organist, the other a choir-
master. The mother, Alice, was a pianist and cellist. Her sister,
who lived with Marcel's parents, was an alto. Marcel's father,
Albert, for seven years a pupil of Guilmant's, taught music at the
Lycée Corneille and was the organist at Immaculate Conception
Church in the nearby town of Elbeuf. He was to become celebrated as the founder-director of a chorus that mounted in Paris as
well as in Rouen such works as Bach's *Saint Matthew Passion,*
Handel's *Messiah,* Haydn's *Seasons,* Mendelssohn's *Elijah,* Berlioz's
Enfance du Christ, Brahms's *German Requiem,* Fauré's *Réquiem,* and

Debussy's *Damoiselle Elue*. Marcel thus grew up in a home filled with music. Invariably someone was practicing an instrument or singing or giving a lesson. Soon the toddler was "inventing" harmonies at the piano, and fashioning his toy blocks into organ pedals.

He was nearly four when Cavaillé-Coll's men came to erect the organ at Saint Ouen. The abbey stood not far from the Dupré home, and often in the early months of 1890 Albert took Marcel to watch the work. At first "petrified" (he would remember) by the sight of the four-manual console, the child was thrilled when he learned that the famous Widor was to play for the inauguration. For weeks he could think of nothing else. He begged to be allowed in the organ loft when Widor came to practice. When Albert gently refused, Marcel accepted defeat with outward good grace but laid secret plans of his own.

On the afternoon of Widor's arrival, after Albert had gone up to the organ loft with Cavaillé-Coll and the local musicians, Marcel, granted permission to listen in the nave, stole away from his nurse, tiptoed up the spiral steps, and found a nook to hide in. He listened entranced while Widor, as ever dour and forbidding in appearance, rehearsed passages from his program and tried out the stops. Till Widor finished playing Marcel hardly breathed. Then he made his way to the console, looked up at the fierce eyes and cavalry mustache, put hands on hips, and said: "You play very well, monsieur, but my papa plays well too!" Cavaillé-Coll and the assembly burst into laughter, to Albert's acute embarrassment, and even Widor smiled as he lifted Marcel to his side on the bench.

As to the instrument, Dupré would recall how "Cavaillé-Coll anxiously awaited Widor's judgment. To his query Widor replied: 'It is worthy of Michelangelo.' And truly it is that. Afterward, Cavaillé-Coll asked my father: 'How much do you think this organ cost me?'—'They say it brought you 90,000 francs.'—'Just so. And it cost me 108,000. But I am not sorry. I wanted to build something beautiful.'" A score of years later, Albert proudly became organist of Saint Ouen. He would preside for a quarter century over the *orgue à la Michel-Ange*.

At age five, having only just begun to learn solfège, Marcel contracted a staph infection of the marrow in his right collarbone. Weeks passed, remedies failed, and he underwent the physical and the emotional trauma of a surgical operation. It too failed. More weeks went by, whereupon a second operation, which excised the collarbone, cured his infection but ruined his health. Bedridden for seven interminable months, arm and shoulder long immobilized, the formerly robust and plucky child grew pale, gaunt, and fearful. He was stricken in mind as in body.

To help him regain his vigor, his godfather, Jules Lesueur, a well-to-do merchant, took him on frequent carriage rides through the woodlands and hills near Rouen. The gentle sway of the carriage, Lesueur's friendly and intelligent mare "Javanaise" whom Marcel found enchanting, and the sweet air of the Norman countryside did much to mend the boy's spirits. To round out the cure, Lesueur, who wanted Marcel to summer by the sea, rented for the Duprés a villa near the beach at Saint-Valery-en-Caux. There Lesueur had a piano installed. And there Marcel, now seven years old and eager to make up lost time, once more began studying music.

His father proposed to give him a half-hour piano lesson every morning, but this pace Marcel found too slow. At the first lesson Albert assigned an exercise from Le Couppey's *Alphabet*, whose pages each were headed by a letter and devoted to a single piece. The next day he asked Marcel to play it. "But I don't need to!"— "No? Why not?"—"Because I know this page already. Let's do the next."—"Play!" ordered Albert, who then watched amazed as Marcel performed by heart and without a mistake. "Good," Albert said, wisely concealing his wonderment. "Take another page for tomorrow." In twenty-five days the child had memorized twenty-five pages. He could play them in any order perfectly.

At the end of summer the weeks of study were rewarded with

a surprise gift. On the family's return to Rouen, an old harmonium was retrieved from the attic, repaired, and placed in Marcel's room. The child was elated. He imagined his room a cathedral, the harmonium a cathedral organ.

· 2 ·

That autumn Marcel performed for the first time in public. His father had been asked to play for a friend's wedding, and he to play a harmonium piece as part of the prelude. He also entered school. After an inauspicious start—his sole interest at first being music— he became an exemplary scholar in every subject but arithmetic.

He began to study the organ during the winter of 1893– 94, continuing his piano lessons the while. As text, Albert chose Lemmens's *Ecole d'Orgue,* which he himself had studied under Guilmant. Marcel's impatience was hard to curb. "I did not want to start with 'easy' scales and exercises. I wanted instead to learn Bach." When at length he was assigned the "Cathedral" Prelude in E Minor, Marcel was crestfallen. He had hoped for something more difficult.

In June he again played in public, this time, unforgettably, in the presence of Cavaillé-Coll. The old man had come to Elbeuf to attend the inauguration of a choir organ in Albert's church. Marcel was to open the program, with his Bach, on the Cavaillé-Coll in the gallery. The honored guest arrived the day before, and the Duprés dined with him at his hotel.

> During dinner, my father worried about what to do with me the next day while he rehearsed the symphony for chorus and orchestra that he was to direct from the chancel. My mother would be playing the cello, my aunt would be singing. "I want Marcel to behave!" my father said.
>
> Cavaillé-Coll immediately interposed: "Confide Marcel to me. We'll take a walk by the Seine." And, turning to me: "All right?"—"Oh, yes, monsieur!" said I, exuberant.
>
> As she put me to bed my mother showered me with orders.

"Remember that Monsieur Cavaillé-Coll is old." (He was eighty-three.) "Don't go off running by the riverbank! Don't cause him any trouble! And be careful not to dirty your shoes!"—"But you take me for an imbecile," I replied, as Mother later told the story; "We shall discuss organs."

And in fact that grand old man, taking small steps, my hand in his, graciously answered all my questions, patiently explaining what he saw I could grasp.

The Duprés spent part of the summer of 1895 in Tréport, where Marcel took his lessons daily on the organ at the village church. By fall he was studying harmony and counterpoint. By his tenth birthday, in May 1896, he had memorized a sonata movement by Guilmant and Bach's "Little" Fugue in G Minor. These he performed in July, at an exposition in Rouen, on an organ of thirty stops in a hall seating one thousand. It was his first appearance on a recital stage. "Mother gave me some lessons in deportment, showing me how to walk without haste and bow without awkwardness, but I was not at all intimidated." Nothing mattered but Guilmant's opinion and Widor's. He knew that each master was kept informed of his progress.

A third began to take an interest as well. Summer vacation in 1896 saw Marcel playing for mass at the village church in Saint-Valery-en-Caux. On leaving the loft one Sunday, he and Albert encountered two men waiting below. One asked Albert if he was the organist. No, came the reply: "My son."—"This nice little chap? How old is he?"—"He just turned ten."—"Astounding! Unbelievable! No mistakes, faultless rhythm, and withal a French pedalboard!" The visitor was Vierne, his brother René with him. He introduced himself as Widor's assistant at the Conservatory and Saint Sulpice.

Vierne continues: "I asked the father's permission to kiss the child, who had stayed at a distance during the conversation. His father summoned him, and I congratulated him and kissed him on the forehead. He blushed when he heard who I was." A few weeks later Vierne too performed at the Rouen exposition, and gave a private recital at Saint Ouen. Young Marcel "came to both, and pulled stops for me with an accuracy the more impressive in that I played without music and he had to memorize the many and tricky changes."

In September Cavaillé-Coll's men once again arrived in Rouen, this time to install an organ in Albert's music room. Marcel, a year or two earlier, had taken part in the planning. On that occasion, Cavaillé-Coll himself had come to town, Dupré would remember, "accompanied by his foreman. Quivering with excitement, I listened to what was being said about the instrument's construction. Then, all at once, during lunch, with the forwardness of children, I spoke up. 'Monsieur Cavaillé-Coll, will the façade have a tower?'—'You want a tower? Very well. For you I'll design two, with three pipes each, and send you the sketch in a few days.' The big eyes my mother made had no effect on me, I was so happy. I lay in wait for the postman every morning. At last, a big package came with my name on it: a lovely framed wash drawing of the proposed façade. . . . Overjoyed, I wrote a nice letter of thanks to Cavaillé-Coll."

The instrument, Dupré adds, took a month to erect: "What magical days those were! Each morning at seven, as soon as I heard the tinkling of the entrance bell, I leapt out of bed, threw on any old clothes, unless Mother caught me in the hall and made me about-face to finish dressing, then took the stairs four at a time to go join the workmen. Under their watchful gaze I would cheerfully render them little services. . . . Most of all, I could not take my eyes off the great voicer Garnier while he was voicing the pipes. I was awed by his patience, his obstinacy with a single note till he obtained the timbre and precision desired."

The instrument done, Marcel exclaimed to his father: "I can really practice the organ now, since I don't need the piano anymore!"—"Don't you believe it!" said Albert. "Your proficiency as an organist depends on your proficiency as a pianist. You may spend fifteen minutes at the organ for every forty-five at the piano."

In this, as in all that concerned Marcel's training, Albert had sought Guilmant's advice—Guilmant, who had traveled to Rouen to see Marcel in his crib; Guilmant, who played for the ceremony when, in May 1897, the eleven-year-old celebrated his First Communion; Guilmant, who backed Marcel's victorious campaign, a year later, to become organist at Saint Vivien de Rouen. Thus from the start, through Albert, Guilmant was Marcel's master. Now began, in 1898, with monthly lessons in Paris, an explicit collaboration that would continue for a decade.

A lesson typically ran to two hours or more, including as it did harmony, counterpoint, and improvisation besides organ and piano, and consisting of the disciplines we know. Rigorous though these were, Guilmant in imposing them was gentleness personified; a mistake would bring the mild injunction: "Put on your glasses, Marcel." But nothing passed unnoticed. "He would stop me almost at each bar for the slightest detail and I had to repeat my bar until he considered every little point was right."

On Sundays at Saint Vivien, Marcel put growing knowledge to use. And though now without direct supervision, Albert having his own services to play, Marcel was required on Sunday evenings to report on his day's work. Had he improvised at the offertory? If so, on what theme? With what solo stop? In the soprano or the tenor? Even at this early stage, his improvising must follow a form. When he embroidered a plainchant, he must do so in strict counterpoint.

Marcel was ten when he made his first attempts at composition; he wrote a "Prière" and a three-voice fugue. Within a year or two he wrote a march and barcarolle for piano, two songs, and a minuet for piano, violin, and cello. He next undertook his first large-scale work, a cantata some thirty minutes long entitled *La Vision de Jacob*. Its inception "went back almost to my First Communion. Among my gifts I had received a superb Bible illustrated by Gustave Doré, and I was captivated, obsessed, by Jacob's dream. What moments I spent contemplating that marvelous ladder, whose top reached heaven and along whose length angels processed up and down!"

Performed at a gathering of family and friends on 3 May 1901, his fifteenth birthday, his cantata brought an unanticipated reward. Present was "Mme. Samson (granddaughter of Boieldieu, the composer of *La Dame Blanche*), who . . . took an interest in me. She put a sum at my father's disposal for the purchase of a grand piano." Albert chose a fine Erard that Paderewski had used on a tour.

The gift was as timely as it was handsome. Guilmant had decided to enter Marcel at the Conservatory, and to enter him in piano.

· 3 ·

From his sixteenth to his twentieth year, though continuing his private lessons with Guilmant, Marcel devoted himself primarily to the piano, sometimes practicing ten hours a day. The teacher to whom Guilmant had presented him was Louis-Joseph Diémer.

Composer, scholar, and performer, Louis Diémer had been the soloist at the première of Franck's *Variations symphoniques*, championed ancient music as vigorously as he did modern, and composed not only solo works but chamber music too, all of which betokens originality of mind and a laudable disregard for shortsighted colleagues. He had taught at the Conservatory since 1887, and the stature of the artists he trained, among them Alfred Cortot and Robert Casadesus, suggests that his skill as teacher equaled his skill as virtuoso.

Bach himself, we are told, held clavier technique to be an indispensable aid to manual technique; Bach disciplined his pupils at the harpsichord before allowing them to approach the organ. So too Lemmens: "To young people destined to become organists," declares the *Ecole d'Orgue*, "one cannot too emphatically recommend that they begin by studying the piano." Guilmant and Widor likewise maintained that the more minutely one cultivated the motions of piano playing, the more exquisite would be one's command of the organ, the piano requiring a diversity of gesture, a precision of movement, and a delicacy of coordination exceeding what is required by the manuals. "That is why the organist takes a wrong path," Dupré was to state, "who does not apply himself passionately and intensely, for several years, to piano study. . . . The organist has no less need than the pianist to master the Etudes of Chopin and the Transcendental Etudes of Liszt."

Young Dupré "learned all the sonatas of Haydn, Mozart, and Beethoven, and much of Schubert, Schumann, Liszt, and Chopin. In fact I learned by heart about three-fourths of the works of Chopin." And though his aim was to master the organ, using the piano as means to an end, he learned to love the piano's own beauty: its union of percussive with singing tone, its varieties of sustained tones controlled by the dampers, its ability to convey emotion of an intimate kind. He came to see that the piano is not more expressive than the organ—the two cannot really be compared—but is more intricate in its shadings, more subtle in its gradations. He realized, as did Vierne at Saint Sulpice, that when one plays large organs in large spaces it is the *grandes lignes* of a work which count, the broad strokes, the curves, vaultings, and buttresses. At the organ, even subtleties are grandiose. At the piano, the emotional canvas can be painted in minuscule detail.

After preliminary work with an assistant, Marcel began to audit the piano class in 1902 and to participate one year later. His progress was swift and sound, which left Diémer pleased and vexed. No doubt to Guilmant's amusement, Diémer grumbled that Marcel was the ablest of pupils but could think of nothing but the organ—a waste of talent in a boy who could become a first-rate concert pianist. And when in 1905 Marcel won a unanimous first prize, with a ravishing performance of a Chopin Ballade and a movement by Saint-Saëns, Diémer's smile gave way to a scowl. "Son, you could have a magnificent career, if only you would forget the organ! You can't possibly make a living at it. You'll end up without a sou."— "*Mon cher Maître*," came the respectful reply, "I could never give up the organ."

In 1905–06, having entered Guilmant's organ class as an auditor, Dupré finished the study of counterpoint and was coached by Vierne in improvisation. Never was there a student easier to teach, Vierne writes, since in Dupré the "sentiment was innate that the more one was gifted the harder one must work." And when in the fall of 1906 Dupré entered the class officially, Vierne, like Guilmant, "urged him on, convinced he could win his *premier prix* at his very first competition." Sure enough, the following spring, Vierne continues:

> The outcome surpassed everything I had foreseen. And this competition, the most remarkable I ever heard at the Conservatory, is worth describing in detail.
>
> Marcel Dupré was the first to perform, and he boldly improvised on the liturgical chant a complete canon between the soprano and the bass at a fourth below, while the two inner parts were treated in third species counterpoint with an audacious musical figure of the smoothest possible kind. With this feat, I knew his cause was won. His fugue seemed like a fugue written down. He dared to maintain the countersubject, which he kept in its usual place even during the entries of subject and answer in the inner voices. His stretto was a masterpiece of assurance and competence. His free improvisation was full of poetry, with an ingenious development in the middle and a wholly unexpected and thrilling return; at the end he also found a nice little canon. Finally, he performed with stunning virtuosity the closing movement of Guilmant's Sonata in A, an appallingly difficult piece, strewn with snares and pitfalls and the pedal part of which . . . contains some terrible passages.
>
> "Were you nervous?" I asked him while the jury was out. "A bit, especially at the beginning," he replied, with the same timidity he had shown years earlier. . . .
>
> "I assure you no one could tell. You were absolutely tremendous."

No teacher could have been prouder than Guilmant, or been more flattered by the query that followed. Dupré asked whether Guilmant, against custom, would continue to give him lessons: "You have told me about your meetings with Franck, and about performing his works for him. Of Franck's twelve pieces, I have played five for you. I would like to study the other seven, and receive the indications Franck gave you." Dupré also requested further instruction in improvising the four-movement symphony, an incomparably exigent form in which Guilmant had no equal. Widor's consent once obtained (since Dupré was to enter Widor's class), Guilmant agreed to coach Dupré for a supplementary year.

Widor too had again broken with custom when, in 1906, he named Dupré his deputy at Saint Sulpice. The appointment startled many, including the twenty-year-old nominee. "But *Maître*," Dupré had stammered, like Vierne fourteen years earlier, "I haven't yet had my prize in organ."—"I know. But you will not be long in getting it."

Already by 1905, Widor had begun inviting Dupré to lunch at the Restaurant Foyot, an opulent haunt of senators and artists where Widor had his accustomed table, and, as Cavaillé-Coll had done for him, was presenting Dupré to the elite that could make or unmake a young man's career. With Dupré's entry into Widor's composition class, the luncheons became frequent indeed. Dupré recalls that during his seven years as Widor's pupil, a hansom would be waiting to take them to the Foyot after class each Monday and Thursday. He never forgot those drives across Paris; they were delectable both for the city's charm and for Widor's conversation. "His intellect, his vast culture, his humor put you under a spell. Music, of course, made up much of his talk, but so did his reminiscences of his own life and of the illustrious men he kept company with." Though Widor was now in his sixties, and Dupré forty-two years younger, the disparity did not stay a friendship "based on an absolute mutual trust, and on a deep affection no shadow ever darkened. To the last, he treated me like a son."

Dupré found no less memorable Widor's pedagogic prowess. Enrolled in the class at about this time were Milhaud, Honegger, and Varèse. That their idioms so greatly differ bespeaks Widor's commendable resolve, Dupré writes, "to guide in its own path the temperament of each pupil." For though the virtue Widor most praised was the dual one of balance and shapeliness of form, insisting as he did that "measured proportions are as necessary in a musical work as in a Greek temple," he well knew that not even Greek temples were built in all respects alike. And though he deemed expressiveness essential, circumscribed always by reason and restraint, he well knew that intellect and heart are one, that no thought can exist without some overtone of feeling. Not surprisingly, the Fugue in Four Voices—in F minor, on a subject by Fauré—with which Dupré won first prize in fugue, in 1909, is a model of form and lyricism.

By 1909, Dupré had submitted to Widor songs, piano works, movements for string quartet, and the violin sonata later published as opus five. There followed, in 1910–12, songs, piano works, and choral music of progressively greater complexity and depth. The songs especially, with their evocative accompaniments adroitly orchestrated, struck Widor as revealing in Dupré a distinct and distinctive gift as composer. Dupré's Fantasy for Piano and Orchestra, a work sufficiently mature to be performed by the Lamoureux Orchestra, confirmed Widor in this judgment. He therefore began to urge Dupré to compete for the Rome Prize itself.

Dupré reluctantly agreed, unwilling to say no to his master, but feeling scant enthusiasm. Recent years had abounded in rewards that made the Rome Prize seem superfluous. He had begun to give private lessons, and discovered that he enjoyed teaching. He had relished accompanying his father's chorus in masterworks by Beethoven, Debussy, and Fauré. With a friend, to their mutual delight, he had presented a two-piano recital. With an orchestra he had played the solo part in a symphony of Guilmant's. And these gratifying events had been crowned by his Parisian recital debut: on 12 March 1912, at the Salle Gaveau, he had delivered a performance that would live on as a triumph, or so proclaimed Vierne, whose Third Symphony, inscribed to his "pupil and dear friend Marcel Dupré," received its première on that occasion.

Alas, the Rome Prize centered on opera, and Dupré wished to devote every moment to instrumental and symphonic techniques.

When Widor suggested that he spend the summer writing arias, recitatives, and duets, he could not steel himself to the task. Instead, he wrote three preludes and fugues and, hoping against hope for remittal, took them to Widor in the fall. That Dupré gave himself heart and soul to these works is attested by their quality and fame: published as opus seven, they stand, by universal consensus, among the finest organ works of the century. But the stratagem failed; Widor praised the works but was adamant. It would be no waste of time, he said, for Dupré to spend a year on opera; he was only twenty-six, and the training would make him "more complete."

In the end, Dupré spent not one year but two, till at length, with his lyric scene *Psyché,* he won the Rome Prize for 1914. Saint-Saëns cast the deciding vote.

· 4 ·

Dupré's Rome Prize, following as it did an acclaimed debut and three acclaimed *premiers prix,* would have assured his renown in Europe. But the First World War erupted soon afterward and robbed Dupré of this kudos. It robbed him too of his sojourn in Italy, instead sending him back to Rouen. There, his childhood bone surgery having disqualified him from the draft, he volunteered to serve in a military hospital, and was put to work in its pharmacy. Witness to an endless procession of stretchers bearing mutilated men, aghast at the irremediable waste, Dupré found his art to be of use chiefly in playing for the funerals of soldiers, some of them his schoolmates and friends. His *De Profundis,* for soloists, chorus, orchestra, and organ, he would compose, in 1916–17, as "an alleviation."

Meanwhile in Paris, where airplanes or zeppelins struck on every cloudless night, a bomb hit Notre Dame and damaged a window and a gargoyle near the organ. Cavaillé-Coll's favorite instrument only narrowly escaped ruin.

Its custodian, Vierne, had begun to fear ruin of a more insidious kind: his eyesight, ever precarious, was being threatened by glaucoma. To protect what vision was left, he decided to seek treatment from a specialist abroad, and to engage Dupré as substitute. Consulted, Widor sanctioned the idea as benefiting both of his protégés: Dupré would find his reputation enhanced by the link with Notre Dame, and Vierne could rest assured that his post was safe in competent hands.

To Vierne, the threat of total blindness came as but one in a new series of calamities. In 1906, a broken right leg threatened to heal improperly and end his career as a player; it caused him weeks of suffering—and put a stop, incidentally, to the improvisation lessons he was giving to Dupré. A few months later, in 1907, Vierne contracted typhoid fever; for days he lay delirious and near death. In 1909, a divorce, in itself excruciating, gave Vierne custody of only one of his children; he moved into his mother's home, so that the child could be reared by its grandmother, but scarcely had a year elapsed before she fell ill and, after months of agony, died. In 1911, Guilmant died, and Vierne, after having for nearly two decades been assistant in the Conservatory class, was denied the promotion he had every right to expect, and saw someone else made professor. In 1913, his son André died. In 1917, his son Jacques died. And in 1918, the being he cherished as his closest friend, his younger brother René, would die in the war only weeks before the armistice.

Vierne, it turned out, was gone from the cathedral not five months, as planned, but four years. He returned with a vestige of sight intact. But the painful and costly treatments left him frail and impoverished.

Released in 1916 from wartime duties, Dupré rented an apartment in Paris, in the relative quiet of Montparnasse, and rented nearby a music studio equipped with a harmonium. There he could teach and practice with greater freedom than at Notre Dame. And there, spurred on by Widor's advice on how best to retrieve his career— "You must bedazzle the public like a beautiful moth emerging from its cocoon"—he embarked on a project so mammoth it would consume a full three years.

The idea of performing all Bach's organ works by heart had first occurred to Dupré in 1907, the year of his organ prize, when he memorized volume two entire, ten difficult preludes and fugues. "I knew eight already, having studied them with Guilmant. So I learned the other two and, one evening at home in Rouen, I put chairs side by side for my parents, and played to mamma and papa, on the organ Cavaillé-Coll built for my father, the whole second volume by heart." Such was the germ of the venture. He had inherited his mother's good memory, he adds, and found it only natural to memorize everything.

But he did not memorize without effort. On the contrary, though his memory was at once auditive, tactile, and visual—he mentally heard the notes, felt them in his fingers, and saw their printed shapes—he learned Bach's music, as he learned all else, by dint of system and hard labor.

Neglecting not the smallest detail, Dupré approached each piece methodically, for though a few bars might be learned at a glance, most put both memory and technique to the test. He would first try fingerings and pedalings to determine those economical of motion. Then, advancing measure by measure, playing in rhythm, at pains not to play faster than he could play perfectly, he would repeat each measure ten, fifteen, twenty times before proceeding to conquer the next; after committing three or four measures to memory, he would repeat them as a group, ten, fifteen, twenty times. "To get perfection in a work," he later explained, "you must first get perfection in a short passage. That is the root of all virtuosity."

It went without saying that virtuosity should serve; it should not abuse. Dupré writes: "One must distinguish the interpreter from the virtuoso. The interpreter is as capable as the virtuoso of bringing off flashy technical acrobatics. But having the beauty of the music as paramount concern, the interpreter never permits himself a lapse of good taste. He wishes only to effect a sharing of the emotion felt when contemplating a masterpiece. . . . If the crushing labors found in acquiring impeccable technique give to those who possess it independence and authority, it remains true none the less that technique is only great if it is conscientious and respectful. . . . To serve Bach means not to exploit him."

Perhaps because this attitude imparts especial eloquence, Dupré's now-famous Bach recitals, at the Conservatory on the ten Friday afternoons from 23 January to 26 March 1920, struck the sensitive among his listeners as something nobler than a tour de force of memory. Had it been only that, announced *Le Monde musical,* not even Dupré could have brought it off; of necessity he had put his whole spirit and heart at Bach's service. The *Courrier musical* likewise chiefly praised, not his memorizing and executing faultlessly the eight hundred closely printed pages of score, but his musicianship: his rhythms at once stalwart and pliant, his unerring choice of tempos, his measured articulations, his refinements in registration—these last held the more astonishing given the mediocrity of the instrument. Dupré's mastery overwhelmed like a force of nature, asserted the *Echo musical,* while the *Revue Critique* saw his rationalism and clarity as faithful to Hesse and Lemmens.

The cheers accordingly turned out louder than even Widor had foreseen. Widor's own quieter and deeper jubilation, as expressed in a letter to Albert Dupré, embraced not just the interpreter but also the improviser and the composer. "I can die content," wrote the seventy-six-year-old master. "I know the French organ school will remain in good hands."

· 5 ·

Dupré's international recital career commenced in 1920–25, its prosperity unexampled and never yet surpassed. His debut in England drew more than five thousand persons to the Albert Hall. His first tours in North America, which nearly everywhere drew multitudes, set a mercurial, indeed unbelievable pace: in 1922–23, ninety-two recitals in six months; in 1923–24, one hundred and ten recitals in six months. Dupré charmed the capitals of Europe, his own not least of all; Parisian ovation succeeded ovation, as he again presented his Bach series, this time at the Trocadéro, and gave recitals devoted, respectively, to Vierne, Widor, Mendelssohn, and Franck. Invariably he played with dash and aplomb. Invariably he played by heart. Invariably he capped his programs, and left his audiences spellbound, by improvising preludes and fugues or chaconnes or passacaglias or trio sonatas or symphonies. His gifts beguiled the more for being accompanied by modest demeanor: he was smiling and unaffected on the stage; in private, courteous and soft-spoken.

During the weeks and months of traveling, Dupré observed, noted down, and pondered. A friend recalls that he "interested himself in everything. To him, nothing was boring. He read much. He questioned his interviewers on their work, their activities. From his foreign tours he brought back numerous observations. He stayed abreast of advances in science. His mind was constantly at work, and, of an evening, he would hasten to enter in his notebooks, faithfully kept, his day's observations, reflections, and meditations on the widest variety of subjects: philosophy, religions, astronomy, architecture, urban planning, painting, sculpture."

He compiled too, in handwriting as meticulous as his thought, lines from favorite poems, translations of musical terms, timings and registrations of works, notes on ancient civilizations, comments on teaching, dates of painters and musicians, populations and mileage from Paris of cities and towns, a volume entitled "Concerts" in which he inscribed the date of every recital, and a dozen tomes of organ specifications in which he pictured in multicolored pencil the consoles and their accessories. Nor, exhilarated by the organs he met, did Dupré neglect to compose, though he must snatch his moments of leisure and write music in hotels and on trains.

Having grown up in the Cavaillé-Coll esthetics, Dupré was surprised, then captivated, by the uses to which electricity had been put by English and North American organ builders. Effortless changes of tone color, key action as reliable as it was facile, timbres born of high wind pressures—such advances, he remarked in 1924, by making possible effects previously unthought of, made necessary a new idiom. But to call the new idiom "orchestral" or "symphonic" struck him as dangerously delusive. "There are no 'symphonic' organs!" Dupré insisted time and again. "The organ is, ought to be, and can only remain polyphonic." The challenge he felt as composer was that of devising "a new artistic formula in modern harmonic feeling and modern orchestral coloring without losing the dignity of the instrument."

Thus challenged and exhilarated, Dupré wrote some of his nimblest works, among them the Symphony for Organ and Orchestra and "Variations sur un Noël." The former he conceived as "a symphony for two orchestras, the whole effect working somewhat like a chemical reaction—that is, producing an entirely new ensemble effect. With the new higher wind pressures, it is possible to oppose any solo stop with the solo instrument in the orchestra." Similarly, as he later specified, the latter work's contrasted hues took inspiration from organs he played in London, Liverpool, Edinburgh, New York, Philadelphia, Montreal, Chicago, Saint Paul, Vancouver, San Francisco, Los Angeles, and San Diego.

Like Guilmant an avid colorist, and as knowledgeable as he about organ building, Dupré relished the lately perfected gambas, French horns, English horns, trombones, clarinets, erzählers, and flute celestes, deeming them sophisticated refinements. To view them as such, needless to add, was no reproof to Cavaillé-Coll, whom Dupré continued to honor as the "greatest genius of the organ that the world has ever seen." Indeed, Dupré held that Cavaillé-Coll, sage and farsighted as always, had considered inevitable and desirable the revolution wrought by electricity. Old age and extraneous factors alone had barred him from that path.

Yet the interpreter of Dupré's fifty-odd opuses for organ will find scant practical use in distinguishing works designed for the old instrument from works designed for the new. Granted, Dupré before

1920 composed for Cavaillé-Coll's organs exclusively. But the early works as readily fit period Willises, Skinners, and Casavants, and the later works as readily fit large Cavaillé-Colls. Disparity among these builders, it is true, and within each builder's work, greatly outweighs likeness; not only is a piece played at Woolsey Hall not the same piece when played at Saint Ouen, a piece played on a 1910 Skinner is not the same played on a 1928. But the difference is of degree, of subtlety rather than essence, as with Chopin on a Steinway compared with Chopin on an Erard. Nor does zest for color keep Dupré from using masses of tone in the manner of his forebears; and when reeds are added *en bloc* to foundations, in, say, the standard crescendo, the ear little cares whether the change is made by ventil or by piston.

A more useful distinction would group the works by purpose: pedagogic, liturgical, and concert. Dupré had the student in mind when writing *Seventy-Nine Chorales* and *Vingt-Quatre Inventions*, as he did when editing the works of Bach, Handel, Mendelssohn, Schumann, Liszt, Franck, and Glazunov. He composed for the Church such works as *Trois Elévations, Eight Short Gregorian Preludes,* and *Entrée, Canzona, Sortie.* He composed for the recital hall such works as the Suite Bretonne, Second Symphony, and *Seven Pieces.* As was also true of his improvising, he drew an unequivocal stylistic line between liturgy and concert; his church harmonies are more austere than their worldly counterparts, his tempos more restrained, his rhythms and forms more sedate, his colors more subdued.

Obviously, some opuses refuse to be pegged. *Le Chemin de la Croix,* devout as it is, was born a concert improvisation; Dupré played its movements in recital, moreover, but also every Lent at Saint Sulpice. The "Choral et Fugue" and *Symphonie-Passion* are by nature secular, their Gregorian themes notwithstanding. *Vision, Evocation,* and *Psaume XVIII,* despite their mysticism, are too long and recondite to fit the liturgy, even used as postludes. Then there is *Les Nymphéas,* a work inspired by the Monet paintings, which is unplayable on any organ but the one for which it was designed, the "organ of the year 2,000," as he called it, that Dupré installed in his home.

To questions of tempo, phrasing, and articulation Dupré himself provides answers, albeit partial and indirect: he writes prefaces to his editions, and occasionally to his works, and gives precept and example in his textbooks, *Méthode d'Orgue,* and *Philosophy of Music.* From these sources, and from his express allegiance to the customs of his masters, we may deduce his preference and practice. This preference and practice applies, furthermore, to works early and late, since apart from the increasing abstractness in his thought that accompanies increasing age, a tendency well known among creators, Dupré's idiom changes hardly at all from the beginning of his career to the end.

More helpful because more explicit, he often incorporates into note values and silences his desired articulation and phrasing; in lieu of drawing a slur, for instance, he will phrase by inserting a rest. And so consistently and thoroughly does he do this, that one need only play what is written in order to grasp and obey his will.

To "play what is written" is the most demanding of tasks, as Dupré reminds us when he insists, as regards organ playing on the whole, that "the legato should be perfect, the rhythm inexorable, the length of rests exact, the simultaneity of the voices impeccable, the attack and release of chords exactly together." And it is not alone in the performance of his own works that he advises discipline and respect:

> People like to say that the organ is devoid of all accent. Accent is what the organist must give it. And this is only possible if one's playing is absolutely clear. Clarity depends first of all on a quasi-mathematical respect for note values. Without this exactitude, the overlapping of notes, given the sustained sound of the instrument, ends in confusion. And phrasing, which makes up so large a part of interpretation, is to be determined not by caprice but by the rules of classical polyphony.
>
> Clarity further consists in knowing how to identify the dif-

ferent levels in a work. Given the tonal masses that the organist must manage, it is indispensable to mark off the beginning of each level by a well-thought-out registration.

It is partly in registration that an organist's individuality is revealed. The tone colors assigned to a classical piece should be restricted to those known when it was written. In modern music, whose range of color is infinitely richer and wider, the organist should be like the good orchestrator who knows how to bestow on each part of the work its proper character and hue.

It is in this way that good organists, though strictly governed by these stern provisos, are plainly differentiated one from another by their taste, lucidity, and imagination.

As to touch, Dupré calculates durations as carefully as did his mentors. His legato is neither sticky nor dry, and is enlivened by respirations. In it he played Franck's works and Guilmant's and Widor's and Vierne's and his own. In it he played early music as well, since to him the older varieties of touch, whether German or French or other, seemed merely precursory, like early organs themselves. Not till the advent of Cavaillé-Coll did the organ come near to perfection, he believed, and not till the advent of Lemmens and his followers did touch become scientific. Dupré well knew that measured legato was a relatively recent development, but on rational grounds defended it as the sum and substance of technique: it being an infallible means to clarity, logic decreed it indispensable to old repertories as well as to modern.

As to tempos, it is no exaggeration to say he was obsessed with the dangers of playing too fast, of speed negating clarity and grace. Though his tempos tended to be quicker than Widor's, they respected the nobility of the organ and its setting. Dupré's judicious tempos intensified rhythm a hundredfold; his rhythmic drive, in his playing and his improvising, was relentless, irresistible, overpowering—as for instance in his tendency to shorten fortissimo chords, as Fleury recalls, "like a 'bang,' or like slapping one's hands together." So too as regards his works: rhythmic drive and imperious accent are among their most conspicuous features.

As to form, Dupré wrote two organ symphonies (the *Symphonie-Passion* his first), then extended the genre by writing the symphonic poems *Evocation*, *Psaume XVIII*, and *Vision*. And his love of the piano, together with his wish to open new paths for the organ, impelled him to write, for piano and organ, a Ballade, a Sinfonia, and Variations on Two Themes, plus a quartet for violin, viola, cello, and organ; a sonata for cello and organ; and a trio for violin, cello, and organ.

Even in such innovative scores as these, his idiom evolves from the traditional. His asymmetrical rhythms may owe something to his interest in Greek music and to Stravinsky's innovations. But apart from the modal harmonies that he uses in both secular and sacred works—harmonies based on Eastern as well as on church modes—Dupré is first and foremost a contrapuntist; his harmonies tend to grow from his counterpoints and to be as linear as his melodies. Though some of his progressions and dissonances might well have set Widor's teeth on edge, he cannot be called daring even so, at least when compared to such innovative contemporaries as Schoenberg, Berg, and Webern. With their harmonic and melodic inventions, with, in short, the tumultuous change these masters were bringing about, Dupré was in fact well acquainted. But he said he felt no need to devise a new alphabet, when so much remained to be written in the old.

❧ 7 ❧

Jean Langlais

BEFORE TURNING OUR ATTENTION TO THE work of one of Music's most remarkable geniuses, we must note some events that took place in the decades of his birth and young adulthood.

In the musico-political Paris of the 1920s, Widor was singularly powerful. To his friends in high places, his successes in ballet and opera, his published instrumental and orchestral music and critical and editorial writings, his half-century at Saint Sulpice, his renown as touring virtuoso, and his professorship in composition— to these wellsprings of influence had been added, in 1914, an appointment as permanent secretary of the Academy of Fine Arts. Thereafter, from his apartment in the Mazarin Palace, Widor could direct state money and prestige to such artists as he thought deserving. A word from him could help decide whether operas would be mounted and symphonies performed, architecture commissioned, painting and sculpture displayed.

No doubt he partook of human foible, and no doubt power tends to corrupt, yet the record shows Widor exercising power with wisdom, selflessness, and humor. Dupré arrived at the Mazarin one day to discover him chuckling over a letter. "Here," Widor said, "read this. I just finished writing it." "Sir," it began, "I do not thank you for your article on my most recent composition. But I take pleasure in informing you that I have ruled favorably on the aid which you requested."

Widor had long since wielded power, if only by his single-mindedness and charm. Thanks to him, Guilmant took over the Conservatory organ class, as we saw, and Vierne gained Notre Dame. Thanks to Widor, Schweitzer wrote a biography of Bach, and collaborated in an edition. Thanks to Widor, Dupré carried off the Rome Prize and pursued a career in America, his first North American booking having come about solely because Widor recommended him.

Not all such endeavors prospered, however, or bequeathed so much to posterity. Widor tried, it seems, but failed to save Cavaillé-Coll's firm from liquidation; it was taken over, in the end, by Mutin. Widor worked long to establish in Spain a cultural center like the Villa Medici, only to see it laid waste by war. And he came within a hairsbreadth of having Vierne succeed Guilmant at the Conservatory; the appointment went instead to Gigout—a loss attributable, Vierne asserts, to Widor's own momentary lapse in tact.

Briefly told, Eugène Gigout, already sixty-seven years old in 1911, the year of Guilmant's death, had declined from the start to give up his own teaching to apply for Guilmant's post; he relented when entreated to apply by Saint-Saëns and Fauré. Now Fauré, the Conservatory director, had at first warmly backed Vierne, having agreed with Widor, who proposed him, that during long years of service Vierne had proved himself worthy. Fauré affirmed, according to Vierne's memoirs, "that he knew how much I had done for the school, and that everyone would be appropriately grateful. . . . Thinking myself the official contender, I made my courtesy calls unworried . . . till Widor committed the grave indiscretion of criticizing Fauré to some mutual friends. These good people, needless to say, hastened to tell him of Widor's remarks. Deeply offended, Fauré felt resentment for which I had to pay the price. . . . Such was the ruin of hopes that were based on seventeen years of unremitting effort, the reward for the disinterestedness with which I had gratuitously served the cause of our art, for I received no salary for the class, and none for my private sessions with auditors."

Whether Vierne's narrative tells all, or whether other factors entered in, Gigout's appointment caused Vierne dismay. But Vierne owed too much to Widor to let bitterness spoil their relation too, and Widor, for his part, tried to make amends. When, soon afterward, d'Indy offered Vierne a post at the Schola Cantorum, Widor, no admirer of d'Indy's, nevertheless counseled Vierne to accept. "It is a pulpit from which you can preach the true gospel," Vierne tells us Widor said. "I will make it known high and low that the genuine organ tradition can be learned nowhere else." Vierne accepted the post, and was to hold it for more than two decades. Eventually, we learn from the memoirs, he made peace with all concerned. He calls Fauré a composer without peer, praises Gigout as upright and excellent, and details with touching warmth his indebtedness to Widor.

The memoirs were Vierne's last work. A page remained in his typewriter, on the evening of 2 June 1937, when Vierne left for Notre Dame to participate in a recital of his music. The crowd was large, and all had gone well, when suddenly, having been handed a slip of paper containing the theme for an improvisation, and having reflected a moment and drawn some stops, Vierne slumped toward the keyboards, his hand clutching his chest, and fell from the bench, hitting a pedal note that reverberated down the nave. In the throes of a heart attack, he began to lose consciousness before the echo faded away. He died a few minutes later.

The year 1937 was lamentable for French music as a whole. It saw Vierne's death and the deaths of Roussel, Pierné, and Ravel. And it saw, on 12 March, the death of Widor, at the age of ninety-three.

Robust health had but recently deserted him. Not till late 1933, Dupré notes, was the old man really unwell. "He continued to climb the steps to his organ loft, but asked me to play for most of the service. . . . Then, at the end of mass on the last Sunday of the year, he took me with him to the Institute. 'Sit down. I am going to write my letter of resignation to the Curé of Saint Sulpice.' I shivered. 'But *Maître*, why? I am beside you—' He stopped me. 'No. I have lost my strength, and consequently I have lost my technique.' He made this declaration with such serenity that I was overcome. He went on: 'I have my reasons for seeing you succeed me while I live.'" Thus in 1934, after having for twenty-eight years served as Widor's deputy, Dupré became his successor.

Schweitzer too, who since the 1890s had been an adoptive son, recalls the close: "Before leaving again for Africa I went to Paris for a few hours to see him once more. He was already very ill (heart and kidneys) and knew that he no longer had much time. He was quite serene. In his armchair he was at work revising some of his compositions that were to be reprinted. He had a presentiment of the war, and was grieved at the thought. We talked again of organ building. He disapproved of the departure by French organ building from the traditions of Cavaillé-Coll, and was sad that his voice was not listened to and that some of his pupils wanted to transform the lovely old organs they had charge of. But he felt certain that his works for the organ would endure and influence organists of the future."

On the evening Widor died, the centenary of Guilmant's birth was being commemorated at Trinity Church. "Widor had taken a keen interest in the preparations for this concert," Dupré writes. "He passed away while it was in progress. So it was that these two great French masters of the organ, these two great apostles of J. S. Bach in France, take their places to the very day within the same one hundred years: 1837–1937."

Guilmant's successor at the Conservatory was, as we saw, Eugène Gigout. Born on 23 March 1844 —the same year as Widor—Gigout was by age ten an exemplary singer and scholar at the cathedral choir school in his native town of Nancy. He came to Paris, in his early teens, to train at the Ecole Niedermeyer. There he studied the piano with Saint-Saëns and the organ with Clément Loret, an apt pupil of Lemmens's, and there learned to play exceedingly well, if less brilliantly than Guilmant or Widor. But then brilliance was not Gigout's aim. Though reviews of his recitals praise his technical command, his passion was for liturgical music, particularly Gregorian chant. In everything touching on church music, Gigout was a master indeed.

As teacher he was also superb. Even before graduating he was teaching solfège and plainsong at the Ecole Niedermeyer, where he later taught harmony, counterpoint, fugue, and organ. Later still, he founded his own academy in organ, improvisation, and plainsong, and saw it prosper for a quarter century. And over a fourteen-year span at the Conservatory he produced some splendid organists. Withal, the stature attained by his pupils attests his dedication and high competence. Fleury, Marchal, and Duruflé count among his last and finest pupils, Fauré among the earliest. Fauré was Gigout's junior by a year. He became a lifelong friend.

Gigout became a friend of Franck's too—a close enough friend that Franck's family entrusted him with preparing *Trois Chorals* for the press—and of Saint-Saëns's; he assisted Saint-Saëns at the Madeleine and shared the older man's conception of church music. As noted above, Saint-Saëns maintained that church music should be grand and serene, should take as its purpose assisting prayer, and should stay aloof from all that was worldly. To this conception, which rejected as inapt even the preludes and fugues of Bach, Widor's secular virtuosity was foreign, if not actually offensive. Only natural, then, that Saint-Saëns should remark to Fauré, endorsing Gigout for the Conservatory, that "quite apart from my great liking for him, I consider him the most capable organist I have ever met."

In 1863, Gigout became organist at Saint Augustin; he remained there sixty-two years. During his tenure he found time to write criticism, revise Lemmens's *Ecole d'Orgue*, and publish some three hundred compositions, in addition to teaching such nascent composers as Léon Boëllmann, who became his protégé and son-in-law, and Roussel. In sum, Gigout attached less importance to execution and technique than to improvisation and plainsong accompaniment, and his organ pupils, though less dexterous virtuosi by and large than those trained by Guilmant and Widor, became adepts in counterpoint and improvisation and in the beauties and disciplines of liturgy.

Gigout's death, on 9 December 1925, left the Conservatory post vacant once more. Vierne applied, but withdrew in favor of Libert, Tournemire, and Dupré, each a former pupil of Widor's. As might be expected, Widor had already resolved to back Dupré, having urged him as early as 1922 to contemplate trying for the succession. Probably Widor had already planned the campaign; it is known, in any case, that he enlisted as allies Pierné, Ravel, and Dukas. Probably Widor, given the recent deaths of Fauré and Saint-Saëns, felt reasonably sure of victory. At all events, Dupré received the appointment, and thus owed to Widor yet another of the great joys of his career.

"All my life and with all my heart," Dupré was to declare, "I have loved teaching." His love took root, he adds, in the example of his forebears, teachers for generations. Their influence approached the mystical: "The moment I awaken in the morning, I feel their presence within me. I continue what they began. And it is that continuity which I try to impart to my pupils." When decades later, having resigned the professorship in order to became director of the Conservatory, Dupré looked back on his achievement, it was to Widor and Guilmant he gave credit, and Guilmant he named as exemplar: "I just followed the path which had been opened by my master, trying to put into practice the precious methods I had been privileged to learn from him." And: "These two great masters brought me up, formed me, as if I were their own child."

Dupré's achievement was prodigious; in twenty-eight years, from the spring of 1926 to the spring of 1954, Dupré produced no fewer than thirty-nine *premier prix* laureates. Prodigious too the number of his pupils who attained international stature. Marie-Claire Alain, Pierre Cochereau, Jeanne Demessieux, Marie-

Madeleine Duruflé-Chevalier, Jean Guillou, Gaston Litaize, and Odile Pierre were among those who won distinction at home and abroad, chiefly as improvisers and performers. Other pupils, though skilled improvisers and performers, won distinction in other ways: Françoise Renet, who served long and honorably as Dupré's deputy at Saint Sulpice; Rolande Falcinelli, who after debuts in France and abroad succeeded Dupré as Conservatory professor; and Jehan Alain, Olivier Messiaen, and Jean Langlais, who wrote works that promise to endure.

To many, Jean Langlais is the most remarkable figure of all. But though high accomplishment has seldom grown from beginnings less auspicious, it is by his work that he should be judged, not by the difficulties he overcame.

· 2 ·

Born in the Breton village of La Fontenelle, on 15 February 1907, the son of a seamstress and of a stone cutter and the eldest of four children, Jean Langlais had by age three, from the ravages of glaucoma, lost every trace of his sight. In after life he could recall nothing more than vague impressions of color, of the yellow and red of some flowers alongside his parents' earthen-floor cottage.

His handicap, like his poverty, at first seemed hardly to matter. Though he was repeatedly wounded by well-meaning neighbors' sympathetic remarks—"Better for him," he overheard, "had he lost an arm or a leg"—his parents so helped him strive for independence that he learned to climb trees, go alone on errands, and even ride a bicycle. It was his further good fortune to be self-reliant by nature, and possessed of about as much wry humor as of typical Celtic pessimism.

At eight he was singing with other children at mass, learning to love the cadences of plainchant as tenderly as he loved Breton folksong. In the village church too, and thanks to a pious grandmother, he acquired a consoling faith. God had been good in making him blind, so he would later reflect: sighted, he would have been deprived of any hope of an education, let alone an education in music.

As it was, he started late. He had attended the village school and learned a bit of arithmetic and history, but there being no provision for teaching the blind, he could neither read nor write, nor had he begun to study music, when at ten on a scholarship he entered the National Institute for Blind Children.

That admirable school had little changed in the quarter century since Vierne's matriculation. The curriculum remained as rigorous, the more so for students specializing in music, who, besides eleven daily hours of classes, must somehow find time to practice. Langlais quickly joined their ranks and, like Vierne, thrived on the discipline: fiercely hard-working, he soon learned braille and began studying solfège and the piano. Like Vierne, he would master the violin. And like Vierne, he was drawn irresistibly to the instrument that would occupy the central place in his life. A cadence in a piano piece, having thrilled him by its sostenuto, turned his thought once for all to the organ.

Franck's spirit, still palpably present in the school, indirectly but ineffaceably touched the future organist of Saint Clotilde. It mainly did so through Albert Mahaut, a favorite pupil of Franck's who for three years taught Langlais harmony; and through André Marchal, the young genius of an organist at Saint Germain des Prés. In October 1923 Marchal, a *premier prix* winner under Gigout at the Conservatory and himself a graduate of the National Institute for Blind Children, became Langlais's instructor in organ. Marchal had as well studied with Adolphe Marty, yet another disciple of Franck's.

But not Franck's supple expressiveness alone did Langlais absorb from Marchal, still less a superlative technique, though these were readily acquired. Rather, he came to emulate in Marchal a certain poetical spirit without which, as Langlais would ever afterward maintain, organ music is mere mathematics.

This spirit was manifest not just in Marchal's way of playing

Franck, but also in his Bach, French classicists, and moderns—in his Vierne, for instance, when, earlier in 1923, in one of four recitals spanning the repertory, Marchal gave, at Vierne's request, the première of Vierne's Fourth Symphony. The poetic spirit was manifest when in that same series at the Conservatory Marchal played Cabezón, Frescobaldi, Buxtehude, Grigny, Daquin, Couperin, Bach, Mendelssohn, Schumann, Saint-Saëns, Gigout, Boëllmann, Guilmant, Widor, Dupré. And together with rare inventiveness and facility, it was manifest whenever Marchal improvised.

The marks of his poetic spirit were Marchal's exquisite rubati, an offshoot, it may be, of Franck's; a plasticity of legato that separated notes not by rule but by expressive need; and refinements of tone color that evolved from a love for old musics and their timbres. In a word, Marchal was an artist. And since Langlais was too much an artist himself to try to imitate the inimitable, he was impelled to seek eloquence of his own.

His study with Marchal thus stands as cardinal event in Langlais's formation. Langlais was sixteen, Marchal twenty-nine, when their collaboration began. It began, unexceptionally enough, with exercises in technique: in pedaling, from a textbook of Marty's, and in legato, from Lemmens's *Ecole d'Orgue*. In time, Marchal would introduce Langlais to counterpoint, fugue, and improvisation, and, though no composer himself, ably coach him in composition. At the beginning, concentrating on repertory, he at once cast Langlais into difficulties by assigning Bach's "Dorian" Toccata, which suggests how swiftly Langlais had progressed from his tenth to his sixteenth birthday.

His progress did not abate, since his love of the art, not to mention his hard work, matched Marchal's demands for perfection. A year or two later sees him assisting Marchal at Saint Germain des Prés, and substituting at another prominent church, Saint Etienne du Mont. Then, at age nineteen, he makes a concert debut: "A very young artist, M. Jean Langlais, gave his first organ recital the other evening. He strikes me as admirably possessed of all the resources of his art. In a well-constructed program, in which were joined works by Bach, Palestrina, Schumann, Dupré, Vierne, he evidenced the most solid technical qualifications as well as a very expressive and very nimble touch, especially in Gigout's Toccata." Langlais hoped soon, the reviewer added, to enter the Conservatory organ class.

It was a class and institution, as the reader will recall, whose prestige and governmental ties determined future employment and distinction, hence a class and institution to which every ambitious young organist craved entrance. Langlais, who might well have preferred to study under Marchal's late master, Gigout, became Dupré's pupil, in 1927, largely by expedience.

"Dupré, for us, was a father," a *premier prix* laureate states, "gentle, encouraging, helpful, patient." Another prize winner asserts that "as a teacher, he was beyond compare: patient, indulgent, encouraging." Another remembers "with what love he directed his class, and how his instruction was clear, methodical, helpful." And another recalls that Dupré adhered to that "fine old pedagogical principle of complimenting what was good in the student's performance before going on to criticize," and that if discipline were the hallmark of the class, it was "quite natural and unforced." Langlais, however, though he would later acknowledge the "deep influence" of Dupré's class, praising its "spirit of order, precision, clarity, . . . its enthusiasm for what is beautiful," and though after leaving the class he would for three years study privately with Dupré, found that some of Dupré's ideals differed unacceptably from Marchal's. Dupré carried discipline too far.

Langlais did not object to rigor in externals: for example, Dupré's dictum that as classes began at 1:30, students arriving at 1:31 would find the door firmly shut; nor to that rigor as regards execution which weekly required new pages to be memorized. Marchal too had been a taskmaster, and few could spend a decade at the National Institute for Blind Children without profiting from discipline of this outward sort—certainly not Langlais, who had left one of the most brilliant records in the history of the school. Nor did Langlais object to rigor in the structures of improvisation, for example Dupré's demand that in fugues the countersubject be kept throughout, though Langlais later held that not every fugue lent itself to such treatment. Nor could Langlais's objections be accounted for by personal dislike, though they perhaps gained strength from disparate background and mores—from the age-old antipathy of Bretons and Normans, it may be, or of pious and worldly Catholics, or of poor and middle class. They grew from artistic dissent so deep-rooted that compromise was unthinkable.

Langlais, nurtured by Marchal's and Franck's warmly poetic spirits, found Dupré's conception of the organist's art rigid to the point of sterility. He found Dupré as creator less detached than Dupré as interpreter, and it was in Franck above all, as we saw, that he deplored Dupré's abstraction. He was puzzled to observe, on the one hand, a composer and improviser whose works brimmed over with feeling: the Dupré of the *Fifteen Pieces,* Three Preludes and Fugues, and *Symphonie-Passion;* and on the other, an interpreter who was a slave to method, an automaton, an icy intellect: the Dupré who when playing the most fervent of scores recurred to articulations and rhythms suited to eighteenth-century polyphony—who applied a procrustean rule to works of every period and style.

For Dupré's Franck was not the only sign of this apparent contradiction. How could so acute a sensibility and so penetrating a mind—we may imagine Langlais asking—find it artistic to play Couperin with the measured legato appropriate to a Widor symphony? Marchal's Couperin breathed elegance; Dupré's was a dead museum piece, so it doubtless seemed to Langlais. There was no use saying in Dupré's defense that musicology was only beginning to announce the principles which ought to obtain, that his style grew from ignorance or misconception: in truth, as Langlais learned, it grew from informed meditation. Nor could ignorance or unconcern explain Dupré's strictness in Franck: Dupré well knew of Franck's pliancy, having questioned Franck's pupils and friends, and having done so because intent on being Franck's faithful interpreter and advocate. The mystery remained. Why such reserve?

In fine, Dupré's style, which like any artist's derived from predisposition and reflection, centered in an all-encompassing love of order to which all things were subordinate, emotion not excepted. Dupré's mind was so given to method, so categorical in both senses of the term, that every impression, artistic or other, must be assigned its place once for all. To the assigning Dupré directed the energy of an exact and critical intelligence. Nothing could have struck him as more natural, though he looked on Widor's and Guilmant's teachings as unimpeachable truth, than to reshape them in much the way early Church fathers turned the gospel into ecclesiastical system: generalities hardened into rule, principles into dogma. As Dupré conceived, so he taught and played. And though receptive listeners lauded his style for its self-effacing objectivity, for constraint that reinforced expressiveness by letting notes speak for themselves, other listeners no less sensitive found it dryasdust, to say the least. To them, notes could only speak for themselves when more freely guided by the heart.

We may recall in passing that the ebb and flow of great artistic trends, those tides spanning decades or centuries, has to do with the need of artists to level the old ground before making a fresh start. Obviously, no artist levels without the animus that grows from offended sensibility; no artist tears down out of indifference, or out of boredom undertakes new construction. The corollary truth is that artistic conviction enjoins a singleness of vision that denies all possibility of merit in others. Thus with Dupré and Langlais, as with Saint-Saëns and Franck and many another irreconcilable pair, a fundamental variance of temperament, of what for each was most inward and peculiar in mood and in manner of apprehending, made mutual comprehension unlikely. At the same time Langlais, together with Marchal and other modernist geniuses, viewed elements of the Lemmens tradition as old ground in want of leveling—the universally applicable legato, for instance, and other vestiges of scientism; Dupré, as tradition's proponent, became *ex officio* an adversary, his style a peg on which to hang repudiation and reform.

Much of this lay in the future. Meantime, young Langlais did what any student may profit from doing: he made himself conform *ad interim* to his teacher's unsympathetic ways, resolving to learn what he could. As a matter of fact, in the beginning, Langlais revered Dupré.

· 3 ·

Dupré's class of eight or ten students met in the Salle Berlioz three times each week, at the two-manual Mutin on which Dupré had played all of Bach. The instrument dated from about 1911, when the Conservatory had moved to the rue de Madrid, and was hardly less mediocre than its predecessor in the rue Bergère. Mondays and Wednesdays were devoted to improvisation—fugue on one day, *thème libre* on the other—and Fridays to execution. Each session lasted two hours. The odd few minutes would be spent on plainsong accompaniment.

Dupré would launch the improvisation sessions by imposing a theme and calling for a volunteer. A classmate of Langlais's recollects how Dupré, "having let us fly off on our own unsteady wings, and noting our perplexities, would take our place on the bench. At once, with sovereign ease and clarity, he would set us on the right path and under his fingers all would look effortless and simple. After such an example, we would resume our place comforted and encouraged." But not always. Another classmate says that Dupré's demonstrations so dazzled as to be inhibiting. And Langlais himself, though he called Dupré a "charming" man and a "marvelous" teacher, found him "daunting" even so: "We were intimidated in the presence of this personage who had toured the world with such great success. . . . His prestige weighed on us heavily."

For the session on execution Dupré would but rarely suggest works to be played, and then only if the student had been playing too exclusively the works of one composer or period. Had one played nothing recently but Bach, Dupré might recommend Franck, Mendelssohn, Liszt, Widor, Guilmant, Dandrieu, or Clérambault. He required every piece to be memorized, even if a student could in consequence perform no more than a page or two. At the outset, Langlais erred by playing in class the same piece two weeks running. He was hurt by Dupré's sarcasm: "If you want to play one piece the whole year long I do not think that will take you very far." Dupré seemed pleased when students learned his own music, but he discouraged its use at examinations, not wishing to vex his colleagues on the juries.

Most students remained in the class three or four years, some being tutored on occasion by their seniors. Once enrolled, the student would receive no private lessons from Dupré, for Dupré would not grant to some what he could not grant to all. He alone decided who might enter his class. None might enter who had not mastered harmony, begun counterpoint and fugue, and passed an informal examination at which Dupré required an improvised fugue exposition and a Bach work played by heart. To Langlais was granted the privilege of auditioning for Dupré at Marchal's studio. Langlais feared he had done badly, but Dupré was sufficiently impressed to promise him admission.

From Dupré, Langlais and his classmates absorbed not merely the history, literature, and technique of the organ and the skills of improvisation-composition, but the essence as well of Dupré's philosophy of music, his conception of the art absolute. "Dupré did not just teach us how to play," a student recalls, "he revealed to us the spirit of the musical forms, indeed of all the arts." Curious, it must have seemed to Langlais, that so cerebral a style should be rooted in views so impassioned.

"Bach was a *monster!*" Dupré would exclaim. "Just think that he improvised as well as he composed! He and Mozart were the greatest 'monsters,' yet Bach would have laughed had anyone told him he would be honored as the greatest of composers. 'Whosoever will use the same concentration as I,' Bach said, 'will compose as proficiently as I.'" Less curious to Langlais, we may suppose, was Dupré's admiration for Descartes, whose method and conclusions "were of capital influence, and applied as aptly to the arts as to the sciences."

Dupré would descant on symbolism, saying that the use of leitmotif seemed a common, if often unconscious, tendency among certain great Germans. "Wagner was not the first. Beethoven used some of Bach's motifs in the last piano sonata." Bach's own use of motifs had been independently detected by Schweitzer and by Pirro, he said, whose researches had been published, with Widor's help, almost simultaneously. And Dupré would cite as an example the organ chorale on "Christ Lag in Todesbanden," in which Bach depicted the "last moment of sorrow before the world beheld the Resurrection," the semiquaver pedal figure representing the "descent by the holy women, step by step, down to the tomb. . . . This I learned from Guilmant."

Or Dupré might compare styles with states of mind, talking of the art of music as "in all likelihood deriving from magic." Among the constituents of music, melody, he would assert, conveys the "greatest emotive force." And always: "The essential mission of music is to express feelings."

He would descant too on the mission of the artist, declaring that "no matter the form in which one expresses oneself, [it is] essential to approach one's task with utter confidence but also with humility." In church, the organist must assist prayer, not disturb it: "Before presuming to induce others to pray, one must first take care not to distract them. Widor taught me this." In concert, the "supreme level" interpreters should strive for is "to regard their life not as a commercial enterprise but as an artistic evangelism," the interpreter's paramount aim being to express the composer's intent.

Whence the importance of tradition. "Take Bach," Dupré would say. "We know how he played, because the living history of music brings his tradition down to us from disciple to disciple. One must play Bach with fidelity to this tradition, for in no other way will we hear his true message. This is so not just for Bach, but for all the music of the great masters." Langlais must have wondered at the gulf dividing principle from application: had not Dupré learned Franck from Guilmant, himself an expressive player?

The lofty was accompanied by the practical. "Do not set pistons during a recital," Dupré would admonish. Or again: "When performing the Bach sonatas," he would say, "be able to play on any combination of manuals, depending on the best registration offered by the organ in question; change manuals with each movement of the work, to prevent fatigue in the arms." Or again: though practicing hands alone or pedals alone might be useful on occasion, "mostly one should practice everything together." One should practice slowly—never faster than one could play perfectly—and let speed come of itself, as it inevitably would. Or again: the common error to avoid when playing in resonant rooms was to play staccato, it being a false belief that this would overcome the muddling effect of echo. Or again: he found it imperative to work "with regularity." One might work by day or night, a matter of mere preference, but the mind functioned best if engaged on the same work at "about the same hours every day." Meantime, "beware of undue self-esteem," which is the "greatest rein on genius."

To safeguard technique, Dupré recommended daily practice at the piano of major and minor scales in octaves, tenths, double thirds, and double sixths; of arpeggios in four and five species; of chromatic scales in double octaves; and of the works of Liszt, Beethoven, and Chopin. He liked to start his own daily routine with an hour spent at the piano. It pleased him that Langlais, already an expert pianist, began coaching with Lazare Lévy, and it would have pleased him that Langlais later told his own students that an organist weak in piano technique was an organist without fingers.

As to practice at the organ, Dupré maintained that whereas three or four daily hours sufficed for the virtuoso, for the student a minimum of seven or eight hours was indispensable, though less if the student were struggling also with counterpoint or fugue. Even so: "At your age," he told Langlais's class, "I practiced twelve hours a day. You will be well advised to do the same!"

To perfect one's pedaling, Dupré recommended mastering all the major and minor scales, first in single notes extending the range of the pedalboard, then in thirds and sixths. He insisted that the key to infallibility lay in the suppleness of the ankle, which must be cultivated like that of the wrist at the piano.

To overcome stage fright, "avoid thinking of what comes later, and concentrate on the moment you are living"; the present would "save" you, the future "unsettle" you. "If you replace stage fright with concentration, you will be amazed at how fast time passes, and how easily and naturally a work unfolds." Attitude was everything. "He that earnestly seeks to make the work he is playing loved will find in this a great source of assurance. He will attain to the inward poise of the great interpreter who, while playing, knows he is there to teach. What does 'to teach' mean, if not to make understood and loved?"

Langlais was still enrolled in the class when he entered on his career. In 1927–29 he composed a Prelude and Fugue, *Six Préludes,* "Prélude sur une Antienne," and "Thème Libre," some of which were later published. In 1929 he began to teach privately. And in April 1930 he joined the faculty of the National Institute for Blind Children, where he was to remain for some forty years.

The competition which decided his appointment was so difficult that the Conservatory competition, in June, seemed easy by comparison. In fact it was very hard, and he was justly proud of his *premier prix.* So too was Dupré, despite one heart-stopping moment. Langlais explains that the fugue "posed no particular problem," but in the *thème libre,* "I decided instead of making the usual transposition to the relative, which would have been C major, to modulate into E minor, which seemed to me much better musically. Well, that was assuredly not how we customarily did it in the class. At the end of the test, when Dupré came up to lead me off the stage, he said: 'My boy, you gave me a turn! What were you thinking of in the *thème libre?* I looked at the jury at that moment, thinking you were lost, but those gentlemen did not bat an eye.

Fortunately, you carried it off well, or it would have ruined your chances of getting a first. Still, I think they will give it to you.'"
Langlais not only won a first, but was granted also, as the *premier prix* laureate ranked highest, the Alexandre Guilmant Prize, with its generous annual stipend.

His post required Langlais to teach organ and also to direct a choir, a choir of fifty-nine members that rehearsed three times weekly and sang twice weekly in chapel. With it he performed quantities of plainsong and works ranging from Dufay to Debussy; in so doing, he learned the techniques of choral composition. For these singers he composed, in 1930–31, "Deux Chansons de Clément Marot," which was his first opus for four-part mixed voices, and "Ave Mundi Gloria," for two voices and organ. These, together with *Poèmes évangeliques*, for organ, were his first works to appear in print.

In 1931, the year he married the lovely and cultivated Jeanne Sartre, Langlais drew acclaim by winning a competition put on by the Société des Amis de l'Orgue. The difficulties were such as could be surmounted by few even among Conservatory graduates: an improvised chorale on a plainchant and on the same theme a fully developed symphonic paraphrase, an improvised prelude and fugue on a given theme, an improvised sonata-allegro on two given themes, the performance by memory of four works of divers periods and styles, and the performance by memory of a modern work chosen by the jury from among three the candidate prepared. No jury could have been more exacting. At its head sat d'Indy— an artist never easy to please—and beside him, among others, Tournemire, Bonnet, Marchal, and Vierne. The candidates were identified by number only, and were invisible to jury and public.

> We have come a long way [reported *Le Courrier musical*] from those competitions in which a single work, too often more pianistic than organistic, is thought an adequate gauge of the complex elements of organ style and technique. On the present occasion, the apt preponderance accorded to works by Bach, the choice of the chorale "O Lamm Gottes," for example, whose

polyphony sets off in relief the organist's ability to phrase—a quality as rare as it is vital—and the obligatory performance of one of Franck's *Trois Chorals*, which are the touchstone of the discerning and sensitive player, together illumine the interpreter's merits or deficiencies. . . .

M. Langlais was easily the victor, thanks in large part to his wonderful paraphrase on "Ave Maris Stella." Jury and audience were captivated from the very first notes of this lovely improvisation, and its charm did not cease till the closing chord. The prelude of his fugue was no less seductive, and his performance of [Bach's] Fugue in D Major and of the finale to M. Vierne's Fourth Symphony revealed a clear, incisive touch and a superior rhythmic sense. The jury awarded the Prix des Amis de l'Orgue to M. Jean Langlais unanimously.

Lessons with Tournemire had helped him to master the subtleties of the Gregorian paraphrase, a technique which, given his love of plainsong, appealed to Langlais strongly.

In 1934 Langlais was named organist at Saint Pierre de Montrouge. He would remain there till his appointment to Saint Clotilde, in 1945. Also in 1934 he returned to the Conservatory to study composition with Dukas. Said that venerable figure at the beginning of their eighteen months together: "You are a born composer. I can teach you nothing but how to orchestrate."

· 4 ·

"Rather short and slender," states a biographer, Langlais in the 1930s and later "displayed surprising agility, covering all alone on foot or by subway great distances in Paris, aided solely by his white cane. His premature baldness and the dark glasses he now wore gave him an air of gravity and seriousness at once belied by his cheerful expression." This duality is present also in his music, for in art as in life his sense of fun was foil to his pessimism. Not that melancholy and mirth coexist in every work; "Scherzo Cats" is not sad or deep, nor *La Passion* humorous. But we find Langlais weep-ing about as often as we find him chuckling to himself, chuckling as he did while sitting in Dupré's class reading Boccaccio in braille.

His wit seemed perennially ready. As students, Langlais and a friend had once disrupted a class by singing at the second a canon written at the third. At an American recital, finding himself encircled by lighted candles, Langlais quipped: "All that is lacking is the coffin." While walking an impetuous dog that suddenly pulled him to the left: "He is becoming a Communist." When that same beloved companion once fell to snoring while its master was practicing, Langlais began to improvise on French lullabies in dialogue with its pitches.

Langlais's output was diverse and prolific. For organ, he wrote ninety-odd opuses that comprise some three hundred pieces, and he wrote orchestral music, chamber music, solo pieces for winds or strings with and without piano, solo piano pieces, suites for cello and orchestra and for piano and orchestra, songs and secular choral music, masses, hymns, anthems, motets, cantatas, and pedagogical works. That he wrote quickly and disliked revising explains a certain unevenness in his catalogue, but nobody would deny that at his best Langlais is superb. Such works as *Hommage à Frescobaldi*, Suite Médiévale, and *Trois Paraphrases Grégoriennes* deserve the renown they enjoy; others as well-wrought, such as his Trio Sonata or First Symphony, ought to be as widely known. The level of his work overall is so high that even his lesser achievements, such as his settings of hymns and Christmas carols, merit admiration.

The organ works, early and late, build on a basically legato touch, presuppose the player's respect for the designated tempo and registration, and range in difficulty from easy to daunting. They are by turns modal and tonal, traditional and daring, but do not so much innovate as synthesize: juxtaposed elements of idioms ranging from Bach's and the French classicists' to Webern's are given unity and strength by Langlais's vitality and vision. "Vision" reminds us that his handicap was no impediment to his art, that if anything it gave added force to his perceptions and depth to their expression. His harmonies are rich, his counterpoints masterly, his timbres multihued and alluring. Emotion ranges from the sublimely detached, as in the "Chant de Paix," to the vehemently engaged, as in the outer movements of the First Symphony—Langlais embracing, like Dupré, the romanticist idea that art must move the beholder. In course of time he becomes a composer of church music primarily, and well over half his organ works are based on Gregorian chant.

After a span of roughly thirty years, in which appear the works that are at present most familiar, come a second thirty years in which works are freer in form, more complex in rhythm and tonality, more variegated in timbre—this we read in the thoughtful biography by Marie-Louise Jaquet-Langlais, the musicologist and former pupil who married the widowed master in 1979.

But though the works can be classed only arbitrarily, their evolution following no unmistakable path, a useful distinction may be drawn between subjective works and objective. Under the former head fall the works lyrical or passionate, among them those based on plainchant; under the latter, the hymn arrangements and the works based on folksong. The subjective pieces require of the player an introspective delicacy, embodied most notably in a pliant legato and rhythm. It is intrinsic to their style, as Langlais said it was to Franck's, that the summits of phrases should be broadened and that repetitions of patterns should be varied. The objective pieces, by contrast, are eloquent in their simplicity. In them Langlais cautioned his pupils not to apply too much rubato, and when playing them himself he would measure repeated notes as meticulously as Dupré.

Whether playing others' music or his own, Langlais in the simpler or the contrapuntal forms was as strict as Dupré in tying common tones in adjacent voices and in measuring repeated notes and phrasings. But whereas Dupré, unlike Guilmant, did not adjust touch to acoustics—it sufficed, Dupré said, to adjust tempo—Langlais did; the less resonant the room, the more legato his touch.

Langlais kept steadily before him Dukas's advice to seek variety in style and in sources of inspiration. Besides the folksong and plainchant he loved, which to him were inseparable from his Breton heritage, he invents original themes that show his gift for shapely melody, and themes derived from proper names, ecclesiastical or Biblical symbolism, hymns, and, long before the fashionable rapprochement of Catholic and Protestant, chorales. He acknowledged Tournemire's influence and Debussy's and Fauré's and once or twice, ruefully, his friend Messiaen's. What is more, he so plainly took Vierne's work as a model, in choral music as well as organ, that he may almost be said to carry on a Vierne tradition. Toward the man he evinced respect and liking that did not go unreturned. *"Mon cheri,"* Vierne once said, "you will learn that everything in life can betray you—health, happiness, money—except for one thing which, believe me, will never let you down. That one thing is music."

Finally, as noted above, the Saint Clotilde organ was so important an influence that Langlais laughingly called it his mistress. "I will never forget the feelings aroused in me the first time I played it. The first chords I played, on the three eight-foot foundations of the récit, were literally overwhelming. For twenty-five years, each Sunday has brought me a renewal of those feelings." And in the 1950s and 1960s, when his hugely successful American tours acquainted him with Aeolian-Skinners, he drew inspiration from these as well. He admired most of all the Mormon Tabernacle organ that Harrison and Schreiner designed; its sonorities were "intensely poetic."

The inspiration that ranked highest of all, however, was his abiding religious faith. With it went a veneration for Mary that was likewise profound and unwavering. She it was, he often said, who inspired the best of his pieces. He liked to add that he was a Breton Catholic who put his gifts at the service of his Church.

The liturgical reforms that preceded and followed the Second Vatican Council put his service to the test. His faith did not waver, nor his love for his Church. But Langlais grew exasperated with clergy who instituted change for the sake of change, and he was appalled by the decline in standards. It was one thing to advocate congregational singing, with its chants on vernacular texts, a reform Langlais approved. In point of fact, few musicians were as eager as he and as qualified to compose such music—witness his French and English masses and canticles. But it was another thing to countenance music so vapid as to be an artistic disgrace.

He grieved to see work of this sort, sung ineptly or played by guitars, supplant plainsong and the organ. Whereas the Church, as he wrote in 1963, had for centuries been mother to the arts, promiscuous reform threatened the continued existence of sacred music worthy of the name: "The most astounding thing about this sad development is that no one seems to understand that a religious ceremony is addressed first and foremost to God, for whom nothing can be too beautiful. We have built magnificent cathedrals to His glory. We have marvelously adorned His ministers in the exercise of their priestly office. We have transcended prayer with music. . . . But for the past few years, genuine composers of sacred art have been replaced by persons who, though sincere, are alone in thinking they have talent." That Rome continued to endorse plainsong and the Latin language officially, and to regard the organ as the sacred instrument of choice, did nothing to undo the damage or cure the mania for experiment.

Then too: "The church was a place into which we were accustomed to enter with reverence, with feeling, in order to meditate devoutly and individually. Nowadays, the big word 'community' is what the clergy lean on exclusively when they organize our public worship, and this deprives the individual Christian of the freedom to pursue the mystical."

At the same time Langlais grew increasingly distressed by trends in the organ world itself. Partisans of the neo-classical, as we saw, were scorning creators and traditions he honored, and he looked on sadly as great numbers of organists, mainly in France, Germany, and the United States, deemed axiomatic ideas he found absurd. He refused to believe that eighteenth-century music had reached a degree of perfection compared to which later music was necessarily inferior, or that early keyboard techniques ought to serve as the model for modern players, or that unequal temperaments were inherently expressive, or that none but tracker action could allow sensitivity in phrasing, or that nineteenth- and twentieth-century works sounded best when played on eighteenth-century organs. He thought it self-evident that such notions betrayed a lamentable ignorance of history.

Still less would he believe in some "ideal" organ perfected during the Baroque. His own fine discrimination let him enjoy the Aeolian at Duke University as much as the Müller in Saint Bavo's or the Clicquot at Poitiers. He relished their distinctive traits. "To me there are but two kinds of organ," he said, with a wisdom that in those troubled decades stands out as unique: "good organs and bad." Or again, in a spirit that could by then have been labeled classic romanticism: "I love everything that is beautiful."

That he continued to play such classicists as Couperin and Frescobaldi, willingly amending his tone colors and ornaments in accord with musicological findings, shows that Langlais opposed extremes, not periods or progress. Possibly for the same reason he took little interest in post-serialism or *musique concrète*, and shunned such techniques as drawing stops part way, holding chords while turning off the wind, and creating tone clusters by depressing keys with the elbows. Perhaps he thought that such devices betokened the end of an era, that resorting to them was tantamount to admitting that a language had been exhausted and everything said. We do know he admired his friend Messiaen and respected Messiaen's discoveries, even though he thought they sometimes verged on the mathematical. What is sure is that his own idiom built on the past unashamedly, incorporating with finesse such innovations as seemed to him musical, and that his late years were as fruitful as his early.

Among the rewards of Langlais's final decades were his organ class at the Schola Cantorum (1960–75), which drew students from North America and several European countries as well as from

France, and which he undertook, he said, in faithfulness to the memory of his predecessor Vierne; accolades from the Academy of Fine Arts and the Legion of Honor; and his frequent classes and tours (more than four hundred recitals in 1952–81) in North America as well as Europe.

Never to be forgotten among the events of his travels were summer sessions at Boys Town, honorary doctorates from four universities, and festivals devoted to his works. A specially memorable event was his appearance in Washington, D.C., in 1969, at one of the most eminent of the world's shrines to Mary, the National Shrine of the Immaculate Conception. There at a pontifical mass for peace, which was attended by several thousand persons, among them seven cardinals, one hundred and seventy-five bishops, representatives of the American government, and dignitaries from the embassies, he heard the choirs of the military academies join those of the shrine and of the Catholic University of America, together with organ and brass—some five hundred musicians—to perform his mass *Orbis Factor,* composed for the occasion. At the close he improvised on the Lourdes hymn, with éclat we may easily imagine.

Though declining health slowed his activity after 1984, Langlais continued teaching and composing almost to the end. His eightieth birthday was observed with a gala concert at the Madeleine—where the Cavaillé-Coll that Saint-Saëns had played had long since been revised—and, in London, with an honorary doctorate conferred by the Royal College of Organists. Nor was he forgotten by his natal village, whose mayor and council organized a reception in honor of its distinguished son.

Langlais died in Paris on 8 May 1991. A Solemn Mass of the Resurrection was celebrated at Saint Clotilde.

⟩⟨ 8 ⟩⟨

Olivier Messiaen

TO LANGLAIS, HE WAS A SCHOOLMATE WHO
ever remained the warmest of friends, and they respected each other's music and played it publicly. To Dupré, with whom friendship
was also lifelong, he was an enigma from the day he enrolled in the
organ class. Not even a request for the father's advice could overcome puzzlement: "Sir," said Dupré to Messiaen *père*, himself a
lycée teacher, "I have not had much experience in teaching, and I
cannot understand your son."—"I don't understand him, either!"
confessed the older man with a smile. "Of all the students I have
had, in twenty-five years of teaching, my son is the only one I
cannot begin to comprehend."

Olivier Messiaen was born in Avignon on 10 December 1908 to
Pierre Messiaen, a Shakespearean translator and scholar, and Cécile
Sauvage, a poet remembered chiefly for the effect her work had on
her son. It was to her, Messiaen maintained, that he owed his interest in music. More precisely, he owed it to what he called her poetic
intuitions, intuitions he said he perceived *in utero*.

　　She made intuition manifest, in the months leading up to his
birth, by composing a set of poems that records her certainty of the

child's being male and an artist, her uneasiness at hearing within her an Oriental music associated with butterflies and bluebirds— "How could she tell I would be an ornithologist and that Japan would fascinate me?"—and her sadness that a colloquy of such high order could but briefly endure.

The poems are not without joy, but their joy is tinged with melancholy. As Messiaen was to observe: "The moment of birth is tragic: tragic for the child whose first gulp of air is brutal, painful, but tragic also for the mother, who loses a part of herself after the longest and most profound of human associations. All these things, so difficult to express, my mother put into words in this book of verse titled *L'âme en bourgeon*. She said them magnificently, with very apt imagery, a keen sense of natural beauties, and, above all, exquisite modesty."

Still, it is sadness verging on morbidity that can compare a child sleeping in the embryonic waters to a god laid out in a transparent bier, or claim a sculptor's authorship of the child's eventual death's-head, pondering how little the dawn knows of the shadows from which it emerges. And in fact Messiaen tells us that his mother was constitutionally unhappy, grieved as she was, he surmises, by the premonition of her early death. At all events: "There is a continuous exchange between mother and child, and the child can pick up exterior emotions. . . . It was my mother who guided me, before I was born, toward nature and toward art."

Though born in Avignon, Messiaen grew up in Grenoble, and even without his mother's guidance would have fallen under the spell of the mountains and meadows of Dauphiné. That region of southeastern France, he would say, was nature at its most imposing, a region "which I have never ceased to love, and in which I live even when far distant from it." There amid valley, crag, forest, and ice cap, beneath a sky whose blue is thick enough to cut, where light and color are constantly changing and where nature's most commanding voice is of sudden storms and rivers in spate—there Messiaen would spend his summers, there write some of his principal works. He would "listen passionately to mountain torrents and waterfalls, and to all the noises made by water and wind," making "no distinction between noise and sound: all this for me always represents music." But he would most love the song of birds, because of all nature's voices theirs struck him as "ultimately the most musical."

The father's influence, in contrast to the mother's, was in large part indirect. Pierre Messiaen went off to the Great War when the boy was only five, and was able to come home on leave fewer than a half-dozen times in four years. But his presence actual or not helped nurture in Messiaen a passion for reading—"I am the offspring of two or three thousand books"—and for English literature especially. Though the lad resisted his father's every attempt to teach him to speak English, he was none the less enjoying Tennyson's poems when he was nine; and acting Shakespeare's villains and heroes, with younger brother as audience or partner, ranked high among childhood games. He was drawn as early and as irresistibly to the theater of Calderón and of Sophocles, whose personages he also acted, and to drama of yet another kind, to Gluck's *Alceste*, Mozart's *Don Giovanni*, Berlioz's *Damnation of Faust*. He taught himself to play the piano sufficiently well to decipher these scores, and learned to sing all the roles.

Messiaen recognized his vocation the day he received as a gift the score to Gluck's *Orfeo ed Euridice*. "I think a true musician ought above everything else to hear with an inner ear. I was quite young, maybe about eight. I went and sat down in the big public park in Grenoble, where there are many beautiful plants and flowers, superb! I sat on a little stone bench, which, incidentally, is still there, and began to look at this score I had just been given. I happened on Orfeo's great aria in F in the first act. And I *read* this aria. At first this did not really surprise me, but little by little I noticed that I was hearing it, that I was hearing the harmonies, that I was hearing within me the melodic line and the rhythms. Hence I had an inner ear, hence was a musician."

Curiously enough, neither father nor mother much influenced Messiaen's religious faith. It was ardent from the beginning, though neither parent was a believer. Art proved the greater impetus to faith, art as refiner of the imagination, for Messiaen soon found correspondence between dramatic truth and dogmatic, between the dramas of Gluck, Berlioz, Shakespeare and the tenets of Roman Catholicism. In Shakespeare especially he was enthralled by "not only the human passions, but the magic too: the witches, sprites, sylphs, ghosts, and apparitions of all kinds. Shakespeare is an author who powerfully develops the imagination. I was partial to fairy tales, and Shakespeare is at times a surpassing fairy tale. It was this aspect that impressed me, much more than certain disillusioned accents of love or death, such as can be found in *Hamlet*, accents that a child of eight obviously could not comprehend. . . . In the verities of the Catholic faith, I found this lure of the marvelous multiplied a hundredfold, a thousandfold, and it was no longer a matter of theatrical fiction but of something that was true."

He was born a believer, he says, and though in later years he read theology from Aquinas to Teilhard, he did so not to dispel doubt—he had none—but to gain understanding that would help him show others by his music the truths of his faith. To the end of his life he believed this to be the noblest, the most valuable part of his work.

· 2 ·

Fast on his father's return from the war and appointment to a teaching post in Paris, Messiaen, now eleven, entered the Conservatory. He had taken some lessons in piano and harmony, had composed his first piece ("La Dame de Shalott," for piano), and had been given another determinative score, *Pelléas et Mélisande*. Like his contact with Gluck, Berlioz, and Shakespeare, this entree into Debussy's and Maeterlinck's world—into eroticism depicted in music and prose each of ineffable harmonies and colors—gripped his imagination. So much so that forty years later, to the astonishment of his pupils, he could still analyze every page of the score by heart. So much so that human passion of the fatal Tristramian sort would become, together with nature and his faith, a preponderant idea in his work.

An artist is more than the sum of his influences but is of course also not less, and Messiaen's decade at the Conservatory brought encounters that were seminal. With Jean Gallon and Georges Caussade, and privately with Noël Gallon, he studied harmony, counterpoint, and fugue; with Georges Falkenberg, the piano; with César-Abel Estyle, piano accompaniment; with Joseph Baggers, percussion; with Maurice Emmanuel, music history; with Dukas, composition and orchestration; with Dupré, the organ and improvisation. Prize followed prize, moreover, and Messiaen was accounted by many the most brilliant Conservatory student of his day. Only the Rome Prize eluded him, though he competed for it twice.

He learned much from each master, he recalls, and to each acknowledged a debt: to the Gallon brothers for his feeling for natural harmony and understanding of harmonic techniques; to Dukas for skill in orchestration and instrumentation, a sense of artistic integrity, a sense of form, a sense of the poetical in music, and insight into color-sound correspondence; to Emmanuel and Dupré for interest in modes and Greek rhythms; to Dupré, who "introduced me to plainsong, registration, and improvisation, and passed on to me organ technique," for help in fathoming the inmost artistic self. This self-knowledge he attributes to Dupré's having made him work at improvisation methodically.

And yet, Messiaen notes, the word *influence* "is not exact. I liked all my teachers very much, respected my teachers greatly, felt for them deep esteem. But I cannot say that I was influenced by them. (Dupré is a wonderful teacher and a wonderful performer. He has always been very good to me, and I love him dearly.) It is hard to say what my influences are. When I was a child I loved Mozart, Berlioz, Wagner. I loved most of all Debussy. But afterward I worked with many other things. I worked with Greek metrics. I worked with the deçî-tâlas [regional rhythmic patterns] of

India. I studied ornithology and wrote down the songs of birds. And I fell in love with stained glass, the great cathedral rose windows and their colors. All this influenced me, plus all the reading I did. And Shakespeare. Don't forget Shakespeare. These are therefore very mixed influences, very, very complex."

One influence is undeniable nevertheless: the idea of time. Time as interval, time as duration, time as point or as speed or as dimension—in all the ways his coalescent mind could manipulate the temporal abstractions, time began to fascinate Messiaen. It intrigued him in H. G. Wells's *Time Machine,* which was always a favorite novel, and in *Pelléas et Mélisande;* Wells showed time as multilayered and traversable, Debussy as linear and ductile. It intrigued him in the sound of the organ, whose unvarying tone symbolized, as Widor and others had said long before, the infinite and the immutable. It intrigued him in the idea of God as in the most literal sense timeless: a Person whose knowing is simultaneous, unconfined by past and future.

Time and rhythm being allied, Messiaen began to develop a rhythmic vocabulary whose complexity resembled time's own, a vocabulary remarkable for its use of irregularly patterned note values, non-retrogradable rhythms (his term for a series of note values that reads identically left to right and right to left), superimposed tempos—in other words, a vocabulary for the most part ametrical that echoed the rhythms of nature as Messiaen perceived them.

For Bach himself is not rhythmic, Messiaen declares, turning a thought-cliché inside out: Bach's music is arrhythmic if rhythm is understood as deriving from the movements of nature. These are free, unequal in length, incessantly multiple and undulating. In Bach's music, by contrast, "one hears an uninterrupted succession of equal durations that immerse the listener in self-satisfied contentment. Nothing intervenes to disturb one's pulse, breathing, and heartbeat, so one is very tranquil, receives no shock, and all this seems perfectly 'rhythmic.'" Not even jazz is truly rhythmic, for its syncopation only exists by virtue of being superimposed on equal note values; these it contradicts, and "despite the rhythm engendered by this contradiction, the listener once again becomes accustomed to equal note values that bring a great tranquility."

By 1930, when Messiaen left the Conservatory, his ideas of rhythm and time were beginning to be manifest in songs, piano preludes, orchestral scores, and organ pieces—notably, among these last, in "Le Banquet céleste" (1928) and in the second panel of his *Diptyque* (1930), his earliest works to be published.

The former title refers to the Eucharist, to that cluster of ideas, that is, two chief of which are the penetration of the eternal into the temporal by way of the mass, and of the temporal into the eternal by way of the soul's entry into heaven. Heaven, in Messiaen's view, is a state of blessedness akin to perpetual feasting, and the mass is not just the remembrance of Christ's sacrifice but also its re-enactment. Messiaen's superscription ("He that eats my flesh and drinks my blood abides in me and I in him") likewise shows that time—timelessness, rather—is his theme. His symbolism is direct and simple: the two dozen bars take fully six minutes to play, the chords attaining near-stasis emblematic of eternity, and Messiaen gains forward motion, in his nearly motionless pace, by starting and ending with a dominant feeling and avoiding the tonic throughout.

But to say this is to attest his genius while misstating his technique. Though he was not yet twenty when he wrote "Le Banquet céleste," he had already turned from prescribed harmony to the modes of limited transposition that were to be a main feature of his early work, and it is these, or, more precisely, his uses of one of these, that create a distinctive harmonic movement dominant and tonic only by analogy.

The modes of limited transposition, which, incidentally, he says bear no relation to church modes or to Eastern, consist of an arbitrary ordering of the twelve semitones of the tempered scale into six groups of two notes, four groups of three, three groups of four, and two groups in which the number of notes varies. Each mode perforce recurs to the same notes after a fixed number of transpositions: the second mode can be transposed three times, for example; the third mode, four.

The modes are further limited by what Messiaen perceives as their colors. Since in a given transposition one mode may be violet and yellow, another blue and orange, the modes are not interchangeable. For to him the colors of these modes, indeed the colors of all musical sounds, are intrinsic and specific. The second mode in its first transposition "revolves around certain violets, blues, and purplish deep reds, whereas the third, in its first transposition, corresponds to an orange with red and green pigmentations, to specks of gold, and also to a milky white with iridescent reflections like opals." It would remain central to his thought that "certain complexes of sound and certain sonorities are linked for me with certain complexes of color, and I use them in full awareness of this."

He hastens to explain that his harmonic vocabulary is by no means restricted to modes: "I also and above all use chords: chords of contracted resonance, revolving chords, chords of total chromaticism, chords of transposed inversions on the same bass note, and thousands of chords invented to reproduce the timbres of bird song." Furthermore, he uses chords in his *Diptyque,* which is inscribed to Dukas and Dupré, in a manner of Dupré's that he found created its own coloristic harmony. And here as elsewhere the color of chords is partly dependent on pitch: a given chord raised by an octave is "shaded toward white"; lowered by an octave, it is "toned down by black."

Though the modes of limited transposition, like other of Messiaen's techniques, lend themselves to harmonic as well as melodic use, they "are not harmonies in the ordinary sense . . . or even classified chords. They are colors, and their force springs up first from the impossibility of transpositions, and then also from the color linked with this impossibility." A magical charm is inborn in such impossibilities, Messiaen contends, referring to the impasse reached when principle or formula exhausts variation; a "technical process" colliding with "an insuperable obstacle" invokes nothing less than "an occult, a cryptic power over one, temporal and acoustic." The phenomenon "has dominated my whole life as musician."

Messiaen says he became fluent in his modes by often improvising on them in Dupré's class. But he takes no credit for contriving them all. The first mode is the whole-tone scale. The second had been used by, among others, Rimsky-Korsakov and Scriabin, both of whom having been, as it happens, coloristic musicians. "There are many other musicians who have been musicians of colors," Messiaen adds. "Mozart was coloristic. So were Chopin, Wagner, Berlioz, Debussy—Debussy was an extremely coloristic musician—all the Spanish musicians, all the Russian. . . . Many musicians were coloristic without saying so, or without being aware of it."

Indeed, Messiaen remarks, the "most radical, the most profound difference between me and other composers—it constitutes a virtual gulf—is that I am a coloristic musician. While I hear music, while I read music, not only do I hear it in my head, but I also see the colors corresponding to the sounds. I do not see them with the eye. I see them with an inner eye. I see them in an intellectual way. But I see them." He explains that

> these are not *simple* colors. They are colors in movement: they are complex and they swirl, just as music is complex and swirls. In music you have certain sounds that vary in register, which are high or medium or low; sounds that vary in intensity, which are loud or soft; sounds that vary in timbre, which are made by an oboe or clarinet or xylophone or piano. Likewise these colors vary in nuance. They intermingle. They turn . . . like superimposed rainbows. It is very beautiful. And it generally recurs: with the same combinations of color come the same complexes of sounds, the same timbres, the same registers; with the same chords or with the same sonorities, it is the same colors that return. And not only in my music, but also in the music of others.
>
> I have put to use, as it were, the inverse phenomenon. That is, being fortunate enough to see colors while I hear music, I have tried in turn to put color *into* my music, so that listeners can have the same impression, obtain the same result. I think all listeners . . . do have this sixth sense, this correspondence be-

tween sound and color, only they are not aware of it. And naturally people are more or less gifted at it, more or less sensitive. Then too, this relation of sound and color is partly objective, partly subjective: there are certain correspondences that are the same for everybody, others that are perhaps the result of musical or literary background, the social stratum in which one lives, the state of one's health, of the climate, of the fact that it is hot weather or cold, spring or winter, and so forth. These things can affect the sound-color relation. But broadly speaking I think this relation exists for everybody, and in roughly the same way for everybody.

· 3 ·

Timbres are deemed colors too, and it is fitting that Messiaen became organist of a church where a masterly colorist preceded him. Guilmant was organist at Trinity Church over the three decades leading up to the turn of the century, and in 1931, at twenty-two, Messiaen became a successor. Like Guilmant, he evinced affection for the church's Cavaillé-Coll. It dated from the late 1860s, the builder's high maturity, and though but three manuals in size, was unexcelled "in power, in majesty" by instruments much larger. So, at least, Messiaen proclaims proudly ("my organ, my child, my son!"), expressly comparing it to Saint Sulpice, Notre Dame, and Saint Ouen, and asserting that it might well surpass even them "in mystery and in poetry." At any rate, its forty-five stops offered him timbres he found bewitching.

On the positif, the sixteen-foot basson, with its rich harmonic development, and the sixteen-foot quintaton, with its gently piquant overtone, counted among his favorites. Not alone for their individual hues, however, did he think such stops essential, but also for their function in the ensemble. He states that the lack of sufficient sixteen-foot manual stops in seventeenth- and eighteenth-century organs, and in their latter-day analogues, unfits such organs for his works. He is adamant that his music "requires the forceful personality of large instruments that possess varied timbres and numerous mixtures and, in particular, that have sixteen-foot stops in the manuals."

It is in vogue, he goes on, "to build organs again in the baroque style. Electrical combinations are dispensed with, on the pretext of baroque authenticity, and we deny ourselves a most useful aid. Sixteen-foot manual foundations are removed, on the pretext that they did not exist in the baroque era, and we ruin the tonal palette. Mixture is heaped on mixture, while the powerful reeds are given up, on the pretext of their being a romantic contribution. In short, we build instruments on which we can no longer play anything but Frescobaldi or Grigny, which is really limiting. I adore these composers, but all the same I want to be able to play other things. On such organs, it is obvious, my own music cannot be played."

Messiaen liked the power and freedom from hardness of the Cavaillé-Coll tutti, and the blaze of a full récit with reeds behind tightly closed shutters. He liked the transparency of the foundations, the floating otherworldliness of harmonic flutes. He especially liked the mixtures and mutations, whose widely scaled, fluty tone made for choice blending. With them he delighted in synthesizing colors without the fundamental; he would laughingly say that only mere custom decreed the drawing of an eight-foot stop whenever one drew a mixture.

In other ways too he put custom aside: in joining nasard and sixteen-foot bourdon to voix humaine with tremulant; in assigning a soprano part to the pedal and exploiting other extremes of register; in pairing tierce and piccolo, bourdon 16 and octavin, quintaton 16 and tierce; in drawing foundations without flutes or gambes; in opposing voix célestes to mixtures—the list could go on and on, since his coloristic imagination was virtually without bounds, and since forty-five stops provide the innovator with abundant permutations. Innovative mixes notwithstanding, Cavaillé-Coll's timbres are Messiaen's palette.

Even so, Messiaen's early works innovate less in timbre than in harmony or rhythm. Registration is as conventional in the *Appari-*

tion de l'église éternelle, completed by 1932, and *L'Ascension,* completed in 1934, as it is in the *Diptyque* and "Le Banquet céleste."

When in his *Apparition de l'église éternelle* Messiaen uses the Cavaillé-Coll tone and mechanism to fashion, in his words, an enormous, granite-like crescendo, it is that standard crescendo which we noted as characteristic of the French masters. True, it is made an apotheosis by his harmonies, rhythms, and the dignity of his program: the crescendo is at once canvas and brush stroke, as it were, in a surrealistic portrait of the holy Monolith. But its origins are plain. Similarly, in *L'Ascension* his use of Cavaillé-Coll's tone and mechanism differs little from its use by predecessors: Saint-Saëns drew flutes and strings in much the same way, Vierne foundations and reeds. Besides that, the work is a suite; and it sufficiently resembles the organ-symphony forms we saw Franck and Widor devise to be considered a near relation. That it was born a suite for orchestra—the third movement alone is originally for organ—does not controvert the kinship.

It is with *La Nativité du Seigneur,* finished in 1935, that Messiaen enters on his maturity. His knowledge of the fact re-echoes in the forthright tone of his preface. In phrases neither apologetic nor boastful, the twenty-eight-year-old states that his subject is the birth of the Lord, that he will treat it with emotion and sincerity from a theological, instrumental, and musical standpoint, and that his means are sure and clear. These he proceeds to illumine: modes of limited transposition; enlarged pedal points, embellishments, and appoggiaturas; half-unit of added value; progressive increase and decrease of intervals; chord on the dominant; and management of timbres by means of combinations differing in color and in degree of density.

Timbre is granted importance on a par with rhythm, melody, and harmony, and proves by its astonishing range as innovative as they. More astonishing still is the cohesion, the unity; disparate elements are at one, thanks to Messiaen's conjunctive mind, and together speak with such aptness and warmth that *La Nativité du Seigneur* remains, with players as well as audiences, the most popular of his works for organ.

Popularity is notoriously unreliable as an indicator of merit but in this instance can hardly be gainsaid. Among his organ works, *La Nativité du Seigneur* is arguably Messiaen's masterpiece by its concision and coalescence, its air of intention achieved, and its poetic rendering of an exalted Biblical theme. To bring unity out of diversity was the cornerstone of Bach's genius too, and the parallel is close. Bach conjoins generations of style, Italian and French styles as well as German, making out of many one and bringing an era to an end. Messiaen conjoins generations of style, fragmented, it is true, and not restricted to Europe, making out of many one and bringing an era to an end. And it is a telling biographical datum that each man's faith, which gave the works topic and impetus, was as matter-of-fact as it was deep.

The trust given voice by the dying Bach in "Before Thy Throne I Now Appear" is thus counterpart to Messiaen's own in yet another of the well-known works: *Les Corps glorieux*. Though intuitive and private, the work's seven "visions" are rooted in Scripture and dogma. Messiaen tells us that he means to show the resurrected as enjoying a life free, pure, luminous, and colorful, qualities he specially means his timbres to represent. Immortal resurrected bodies, he continues, manifest glory, impassability, agility, and refinement: they supply their own light, being luminous; they no longer suffer, being beyond all possibility of distress; they pass freely through obstacles; and they no longer need food or sleep. This beatitude he describes in three of the movements. In another movement he portrays the resurrected enjoying a life of prayer and contemplation, in another their grasp of the mystery of the Trinity, and in another the waters of grace. Central to the work in placement and importance is a movement that depicts the struggle of life and death, death a gate into the timeless. The issue, in both senses, is Christ's own Resurrection:

> A long piece in two parts. The first, noisy and agitated, is the actual combat, which is to say: the sufferings and cries of Christ's Passion, death being the foregone result. The second part is life.

One would have expected it to be fast and loud; it is, on the contrary, soft, calm, serene. This is because it represents the highest, most moving, most secret moment of the life of Christ. This moment is not described in the Gospels; of it we know only the outcome—the earthquake, the sudden light, the angel who rolls the stone from the entrance, the many appearances of the risen Jesus in various places. But Psalm 138, which in the introit for Easter the Church applies to Christ, described for us in advance the sublime moment in which Jesus rises, living, luminous, first-born of the dead, and, in the sunlit peace of his Resurrection, addresses this homage of love to his Father: "I am again with You."

We may note in passing that Messiaen embraces a romanticist conception of program music, undertaking moreover a program to which, as with *La Nativité du Seigneur,* Liszt himself might have given a blessing. Liszt defines a program as any preface in intelligible prose affixed to a piece of pure instrumental music. One purpose of a program is to keep the listener from making an arbitrary poetical interpretation and to direct the attention in advance to the poetical idea of the whole; another is to indicate the "spiritual moments" that drove the composer to create the work.

In conforming to Liszt's definition, and in maintaining as he does that music "ought to be beautiful to hear and it ought to touch," Messiaen affirms his declaration that he is "not ashamed of being a romantic."

· 4 ·

Completed in 1939, *Les Corps glorieux* crowned the decade that saw Messiaen progress from student to acknowledged master. He first won public acclaim in the performance by Walter Straram, at the Théâtre des Champs-Elysées, in 1931, of the orchestral *Offrandes oubliées.* The audience was apparently unperturbed by the novelty of the work—by the portrayal in a secular concert of Christ's "forgotten" offerings of His life on the cross and of that life continued in the Eucharist; by the rhythmic alternations of twos and threes, sevens and elevens; and by the peculiarities of orchestration. This was Messiaen's first great public success, and his last for many years.

The decade also saw his affiliation with a group of avant-garde composers who styled themselves La Jeune France. His *Hymne au Saint Sacrement,* for orchestra, finished in 1932, another meditation on the Eucharist, received its première four years later at the first of the group's concerts.

The decade saw his marriage, in 1932, to Claire Delbos, a violinist and composer, and his addressing to her, in 1936 and 1938 respectively, two song cycles inspired by the idea of marriage. *Poèmes pour Mi* ("Mi" his pet name for Claire) treats of the spiritual states evoked by the conjugal sacrament. The cycle begins by thanking God for the gifts of nature, a woman's love, an immortal soul, and a body that will rise again, as well as of truth, grace, redemption; the cycle ends by depicting a day of glory and resurrection whose bliss is foreshadowed by the joy of married life. In like manner, the cycle *Chants de terre et de ciel* treats of marital love in a spiritual context, closing with a section on Christ's Resurrection. Aptly, Messiaen and Claire would decide to name their son Pascal.

In these years too Messiaen began his long career in teaching: in 1936 he joined the faculties of the Schola Cantorum and the Ecole Normale de Musique. It would be a career made prosperous by his superlative ability as teacher, and by the accomplishment of such of his pupils as Stockhausen, Xenakis, and Boulez.

And the decade saw a first performance abroad of some of his music. At a London recital in 1938 he played parts of *La Nativité du Seigneur.*

The Second World War broke out in 1939, and Messiaen was serving as a hospital orderly when, following the 1940 invasion, he was captured and sent to a prison camp. His guards were not unkind, he recalls; his morning duties once completed, he could spend the day writing music. But the camp lacked heat and food. Over the winter he came near to freezing, and for eighteen months nearly starved.

> We had a bit of soup at noon, that was all—adequate to sustain life, not to sustain health. Had I remained another year, I think I would probably have died. . . .
>
> It happened that I had with me as companions in captivity a violinist, a clarinetist, and a cellist . . . all three in the same stalag as I. So I had the idea of writing a piece for them and myself, a work, that is, for clarinet, violin, cello, and piano. A German officer had kindly given me some music paper, pencils, erasers. . . .
>
> The same officer decided to have the work heard by all the prisoners in the camp, and he gave us the instruments we needed. They were ghastly. The violin was cracked. The cello had three strings instead of four. The keys of the clarinet were broken. As for the piano, it was an upright whose keys had no springs; the keys would stay down and had to be pulled back up by hand to continue. It was dreadful.
>
> And we were grotesquely dressed. I had a big fur cap on my head, wooden shoes, a green checked suit in shreds. You could see my arms and legs through the tatters. But nobody laughed. We were too miserable to feel like laughing.
>
> And so this work was performed for an audience of—I don't know—maybe ten thousand people, all prisoners, all different. There were doctors, lawyers, priests, farmers, laborers, men from every class of society. And they were obviously very moved. After the war, the work was performed for audiences it greatly shocked, a reception unfortunately much different. But at that first performance it was very beautiful because we were all in misery, we were all brothers.

Such were the origins of the *Quatuor pour la fin du temps*, music inspired less by his captivity, he notes, than by his rereading during it of the Book of Revelation. The score is inscribed: "In homage to the Angel of the Apocalypse, who raises his hand toward heaven, saying: 'Time will be no more.'"

Released some months after that singular première, Messiaen returned to Paris and was in 1942 named professor of harmony at the Conservatory. As had happened with Franck, the title belied the fact that he was teaching composition. As had unfortunately not happened with Franck, he later received title, salary, and prestige in accord with the actuality.

Some of Messiaen's chief works from the war years and just after show his preoccupation with the piano, with an orchestra enlarged by novel percussion timbres, and with new uses of the voice: *Visions de l'Amen* (1943), a large work for two pianos; *Trois petites liturgies de la Présence Divine* (1944), for orchestra and women's voices, which thirty years later Messiaen would call his "best religious work"; *Vingt Regards sur l'Enfant-Jésus* (1944), for piano; *Harawi* (1945), for soprano and piano; *Turangalîla-symphonie* (1946–48), for orchestra; and *Cinq Rechants* (1948), for SATB soloists.

The three works last named form a trilogy on the Tristramian motif, which Messiaen conceives as "a fatal love, an irresistible love, a love that as a rule leads to death, that to some extent invokes death, since it is a love that transcends the body, transcends even the confines of the mind, and grows to a cosmic scale." Such a love does not contradict faith, "because a great love is a reflection, a pale reflection, but still a reflection, of the only true love: divine love," and leads to "an initiation through death" into that "greater and purer love."

Messiaen did not turn again to the organ till 1949–50, when he wrote his *Messe de la Pentecôte*. It was his first liturgical organ work properly so called, his earlier suites having been in the main—notwithstanding their religious programs—concert works as outwardly secular as any organ symphony of Widor's. The work comprises five movements designed to accompany a spoken liturgy. He does not set the Kyrie, Gloria, Credo, Sanctus, and Agnus Dei, but sets liturgical acts: the entry of the celebrant, Offertory, consecration, Communion, and recessional.

The *Messe de la Pentecôte* is somewhat loosely structured, having been inspired by improvisations notably flexible in form. At Trinity Church, over two decades, Messiaen had felt duty-bound to improvise Sunday after Sunday. Quantity varied by circumstances. He typically improvised less at the ten o'clock high mass, when he would recur to plainsong, and at eleven o'clock, when he would play from the repertory, and at noon, when he would play his own pieces, than at vespers, when he would improvise much. His style grew from the appointed texts, which might lead him to imitate Bach, or Mozart, Schumann, or Debussy, or to devise commentaries more radical. At length he saw that this *extempore* was draining his creative substance, expending his ideas. Accordingly, he composed his *Messe*, he says, as a résumé of his improvisations, and later on, to his great relief, in general no longer improvised.

Loosely or not, the work apposes any number of innovations. Bird song, plainchant, serial techniques intermingle to form its melody. Greek and Hindu patterns, among others, go to form its rhythm—adjusted, as we might anticipate, by chromatic durations, irrational values, and other new-wrought devices. Harmony is noteworthy for resonance chords and added-note sonorities; timbre for such colors as a combined quintaton 16, clarinette, and nasard; bourdon 16, gambe, and octavin; flute 4 and cymbale; bourdon 16 and hautbois; and bourdon 32 and piccolo.

The more tightly structured *Livre d'Orgue* followed in 1951. Five of its seven movements are given liturgical associations, but it is at heart an essay on rhythmical relation. Among the most striking relations are what Messiaen describes as "sixty-four chromatic durations, from one to sixty-four thirty-second notes—inverted in groups of four, from the extremities to the center, straight and retrograde by turns—treated in retrograde canon." He expects the listener to discriminate lengths whose difference is razor-edged, though he admits that to counterpose such niceties is perilous indeed. "We are creatures of the mean," he contends. "We are average in size, and, alas, average in our thinking, and we evolve in an average length of time. We are midway between microcosm and macrocosm. Hence we find it hard to perceive very long durations, and even harder to discern the minute values by which these long durations differ." But since he himself could discriminate all sixty-four, he sees no reason why the listener should not be asked to do so as well.

He was guided in addition by ideas less stringent. Present in the work also are "violent colors and new effects" redolent of nature and of God. The first movement, for instance, was written "while gazing at the Romanche winding through the terrifying mountain gorges of the Infernet Pass. It is a truly impressive chasm. I wanted to pay homage to this feeling of vertigo and at the same time, symbolically, to the two gulfs of human misery and divine mercy."

To express the sensation of dizziness, Messiaen "juxtaposed the organ's extreme limits . . . : I caused to sound at the same time a very low voice that represents the depths of the abyss of human misery by a deep and terrifying resonance a bit like the cavernous horn calls and chants of Tibetan priests, and, above, the voice of God in reply—not a terrible voice of thunder and lightning flashes, but a voice mysterious, distant, very high-pitched, almost tender, barely audible. So low is the one voice, and so high the other, that you understand absolutely nothing of what you are hearing. And the timbres are so strange it is impossible to make out the notes. This seems to me to render marvelously the ideas of penitence, reverence, and a sensation of dizziness in the presence of the Holy."

The absence of development, which is characteristic with Messiaen, and the absence of a program make the *Livre d'Orgue* eminently resistible to many, as Dame Gillian Weir points out. "But Messiaen is not concerned," she writes, "to present an argument, or explain, or even describe; he evokes, and when the listener has learned in what manner to respond, the pull is infinitely compelling. . . . [It is] gentle as the forming and reforming of clouds but as inexorable as the tides."

It need hardly be added that to convey Messiaen's message, in this work or any other, the performer must scrupulously respect every slightest signal of intent. All that has been suggested on previous pages in behalf of fidelity and subdual of self applies here with special emphasis. That Messiaen expects nothing less of his interpreters is implicit in his actions: he spares no pains to make intention unmistakable by elucidating his techniques—whether in preface to individual works, or in lecture, interview, and treatise— and by trying to bar ambiguity from his scores. Because he is a rhythmist first and foremost, as he himself maintained, respect for the durations by which rhythm is measured is an imperative de- mand. Its twin is fidelity to timbre.

Messiaen's international reputation grew apace in the immediate postwar years. In 1947–49, North America saw Stokowski con- duct the *Hymne au Saint Sacrement*, Koussevitzky *L'Ascension*, and Bernstein the *Turangalîla-symphonie*, and saw Messiaen teaching for the first time at Tanglewood. Hungary and Germany honored him with invitations, and he gave classes or supervised premières in Darmstadt, Donaueschingen, and Budapest. And modernists hailed it as a milestone in twentieth-century music when in 1949– 50, with one of his *Quatre études de rhythme*, for piano, Messiaen extended serialism beyond pitch to other elements. But he himself came to believe serialism a dead end, and for that reason among others the 1950s saw him turn the more resolutely to bird song. The hours he spent in woodland and meadow transcribing bird song in notation produced *Revéil des oiseaux*, *Oiseaux exotiques*, and *Catalogue des oiseaux*—and helped produce one of the most scandal-making of his pieces, *Chronochromie*, for orchestra.

In *Chronochromie* bird song is one element among many, but it was the element that most angered audiences, in a passage for eigh- teen solo strings that makes use of the songs of eighteen kinds of bird. The songs enter successively in fugue-like manner, and effect a counterpoint that some found outrageous. Messiaen did not in- tend to affront, but to be true to his daemon. Were listeners to repair to forest or park, he explained, the beauty of the lights, scents, and colors would render the aural phenomenon natural. "I separated this extraordinary counterpoint from its context . . . and this is what provoked the outcry." His joy in creating was tinged with sadness whenever he encountered antagonism.

Sadly too the decade saw the long illness of Messiaen's wife. Claire, we learn, lost memory and function as the result of an operation. By one account, she "had to be put into a home where everything was done for her. From that time Messiaen brought up his son by himself. He did all the housework and all the cooking and he would get up at 5 o'clock in the morning to make the coffee and get breakfast for his son before he went to school. Eventually, in 1959, his wife died." The recollection is that of Yvonne Loriod, the superb pianist and interpreter of his music whom Messiaen married two years later.

Apart from the brief "Verset pour la fête de la Dédicace," which Messiaen in 1960 wrote as a test piece for the Conservatory organ class, two works remain to be noticed: *Méditations sur le mystère de la Sainte Trinité*, completed in 1969, and *Livre du Saint Sacrement*, completed in 1984.

Messiaen intended the nine *Méditations* to be an essay in language and communication. Music, he reminds us in his preface, does not express anything directly. Though music can evoke a mood or feeling, touch the subconscious, and expand the imagination, music can do no more than suggest; it cannot inform. Not even leitmotif can convey ideas independently of convention. To exchange information without need of the conventions of language is reserved to the angels, whose thought-transference, an intellectual operation, is unrestricted by time and locale. With due deference to angelic example, Messiaen nevertheless resolved to invent "as an amusement and as a renewal of my thinking" a "communicable musical language."

He began by devising an alphabet in which his words might be transcribed. He turned first to the traditional note-letter equivalents, of which B-A-C-H is an instance, and widened their scope by grouping letters according to phonic type. He assigned each letter "a sound, a register, a duration." He dispensed with article, pronoun, adverb, and preposition, in order to avoid clutter, and confined himself to verb, adjective, and noun, indicating their activity by way of symbols for inflection. He gave the auxiliaries, "to be" and "to have," specific rhythm and interval, and assigned a theme to what he called "the single most important word in all languages," the name of the King of Kings. "Wagner would have called it a leitmotif," he adds, and with it Messiaen intended to express, "stammering though the expression be, the fact that God is immense as well as eternal, with neither beginning nor end in space, as well as in time."

His subject he declares to be "the greatest mystery of the Christian religion. It is hardly ever talked about, even in my church. When the Trinity Church organ was inaugurated after its great rebuilding, I invited Monsignor Charles, the well-known rector of Sacré-Coeur de Montmartre, to come and deliver a sermon on the Holy Trinity. We agreed that his sermon would be divided into three parts, after each of which I would improvise. It was from that sermon and those improvisations that the work was born." None of the nine sections has a title. A preface to each specifies which aspect of the mystery is referred to.

Yet another mystery, of the Blessed Sacrament, serves as subject of his final organ work, written when Messiaen was in his mid-seventies. It had served as the subject of his first organ work. But whereas "Le Banquet céleste" is brief enough to be played at Communion—was in fact meditated for the Feast of Corpus Christi with that option—the eighteen sections of the *Livre du Saint Sacrement* take two hours to perform, thus qualifying, it may be, as the longest piece ever written for the organ. The movements range in length from two minutes to fifteen, and though less closely related by program or technique than the movements of previous collections, present the clearest of plans: four revere Jesus in His presence in the sacrament; seven ponder events of His ministry on earth; and seven treat the acts of communion—the miracle that turns bread and wine into the Lord's Body and Blood, and the grace given to the right-minded communicant.

Even in this late afternoon of his career, when his desire to stop composing was express, Messiaen's imagination is free-flowing. In the *Livre du Saint Sacrement* is found bird song noted down during visits to the Holy Land—one page is unique in his organ works for being devoted exclusively to bird song—together with numberless colors and varieties of rhythm, chord, melody, and timbre, some of them unexampled. A cymbale used alone evokes the desolation of the desert where manna, that earlier Bread of Life, sustained the wandering Hebrews. A cluster of all the semitones of the octave, pitched low and exquisitely shaded, depicts the absence of light. A C major triad resounds that by its very consonance seems an innovation. And it is by means of his communicable musical language that Messiaen closes the work, and with it his career as composer for the organ, with a grand fortissimo alleluia in which he spells the word "joy."

· 5 ·

That Olivier Messiaen's organ music is the product and summit of a hundred-year evolution is an idea which many performers and listeners would categorically reject. Surely no precedent can be found, they would say, for his mix of bird song, color-sound synesthesia, and Eastern rhythm and mode, not to mention other elements less outré, such as plainsong and dogmatical reference. But the fact is even the more novel of these elements had interested earlier composers, and the romanticist intentions enumerated in the Introduction to our survey are not only basic to his idiom, but within it achieve a sophistication unlikely to be surpassed.

For with Messiaen, as with our other six masters, keyboard technique obtains that is transcendental in difficulty and scope; timbre derives from the tone and mechanism perfected by Cavaillé-Coll; form enlarges on established forms; and serious purpose, individualism, belief in the excellence of art, love of nature, susceptibility to the supernatural and to correspondence among the arts—these traits and praxes, romanticist all, go to fill the retort in which also distill the more novel of his elements.

The distillate is of singular purity. Certain qualities inhere in romanticist work of any era—self-reliance, recurrent innovation, concern with psychological and dramatic truth, regard for nuance and contrast and for tension and oppositions—and these Messiaen brought to their zenith. More precisely, Messiaen brings timbre, as we saw, to a pinnacle of expressive subtlety: what tonal shading did he leave unexploited that could convey a degree of meaning? Messiaen brings duration, crucial though it was with Lemmens and the others, to a level of refinement compared to which their minute calibrations are coarse; exacting as were Guilmant and Widor and Dupré in their repeated notes and legato, they could scarcely have imagined gradation so slight as the sixty-four chromatic durations. For that matter, can anything remain to be imagined that could elaborate this subtlety without exceeding the human capacity to perceive?

Then too, Messiaen harks back in his suites to the form Franck and Widor developed, and brings the earlier masters' views of the symphonic to new heights of finesse. And Messiaen brings to culmination by his meticulous scoring a change that had taken centuries: the change from music considered a canvas on which to improvise ornaments, harmonies, and timbres to music considered a text fully noted in advance and imposed on an interpreter. And Messiaen so manipulates harmony as to put paid to the fascination felt by French composers for modes, an entrancement that dated from at least the 1830s; indeed, he has the last word by virtue of inventing modes of his own. And Messiaen as it were cuts up rhythm into fragments, so as to reunite each in new patterns, patterns arguably issueless.

No need to labor the point. The evidence is persuasive that with Messiaen's death, on the night of 27 April 1992, a tradition ended that had begun with the young Cavaillé-Coll's journey to Paris. To say this is not to deny that Cavaillé-Coll himself built on precedent, or that music worthy of the organ might in future be composed. Nor is it true that the great summarizers leave nothing to be said; they leave plenty to be said in description, analysis, commentary, or concordance; Darwin's work and Freud's spawned lecture and dissertation by the hundred, not to mention the accounts in the popular press, and what composer equals Bach in sheer quantity of studies? But the original messages cannot be restated except less eloquently or less fully. And when the once-startling discovery has become a commonplace, when the mine of a given style seems exhausted of its ore, what remains to new generations of creators but to copy or destroy?

Such is the dilemma faced by Messiaen's successors, and faced too by painters, sculptors, choreographers, architects, poets, novelists, dramatists. What is more, creators of every stamp are seeing as depleted not just their fields, but also the culture as a whole. Or make the metaphor literal: envision fields so teeming with life that not a square inch is left in which new growth can spring up. It is consequently believed by some that five hundred years of creation are ending—our whole heritage since the Renaissance—and that a successor evolution has simply not yet come into view. Meanwhile, artists tend to imitate the masterpieces that surround us, or devote themselves to such parodies and shocks as minimalist art, anti-art, disposable art, and the art-less. And organists, to bring the point home, are confronted by scores that ask them to hold down the keys with elbow or arm, "play" from within the chambers, and turn off the wind while stops sound. Whether it is a misapprehension or not, the idea that everything worth doing has been done is a paralyzing idea indeed.

Whatever the centuries may bring, it is hardly likely that the romantic and classic will ultimately cease to rule, that we shall see the last of those successive tides of absorption and elimination, for they embody human traits as nearly permanent as anything can be. And even if it were possible to replace this systole and diastole, a new art would no doubt arise that would reflect the new human attributes. Of the new art we should ask the old questions, as

Jacques Barzun happily phrases them: "Do we find the substance rich, evocative, capable of subtlety and strength? Do we, after a while, recognize patterns to which we can respond with our sense of balance, our sense of suspense and fulfillment, our sense of emotional and intellectual congruity?" At its best, one hopes, the new art would resemble the old in enriching our experience, by broadening our imaginations and by raising our thought to the heavens.

Bibliography

INTRODUCTION

On the art and duty of the interpreter, see Bruno Walter, *Of Music and Music-Making* (New York: Norton, 1961); Roger Sessions, *The Musical Experience of Composer, Performer, Listener* (Princeton: Princeton University Press, 1950); and *Landowska on Music*, Denise Restout and Robert Hawkins, eds. (New York: Stein and Day, 1964). On intention and authenticity, see Richard Taruskin, *Text and Act: Essays on Musical Performance* (New York: Oxford University Press, 1995). Among the Toscanini biographies, Harvey Sachs's (Philadelphia: Lippincott, 1978) is bold and exhaustive.

See also my *Albert Schweitzer, Musician* (Aldersgate, England: Scolar, 1994), and *Marcel Dupré: The Work of a Master Organist* (Boston: Northeastern University Press, 1985; German ed., with additional photographs, *Marcel Dupré: Leben und Werk eines Meisterorganisten*, trans. Hans Uwe Hielscher, Langen bei Bregenz, Austria: Lade, 1993).

Dupré's words about piano practice are quoted from his *Cours complet d'improvisation à l'orgue* (Paris: Leduc, 1937), vol. 2, pp. 1, 5; and "Marcel Dupré: Interview and Improvisations" (phonodisk, Cleveland: Telarc [5011], 1975). Nadia Boulanger's remarks were made to me in a taped conversation, 26 July 1969.

On style and period, see Jacques Barzun, *Classic, Romantic and Modern* (Boston: Little, Brown, 1961), and *Critical Questions*, Bea Friedland, ed. (Chicago: University of Chicago Press, 1982); Friedrich Blume, *Classic and Romantic Music: A Comprehensive Survey* (New York: Norton, 1970); and Cecil Gray, *The History of Music* (New York: Knopf, 1935), and *A Survey of Contemporary Music* (London: Oxford University Press, 1927). The last-named work offers helpful discussions of romanticism and of the art of the critic, as does Walter Pater, *Appreciations, With an Essay on Style* (London: Macmillan, 1889), from which essay the long quotation is taken. See also Charles Rosen, *The Romantic Generation* (Cambridge: Harvard University Press, 1995), and *The Classical Style: Haydn, Mozart, Beethoven* (New York: Viking, 1971).

For splendid assessments of period and personage, see *French Organ Music from the Revolution to Franck and Widor*, Lawrence Archbold and William J. Peterson, eds. (Rochester, N.Y.: University of Rochester Press, 1995), and Orpha Ochse, *Organists and Organ Playing in Nineteenth-Century France and Belgium* (Bloomington: Indiana University Press, 1994). Ochse's account (pp. 121–35) of liturgical practice and of the reforms of Gregorian plainsong should be read by every student— as should Wallace Goodrich's *Organ Music in France* (Boston: Boston Music Company, 1917).

On French life generally, the student will find useful Theodore Zeldin, *France: 1848–1945*, 2 vols. (Oxford: Clarendon Press, 1977), and François Nourissier, *The French* (New York: Knopf, 1968).

Among the factors contributing to the organ's present isolation from the musical mainstream: organs are located in churches, a locale that to many persons is redolent of corruption, prejudice, and arrogance; organs are more often than not played badly; good organs are few; and the tones of an organ, merely to be sorted out, require an attentiveness that is demanding—their cascade reminding many listeners, sensitive listeners at that, of a shower beneath Niagara.

Widor's words to Schweitzer are quoted from Charles R. Joy, *Music in the Life of Albert Schweitzer* (New York: Harper, 1951), pp. 168–

Bibliography

69, and Widor's preface to Schweitzer's *J. S. Bach,* trans. Ernest Newman, 2 vols. (1911; reprint, New York: Dover, 1964).

On the evolution of timbre from extrinsic to constituent, see Alfred Einstein, *Music in the Romantic Era* (New York: Norton, 1947), pp. 7–8, and Jacques Barzun, *Berlioz and the Romantic Century,* 3d ed. (New York: Columbia University Press, 1969), vol. 1, pp. 10, 80–81, 450–56.

CHAPTER ONE. ARISTIDE CAVAILLÉ-COLL

My prime source is Emmanuel and Cécile Cavaillé-Coll, *Aristide Cavaillé-Coll, ses origines, sa vie, ses oeuvres* (1929; reprint, Paris: Fischbacher, 1982); the quoted letters may be found on pp. 31, 34, 37, 39, 66–67, 74, the 1878 encomium on pp. 130–32. The passages excerpted from the first Saint Denis specification may be found untranslated in Fenner Douglass, *Cavaillé-Coll and the Musicians* (Raleigh, N.C.: Sunbury, 1980), vol. 2, pp. 1106–21.

Fenner Douglass, *The Language of the Classical French Organ: A Musical Tradition Before 1800* (rev. ed., New Haven: Yale University Press, 1995), provides a helpful background to Cavaillé-Coll's developments. Also valuable are Claude Noisette de Crauzat, *Cavaillé-Coll* (Paris: La Flûte de Pan, 1984); Pierre J. Hardouin, *Le Grand Orgue de Notre-Dame de Paris* (Tours: Bärenreiter, 1973); and Aristide Cavaillé-Coll, *Complete Theoretical Works* (Buren, The Netherlands: Knuf, 1979)—whence in the final section (the book is unpaginated) the 1863 quotation on wind supply.

On stops, see Stevens Irwin, *Dictionary of Pipe Organ Stops,* 2d ed. (New York: Schirmer, 1983). On terms, with equivalents in ten languages, see Wilfried Praet, *Organ Dictionary* (Zwijndrecht, Belgium: Ceos, 1989).

Albert Dupré's brief *Etude sur Aristide Cavaillé-Coll* (Rouen: Académie des Sciences, Belles-Lettres et Arts, 1919) tells us most of what little we know about Cavaillé-Coll's voicers.

Lemmens's influence on Cavaillé-Coll is described in Charles-

Bibliography

Marie Widor, "L'Orgue moderne" (*Les Nouvelles musicales*, 1 Mar. 1934, pp. 5–6), whence the "proper dose" quotation.

The Cavaillé-Coll Association (5 rue Roquépine, Paris 75008) at intervals publishes *La Flûte harmonique;* the editor of this periodical, Kurt Lueders, is a distinguished expert whose writings should be consulted by every serious student. See, to begin with, his "Reflections on the Esthetic Evolution of the Cavaillé-Coll Organ," in *Charles Brenton Fisk, Organ Builder*, Fenner Douglass et al., eds. (Easthampton,Mass.: Westfield Center for Early Keyboard Studies, 1986). See *La Flûte harmonique*, no. 59–60 (numéro spécial, 1991), on Saint Sulpice; on Cavaillé-Coll's uniting of old styles with new see the postscript by Daniel Roth, pp. 56–58.

Seating capacity is discussed in Ronald W. Clark, *The Royal Albert Hall* (London: Hamilton, 1958), pp. 40–42.

The student will perhaps already have learned that scholarship is never disinterested, but that an author's bias by no means renders books and articles valueless. Two able writers, whose works can be profitably read and reread, provide a case in point. William Leslie Sumner (*The Organ: Its Evolution, Principles of Construction and Use* [4th ed., New York: St. Martin, 1973], and many articles in *The Organ*) and Norbert Dufourcq (*L'Orgue* [Paris: Presses Universitaires de France, 1964] and *L'Orgue* [numéro spécial, 1961], p. 149) reproach Cavaillé-Coll for departing from the principles of classic design. Sumner laments the "inadequacy of the romantic organ for giving proper expression to these works of the greatest periods of organ composition," and Dufourcq goes so far as to say that if Cavaillé-Coll "took a false path in the building up of a tonal universe placed at the service of that polyphony which is at the heart of so many masterpieces" a good many "extenuating circumstances" excuse him, among them his ignorance of classic techniques. That Sumner and Dufourcq consider eighteenth-century principles appropriate for measuring nineteenth-century ideas, and overlook Cavaillé-Coll's knowledge of classic organs, smacks of the era in which the two scholars were at work. They placed themselves in the front lines of an anti-romantic war, and were

Bibliography

blinded by the smoke. This does not make their work less salutary reading for the thoughtful.

Schweitzer's tributes are quoted from Charles R. Joy, *Music in the Life of Albert Schweitzer* (New York: Harper, 1951), pp. 151, 157.

CHAPTER TWO. CAMILLE SAINT-SAËNS

Saint-Saëns on form *versus* feeling is quoted from his *Outspoken Essays on Music* (New York: Dutton, 1922), pp. 4–5; for the recommendation of Franck as professor of organ, see p. 46; on Liszt, see pp. 74–79. The nostalgic reminiscence of the Conservatory is quoted from Camille Saint-Saëns, *Portraits et Souvenirs* (Paris: Lafitte, 1909), p. 14. On the pleasure of simple chord progressions, and on childhood and youth, see his *Ecole buissonnière: Notes et souvenirs* (Paris: Lafitte, 1913), p. 189, *Musical Memories* (1919; reprint, New York: Da Capo, 1969), and *Harmonie et Mélodie*, 7th ed. (Paris: Lafitte, 1907).

On his activity as church musician and reformer, even the exhaustive biographies, such as Jean Bonnerot, *C. Saint-Saëns, sa vie et son oeuvre* (Paris: Durand, 1922), and Emile Baumann, *L'Oeuvre de Camille Saint-Saëns* (Paris: Ollendorff, 1905), offer little. The standard work is Rollin Smith, *Saint-Saëns and the Organ* (Stuyvesant, N.Y.: Pendragon, 1993). On style, see Michael Stegemann, *Camille Saint-Saëns and the French Solo Concerto from 1850 to 1920* (Portland, Ore.: Amadeus, 1991), and Fauré's perceptive summary in "Camille Saint-Saëns" (*La Revue musicale*, 1 Feb. 1922, pp. 99–100). Loretta Fox Scherperel, "The Solo Organ Works of Camille Saint-Saëns" (D.M.A. diss., Eastman School of Music, 1978), compares published scores with manuscripts.

On the Revolution, Benoist, and Boëly, see Orpha Ochse, *Organists and Organ Playing in Nineteenth-Century France and Belgium* (Bloomington: Indiana University Press, 1994), pp. 3–6, 10–25, and 30–31. A revealing article on Boëly—my source for his effect on Saint-Saëns and Franck—is Amédée Gastoué's in *The Musical Quarterly* for July 1944, pp. 336–44.

Schweitzer's comparison of rice with Bachian touch may be found

Bibliography

in *Albert Schweitzer: Etudes et témoignages*, Robert Amadou, ed. (Paris: Main Jetée, 1951), pp. 232–33.

Saint-Saëns's pedaling is described in Charles Tournemire, *Précis d'exécution, de registration et d'improvisation à l'orgue* (Paris: Eschig, 1936), p. 33. Gigout on Saint-Saëns's tempos is to be found in Rollin Smith, *Saint-Saëns and the Organ* (Stuyvesant, N.Y.: Pendragon, 1993), p. 190, as are the old organ-blower's verdict (p. 191) and the description of Saint-Saëns's duties at the Madeleine (pp. 53ff.). The liking for old timbres is cited in Jean Huré, *Esthétique de l'orgue* (Paris: Senart, 1923), p. 167n, and the quip about fugues making apt postludes is in Bernard Gavoty, *Louis Vierne: La vie et l'oeuvre* (Paris: Michel, 1943), pp. 279–80.

CHAPTER THREE. *CÉSAR FRANCK*

Vincent d'Indy's account of his master's life is at once revealing and helpful, adulatory and inaccurate, it being shaped by d'Indy's political and artistic prejudice and propagandistic intent. From it I have taken only the occasional description, and no datum that could not be corroborated.

The most reliable of the many Franck biographies (my source for the troubled paternal, matrimonial, and professional relations) is Léon Vallas, *César Franck* (New York: Oxford University Press, 1951). Franck's words on program music may be found on pp. 245–46, and on his sorrow at the death of his children, p. 98; his methods of teaching and his going in search of tardy pupils are described on pp. 253–56; his marriage is described on pp. 81ff. The Zimmermann, Reicha, Cherubini, and Liszt evaluations may be found on pp. 20–21, 30, 74–75; the announcement of the teaching studio, p. 36; the father's threatened abuse of the mother, p. 38.

Another trustworthy life is Charles Van den Borren's brief *César Franck* (Brussels: La Renaissance du Livre, 1950), which offers a fine bibliography.

Vierne's description of Franck's improvising is taken from Robert Delestre, *L'Oeurve de Marcel Dupré* (Paris: Musique Sacrée, 1952), p. 20.

Bibliography

Bernard Shaw on spavined battle horses is quoted from his remarks (in *The World*, 1 Nov. 1893) on Wagner's *Opera and Drama*, reprinted in *Music in London*, vol. 3 (London: Constable, 1932).

As in his *Saint-Saëns*, Rollin Smith gives us much helpful information in *Toward an Authentic Interpretation of the Organ Works of César Franck* (New York: Pendragon, 1983); see pp. 173–75 for additions to the thematic catalogue devised by Wilhelm Mohr in *Caesar Franck* (Tutzing, Germany: Schneider, 1969). On Franck's recital at the Trocadéro, see Rollin Smith, "The Organ of the Trocadéro and its Players," in *French Organ Music from the Revolution to Franck and Widor*, Lawrence Archbold and William J. Peterson, eds. (Rochester, N.Y.: University of Rochester Press, 1995).

On the Franck traditions, see Marie-Louise Jaquet, "L'Oeuvre d'orgue de César Franck et notre temps" (*L'Orgue*, July–Sept. 1978, pp. 5–41), and Ann Labounsky Steele, "Jean Langlais: The Man and His Music" (Ph.D. diss., University of Pittsburgh, 1991), pp. 168–80. It bears emphasis that Langlais and Dupré were superb artists who each played Franck lyrically and poetically; the amazing thing is that after hearing Langlais play Franck at Saint Clotilde, and Dupré play Franck at Saint Sulpice, it was possible to think Franck's music confinable to a single bona fide style. One is reminded that the thoughtful artist of today treasures multiplicity—can commend one sort of romanticism or classicism without disparaging others, not delighting in Dupré at the expense of Langlais, Bach at the expense of Couperin, Cavaillé-Coll at the expense of Clicquot. This all-encompassing, all-accepting view is a new phenomenon in history, one result of our having at our fingertips, thanks to photographic and phonographic reproduction, practically all the art of previous eras.

Paul de Wailly, in a lecture given at Abbeville, 30 Apr. 1922, "La Vie et l'âme de César Franck" (Amiens: Breton, [1922]), offers the reminiscence of a devoted student, illumines briefly but vividly Franck's habits and preferences as teacher, and asseverates Franck's Frenchness via Picardy. Franck is recalled as an uncomplicated man, careless of his outward appearance, ignorant of current political events, modest but aware of his worth, and of heavy tread. Vallas, from a different vantage point, sees Franck as careless of externals, as anything but uncomplicated, as having a temper and a lively interest in politics, and as denying all claim to modesty, and shows conclusively that Franck was the son of a German mother and that the paternal origins too were Germanic.

Norbert Dufourcq's and Norman Demuth's well-known books (respectively *César Franck; Le milieu, l'oeuvre, l'art* [Paris: Vieux Colombier, 1949] and *César Franck* [London: Dobson, 1949]) offer much that is valuable but contain important errors: Demuth overlooks the father's application for French citizenship and states that the son was admitted to the Conservatory without opposition, this in the teeth of the evidence of Cherubini's denying admission to foreigners; and Demuth accuses Berlioz—a critic as honest as he was perceptive—of coloring the accounts of "every experience which suggested hostility to himself." François Sabatier, *César Franck et l'orgue* (Paris: Presses Universitaires de France, 1982), offers a brief exposition of Franck's life and work, based in part on Dufourcq.

See Julien Tiersot, "Les Oeuvres inédites de César Franck" (*La Revue musicale,* 1 Dec. 1922, pp. 97–138), for a scrutiny of unpublished manuscripts of Franck's student exercises and compositions. Franck's training in harmony and counterpoint is described with the aid of student exercise books that were meticulously copied, signed, and dated. We learn that Franck was talented at sketching and drew the staff paper himself. Tiersot argues that Franck composed a symphonic poem in c. 1846–48, a decade before the form was invented by Liszt, the date having been ascertained from the signature "C. Franck"—it being known that after the break with his father, in c. 1848, Franck no longer signed his name "César-Auguste." But see also Vallas, who shows that Liszt was indeed at work on a symphonic poem at about the same time. (A case can be made for Berlioz's invention of the form, in the *Symphonie fantastique* and "La Captive.") Franck and Liszt had several encounters, but Franck had little contact with Berlioz, according to Tiersot, and rarely heard Berlioz's concerts; the two determinative figures of French nineteenth-century music interacted hardly at all. On the autograph of the Piano Quintet, Tiersot notes Franck's inscription "à mon bon ami Camille Saint-Saëns."

Robert Donington's indispensable work is *The Interpretation of Early Music* (rev. ed., London: Faber, 1974; reprinted with corrections, 1977); see pp. 382ff. for the discussion of tempo, and p. 383 for the comments I paraphrase.

On Franck as improviser, the efficacy of formal constraint has never been more concisely explained than by Jacques Barzun in his *Berlioz and the Romantic Century*, 3d ed. (New York: Columbia University Press, 1969), vol. 1, pp. 145–46: "When we speak of the healthful discipline of strict form . . . we think of the desirable pressure which makes the artist squeeze all the significance out of his ideas. Rime, for example, compels the fledgling poet to try a dozen permutations instead of being satisfied with his first line, and leads him to pack his couplets with sense while enhancing their felicity and force. But this only proves that a set form makes it easier, not harder, to achieve merit. Rime is a parapet which keeps the versifier from going over the edge into feeble nonsense, whereas blank verse lets him and his ideas slide. The stiff outlines of the form moreover give a decent starched look to the final product, even if it is internally weak."

On the *thème libre* and Franck's work as teacher see Orpha Ochse, *Organists and Organ Playing in Nineteenth-Century France and Belgium* (Bloomington: Indiana University Press, 1994), pp. 149, 155–60, 257 (n. 8), and 258 (n. 12).

CHAPTER FOUR. CHARLES-MARIE WIDOR

John R. Near, "The Life and Work of Charles-Marie Widor" (D.M.A. diss., Boston University, 1985), includes a comprehensive bibliography; see also Near's "Charles-Marie Widor: The Organ Works and Saint-Sulpice" (*The American Organist*, Feb. 1993, pp. 46–59) and his edition of Widor's symphonies (Madison, Wis.: A-R Editions, 1991). Also illuminating are Andrew Thomson, *The Life and Times of Charles-Marie Widor* (New York: Oxford University Press, 1987); John R. Wilson,

"The Organ Symphonies of Charles-Marie Widor" (Ph.D. diss., Florida State University, 1966); and Jimmy Jess Anthony, "Charles-Marie Widor's Symphonies pour orgue: Their Artistic Context and Cultural Antecedents" (D.M.A. diss., Eastman School of Music, 1986).

The Callinet family is described in P. Meyer-Siat, *Les Callinet, facteurs d'orgues à Rouffach* (Strasbourg and Paris: Istra, 1965). The "Paris" Callinet, who worked on the Clicquot at Saint Sulpice and helped build the Saint Eustache organ that Hesse inaugurated, was Louis Callinet, a cousin to the Callinet brothers of Rouffach, Joseph and Claude Ignace. Widor, notwithstanding his grandfather's ties to the Callinets, apparently cared little for their work in Alsace, perhaps finding it intolerably old-fashioned.

On Lemmens, Hesse, and Rinck, see my *Albert Schweitzer, Musician* (Aldersgate, England: Scolar, 1994), pp. 14–29. Stephen Morelot is quoted from "L'Inauguration de l'orgue de Saint-Eustache," *Revue et Gazette musicale* (7 July 1844, p. 231), Berlioz from "Exposition de l'Industrie," *Journal des Débats* (23 June 1844, p. 3). Widor's assessment of Lemmens may be found in Charles-Marie Widor, "L'Orgue moderne" (*Les Nouvelles musicales*, 1 Mar. 1934, pp. 5–6), and "Souvenirs sur Ch.-M. Widor," an address given by Dupré before the Institute of France, 26 Oct. 1959 (Paris: Firmin-Didot, 1959), p. 5.

Accounts vary as to the length of Widor's stay in Belgium, and his own recollection seems shaky. Widor may have studied with Fétis and Lemmens for as long as one year, but Professor Near shows that four months is a more likely estimate.

For thoughtful essays on Lemmens, see William J. Peterson's chapter in *French Organ Music from the Revolution to Franck and Widor*, Lawrence Archbold and William J. Peterson, eds. (Rochester, N.Y.: University of Rochester Press, 1995), pp. 50–100, and Orpha Ochse, *Organists and Organ Playing in Nineteenth-Century France and Belgium* (Bloomington: Indiana University Press, 1994), pp. 174–82. See also Ewald Kooiman, "Jacques Lemmens, Charles-Marie Widor, and the French Bach Tradition" (*The American Organist*, Mar. 1995, pp. 56–64).

Among Lemmens's prominent pupils, besides Widor and Guilmant, were Alphonse Mailly (who also studied with Girschner), Joseph Tilborghs, and Clément Loret.

Cavaillé-Coll's letter to Fétis appears untranslated in Fenner Douglass, *Cavaillé-Coll and the Musicians* (Raleigh, N.C.: Sunbury, 1980), vol. 1, pp. 710–12. Joseph d'Ortigue is quoted from *La Musique à l'église* (Paris, 1861), pp. 174–75. Lemmens is quoted from his *Ecole d'Orgue basée sur le plain-chant romain* (Brussels: Schott, 1862), pp. 1–3; see also his posthumous *Du Chant grégorien: Sa mélodie, son rhythme, son harmonisation* (Ghent: [Hoste], 1886), which includes a detailed biographical essay by the Rev. Joseph Duclos. Many of Cavaillé-Coll's and Lemmens's letters are reproduced in Norbert Dufourcq, "A propos du Cinquantenaire de la mort de Cavaillé-Coll" (*L'Orgue*, nos. 53–65, 1949–52).

Correctly pronounced, incidentally, the second syllable of "Lemmens" rhymes with that of the English word "immense," though of course without the accent. The final "s" is sounded, as are the final "s" of Saint-Saëns and "z" of Berlioz, all Parisians to the contrary notwithstanding.

In his *Initiation musicale* (Paris: Hachette, 1923), pp. 126–27, Widor recounts his appointment to Saint Sulpice, and contends that the Conservatory was indeed represented at Franck's funeral—d'Indy and Wailly, among others, having said the opposite. Included are brief chapters on the fundamentals of music (from aural perception, acoustics, timbre, harmony, counterpoint, and composition to the instruments and their development and use) and on the history of music from ancient times.

Widor's remark on the effects of timbre is taken from Charles-Marie Widor, "L'Orgue moderne" (*Les Nouvelles musicales*, 1 Mar. 1934, pp. 5–6); the anecdote about the disagreeable countess, Isidor Philipp, "Charles-Marie Widor: A Portrait" (*The Musical Quarterly*, Apr. 1944, pp. 125–32); and the philippic against d'Indy, Andrew Thomson, *The Life and Times of Charles-Marie Widor* (New York: Oxford University Press, 1987), p. 59.

Bibliography

Dupré's remark about the contemplation of beauty may be found in Juliette Hacquard, "Marcel Dupré" (*Rive Gauche: Mensuel catholique du Quartier Saint-Sulpice*, May 1966), p. 21.

CHAPTER FIVE. LOUIS VIERNE

The standard biography is Bernard Gavoty, *Louis Vierne: La vie et l'oeuvre* (Paris: Michel, 1943). See also Henri Doyen, *Mes Leçons d'orgue avec Louis Vierne* (Paris: Musique Sacrée, 1966), and Steven George Young, "The Life and Work of Louis Vierne" (Mus. A.D. diss., Boston University, 1994). Vierne's recollections may be found in "Mes Souvenirs" (trans. Esther Jones Barrow in thirteen monthly installments as "Memoirs of Louis Vierne; His Life and Contacts with Famous Men," *The Diapason*, beginning Sept. 1938) and in fragments from his private "Journal" published, together with "Mes Souvenirs," in a commemorative issue of *L'Orgue* (supplement to vol. 134, 1970). Vierne recounts his meetings and relation with Franck on p. 144 and *passim;* Widor's instruction is described on pp. 28–51, Guilmant's on pp. 52–83. "Mes Souvenirs" also appeared in *In Memoriam, Louis Vierne* (Paris: Brouwer, 1939), together with tributes by pupils and colleagues. Vierne quotes Widor and others at such length that scholarship rightly questions his memory, which was exceptional but not disinterested; in general, I have taken him at his word.

Widor on tempo in Bach and on conveying the composer's intentions is quoted from the preface to Albert Schweitzer, *J.-S. Bach, le musicien-poète* (Leipzig: Breitkopf and Härtel, 1905). Schweitzer on Franck's *Trois Chorals* is quoted from a letter to Melville Smith, Lambaréné, 11 Feb. 1962 (Archives Centrales Albert Schweitzer, Gunsbach, France, by permission of Rhena Schweitzer Miller). The National Institute for Blind Children served as model for institutions in many countries and as a center for research on teaching. See Edgard Guilbeau, *Histoire de l'Institution nationale des jeunes aveugles* (Paris: Belin, 1907).

André Fleury, who studied with Vierne for half a dozen years in the 1920s, describes Vierne's teaching and playing in Rulon Christiansen, "Hommage à Louis Vierne: A Conversation with André Fleury" (*The American Organist*, Dec. 1987, pp. 60–64).

Widor's practice of slightly retarding before each entrance of the subject in Bach's fugues was brought to my attention by Daniel Roth, in a conversation on 19 Nov. 1994.

The Vierne observations on musical tendency may be found in Bernard Gavoty, *Louis Vierne: La vie et l'oeuvre* (Paris: Michel, 1943), pp. 208ff. For Barzun on nuances of feeling, see Jacques Barzun, "Overheard at Glimmerglass," *Berlioz Studies*, Peter Bloom, ed. (Cambridge: Cambridge University Press, 1992), p. 255, and "The Meaning of Meaning in Music," *Critical Questions*, Bea Friedland, ed. (Chicago: University of Chicago Press, 1982), pp. 75–98. For discussions of mind and sensibility that should be required reading for every musician, see William James, *The Principles of Psychology* (1890; reprint, New York: Dover, 1950).

CHAPTER SIX. MARCEL DUPRÉ

The chapter is largely based on my recollections and on private interviews. Dupré's remarks on the organ at Saint Ouen may be found in his *Marcel Dupré raconte* (Paris: Bornemann, 1972), pp. 20–22; on Cavaillé-Coll, pp. 37–38, 40–43; on piano study, p. 44; and on the Rome Prize, pp. 75–76. The anecdotes about Cavaillé-Coll, Diémer, and Vierne are quoted from *Marcel Dupré par lui-même* (phonodisk, Paris: Productions MF [AS-723021], 1965). The cities and organs Dupré associates with "Variations sur un Noël" are listed in an autograph program note in the Dupré papers at the Bibliothèque Nationale.

On Guilmant, see Marcel Dupré, "Alexandre Guilmant" (*La Revue musicale*, Feb. 1937, pp. 73–83), "Alexandre Guilmant" (*The Diapason*, Mar. 1962, p. 8), and *Marcel Dupré raconte* (Paris: Bornemann, 1972), pp. 47–51. See also Michel d'Argoeuves, "Alexandre Guilmant" (*L'Orgue*, Apr.-June 1965, pp. 60–68); William C. Carl, "Some Reminiscences of Alexandre Guilmant" (*The Diapason*, May 1924, p. 6), and Carl's series on Guilmant in *The Diapason* for June, July, and Aug. 1936; Rollin Smith, "Alexandre Guilmant, Commemorating the 150th

Anniversary of His Birth" (*The American Organist*, Mar. 1987, pp. 50–58); and Agnes Armstrong, "Alexandre Guilmant: American Tours and American Organs" (*The Tracker*, vol. 32, no. 3, 1989, pp. 15–23). Kurt Lueders's research suggests that Guilmant studied in Belgium with Lemmens for at most one month, probably in March or April 1860 (conversation with the author, 22 June 1996).

Dupré distinguishes the interpreter from the virtuoso in his *Philosophie de Musique* (Tournai, Belgium: Collegium Musicum, 1984), pp. 42–43; see also his preface to François Florand, *Jean-Sébastien Bach: L'oeuvre d'orgue* (Paris: Cerf, 1947), p. 8. For Widor on the future of the French organ school see Pierre Lafond, "Mon Cousin Marcel" (*Notre Vieux Lycée*, bulletin of L'Association des anciens élèves du Lycée Corneille, Dec. 1971, p. 10). The quotation on North American builders is taken from Ralph A. Harris, "Dupré Sees New Field for Organ Composers" (*The Diapason*, 1 Dec. 1924, p. 8); on the symphonic organ, Dupré's unpublished essay "L'Orgue de demain"; and on playing what is written, the preface to *Seventy-Nine Chorales*. The long quotation is from Bernard Gavoty, *Les Grands Interprètes* (Geneva: Kister, 1955), p. 28.

CHAPTER SEVEN. JEAN LANGLAIS

For Dupré on Widor's kindness, see "Souvenirs sur Ch.-M. Widor," an address given by Dupré before the Institute of France, 26 Oct. 1959 (Paris: Firmin-Didot, 1959), and on Widor's resignation and death, *Marcel Dupré raconte* (Paris: Bornemann, 1972), pp. 68–69. The Schweitzer quotation is taken from a letter to A. M. Henderson, Lambaréné, 24 Aug. 1945 (Archives Centrales Albert Schweitzer, Gunsbach, France, by permission of Rhena Schweitzer Miller).

Gigout's life is surveyed in William C. Carl, "Reminiscences of Eugène Gigout, Organist, Teacher and Improviser" (*The Diapason*, Apr. 1926, p. 28); A. M. Henderson, "Memories of Gigout, 60 Years at Church of Saint Augustin in Paris" (*The Diapason*, Apr. 1951, p. 8); and Charles A. H. Pearson, "Jubilee of M. Gigout Celebrated in Paris"

Bibliography

(*The Diapason,* Jan. 1924, p. 3). See also Clarence Eddy, "Great Frenchmen of Organ World in 1897 Are Pictured by Eddy" (*The Diapason,* May 1937, pp. 14–15); Mark D. Bailey, "Eugène Gigout and His 'Course for Organ, Improvisation, and Plainchant'" (*The American Organist,* Mar. 1994, pp. 76–80); and Bailey's "Eugène Gigout (1844–1925), Performer and Pedagogue" (D.M.A. diss., University of Cincinnati, 1988). Saint-Saëns's recommendation of Gigout to Fauré may be found in Camille Saint-Saëns and Gabriel Fauré, *Correspondence* (Paris: Heugel, 1973), letter of 1 May 1911.

For authoritative, indeed definitive, information on Langlais, see Ann Labounsky Steele, "Jean Langlais: The Man and His Music" (Ph.D. diss., University of Pittsburgh, 1991), which is the basis of a forthcoming biography, and the many articles, liner notes, and lectures by this favorite pupil and protégée. Labounsky remains Langlais's peerless interpreter, as attest her recordings of his complete works, undertaken with his approbation. The humorous quips are from her recollection (conversations with the author, 16 Apr. and 25 May 1996).

Also indispensable is *Ombre et Lumière: Jean Langlais, 1907–1991* (Paris: Combre, 1995), by Marie-Louise Jaquet-Langlais, Langlais's pupil, co-organist at Saint Clotilde, and devoted wife. Langlais's remarks on Vierne's encouragement may be found on p. 55, on his prize competition under Dupré, p. 56, on the decline of church music, p. 221, and on the neo-baroque, pp. 229–36; the review from *Le Courrier musicale* is quoted on pp. 60–61. Another loving and comprehensive piece of scholarship is Kathleen Thomerson, *Jean Langlais: A Bio-bibliography* (New York: Greenwood, 1988). Langlais speaks of the influence of the Saint Clotilde organ in his "Quelques souvenirs d'un organiste d'église" (*L'Orgue,* Jan.-Mar. 1971, pp. 4–6).

Langlais's censure of the neo-baroque leads one to ask whether any idea has ever been more often misapplied, and in consequence more often wreaked havoc on the beautiful and true, than the idea of authenticity.

Bibliography

CHAPTER EIGHT. OLIVIER MESSIAEN

Dupré's puzzlement and the ensuing parental conference were reported to me by Mme. Dupré, in a conversation on 16 Apr. 1975.

My chief sources for Messiaen's words are *Musique et couleur: Nouveaux entretiens avec Claude Samuel* (Paris: Belfond, 1986), which has been beautifully translated by E. Thomas Glasow as *Olivier Messiaen, Music and Color: Conversations with Claude Samuel* (Portland, Ore.: Amadeus, 1994), and a taped conversation with Messiaen, 3 Nov. 1970. In *Music and Color* the reader will find Messiaen's remarks on his birth and childhood on pp. 13–15; on organ building, pp. 24–25; on Tristramian love, pp. 30–31; on Dauphiné, pp. 35, 119; on color, pp. 40–42, 64; on impossibilities, pp. 47–49; on bird song, pp. 64, 133; on rhythms and durations, pp. 68, 118–19; on being a romanticist, pp. 47, 120; on Dupré, p. 111; and on the mystery of the Trinity, p. 125. Messiaen on music as language is quoted from the preface to *Méditations sur le mystère de la Sainte Trinité*, pp. 3, 5; on the power, majesty, and poetry of the organ at Trinity Church, and on the combat of life and death in *Les Corps glorieux*, from the booklet accompanying the reissue (EMI CZS 7–67400–2) of his 1956 recordings of his organ works; and on the sixty-four chromatic durations, from his *Livre d'Orgue*, p. 33.

Invaluable are Madeleine Hsu, *Olivier Messiaen, the Musical Mediator: A Study of the Influence of Liszt, Debussy, and Bartók* (Madison, Wis., and Teaneck, N.J.: Fairleigh Dickinson University Press, 1996), and Antoine Goléa, *Rencontres avec Olivier Messiaen* (Paris: Julliard, 1960); from the latter work (p. 19) comes Messiaen's remark on his love for Dauphiné.

Also indispensable is *The Messiaen Companion*, Peter Hill, ed. (Portland, Ore.: Amadeus, 1995); Yvonne Loriod's words are quoted from p. 294, Dame Gillian Weir's, p. 366. In an appendix by Jean-Louis Coignet, we read that the Cavaillé-Coll at Trinity Church, whose renovation at the turn of the century became a *cause célèbre* when it occasioned Guilmant's resignation, remained largely unaltered till 1934, when Messiaen added seven stops and a Barker lever, and that in 1962–65 a new console and combination system were installed, the stop and key actions electrified, eight stops added, and seven positif stops enclosed. Messiaen was organist at Trinity Church for some sixty years.

See also Paul Griffiths, *Olivier Messiaen and the Music of Time* (London: Faber, 1985); Robert Sherlaw Johnson, *Messiaen* (Berkeley: University of California Press, 1975); Roger Nichols, *Messiaen* (Oxford: Oxford University Press, 1986); *Messiaen on Messiaen: The Composer Writes About His Works*, trans. Irene Feddern (Bloomington, Ind.: Frangipani, 1986), drawn from liner notes to recordings and prefaces to scores; and Clyde Holloway, "The Organ Works of Olivier Messiaen and Their Importance in His Total Oeuvre" (S.M.D. diss., Union Theological Seminary, 1974).

Not to be overlooked is Messiaen's *Technique de mon langage musical* (Paris: Leduc, 1944; rev. ed., 1955). His multivolume *summa* on rhythm, color, and ornithology is forthcoming. The modes of limited transposition and their use are explained in the preface to his *Nativité du Seigneur*. See also John Philips, "The Modal Language of Olivier Messiaen: Practices of *Technique de mon langage musical* as reflected in *Catalogue d'oiseaux*" (master's thesis, Peabody Conservatory, 1977).

The Liszt quotation is taken from Humphrey Searle, "The Orchestral Works," in Alan Walker, *Franz Liszt: The Man and His Music* (New York: Taplinger, 1970), pp. 280–81; the Barzun quotation, Jacques Barzun, *Critical Questions*, Bea Friedland, ed. (Chicago: University of Chicago Press, 1982), p. 66.

It remains to thank for their encouragement and help G. Dene Barnard; Jacques Barzun; Cristina Brawner, of the Upper Arlington, Ohio, Public Library; Joseph F. Dzeda; Richard Fettkether; Gary L. Garber; Harry Haskell, music editor, Joyce Ippolito, production editor, and Noreen O'Connor, manuscript editor, at Yale University Press; Thomas F. Heck, director, and the staff of the Music Library, Ohio State University; Michael Herzog; Charles Krigbaum; Herbert Livingston; Kurt Lueders; William Parsons, of the Music Division, Library of Congress; William J. Peterson; Christian Schoen; Alexander Schreiner; Ann Labounsky Steele; and Erik Wensberg.

Index

Index

Index

Index

Dupré, Marcel (*continued*)
and Saint Clotilde, 78
and Saint Ouen, 134–35, 138
and Saint-Saëns, 84, 145
and Saint Sulpice, 2, 143, 151, 157–58, 161, 213
and Saint Vivien de Rouen, 139
and Schumann, 141, 151
Second Symphony, 151, 154
and self-esteem, 170
Seven Pieces, 151
Seventy-Nine Chorales, 151
Sinfonia for Piano and Organ, 154
Sonata for Cello and Organ, 154
and stage fright, 171
style and idiom, 57, 148, 149–50, 150–54, 165–66
Suite Bretonne, 151
Symphonie-Passion, 17, 151, 154, 165
Symphony for Organ and Orchestra, 16, 150
as teacher, 144, 160–61, 164–65, 167–71, 184
and technique, 56, 147–48, 153, 170, 171
and tempo, 148, 151, 153
Three Preludes and Fugues, 16, 145, 165
and timbre, 149–50, 151, 153
and tradition, 83, 98, 152, 160, 167, 169–70, 213
Trio for Violin, Cello, and Organ, 154
Triptyque, 16
and the Trocadéro, 40, 149
Trois Elévations, 151
"Variations sur un Noël," 16, 150
and Vierne, 75, 133, 137–38, 142, 144, 146, 149, 153, 160
Vingt-Quatre Inventions, 151
Vision, 151, 154

and Widor, 84, 92, 98, 107, 133–66 passim
Dupré-Chauvière, Alice (mother), 133, 136–37, 138, 147
Durand, Auguste, 76
Duration. *See* Style(s), legato; *individual composers*
Duruflé, Maurice, 2, 78, 83, 159
Duruflé-Chevalier, Marie-Madeleine, 2, 161

Ecole Monceau, 109
Ecole Niedermeyer, 54, 158–59
Ecole Normale de Musique, 194
Electricity, use of, in organ building, 103, 149, 150, 190
Emmanuel, Maurice, 184
Emotion, expression of. *See* Feeling(s), expression of
Erard firm, 25, 113, 120, 140, 151
Estyle, César-Abel, 184

Falcinelli, Rolande, 161
Falkenberg, Georges, 184
Fauré, Gabriel, 49, 133, 144, 160
and Langlais, 176
and Saint-Saëns, 54, 62, 156, 159
and Vierne, 126–27, 156, 157
and Widor, 107, 156
Feeling(s), expression of, 13–14, 15, 43, 64–65, 74, 80–81, 94, 127–28, 141, 144, 166, 169, 174, 175
Fénelon, François, 21
Fessy, Alexandre, 51, 90, 91
Fétis, François-Joseph, 15, 75, 92–94, 95, 96, 216
Flaubert, Gustave, 107
Fleury, André, 120, 126, 128, 153, 159
Flutes. *See* Cavaillé-Coll, Aristide, and flutes; *individual composers*, registration

Index

Fonds. See Cavaillé-Coll, Aristide,
  and foundations
Form, 59, 80, 117, 139, 184
  classic, 11, 14, 42, 57, 144
  concerto, 61
  and constraint, 215
  vs. content, 126
  and feeling, 43, 64, 74, 128
  and history, 13
  organ symphony, 17, 101–03, 104,
    124–25, 143, 154, 174, 175, 191,
    203
  and the romanticists, 17, 202
  sonata, 17, 87, 102, 125, 131
  Thème libre, 87, 142, 171–72
Foundations. See Cavaillé-Coll, Aristide, and foundations; individual
  composers, registration
Franck, César, 4, 10, 12, 13, 15, 19,
    60, 128, 168
  and animosity of colleagues, 86,
    109, 113, 217
  and Bach, 42, 75, 79, 85, 87
  and Benoist, 51, 67
  and Berlioz, 70, 75, 76, 88, 214
  and Boëly, 48, 87
  "Cantabile." See Franck, César,
    Trois Pièces
  and Cavaillé-Coll, 16, 32, 36, 73,
    75–100 passim
  and "César-Auguste," 70, 214
  character and mien, 64–111, 213–14
  childhood and schooling, 65–66
  children, 72
  death, 65, 111, 113
  and Dupré, 3, 75, 80, 83, 84, 133,
    142–43, 149, 151, 153, 165–66,
    170, 213
  and early music, 74
  Fantasy in A. See Franck, César,
    Trois Pièces

Fantasy in C, 80
"Final," 79–80, 81
Germanic origins and leanings, 42,
    65, 66, 74–75, 86
"Grande Pièce symphonique," 16,
    17, 80, 101, 102
and Guilmant, 83–84, 142
and improvisation, 67, 74, 75, 86,
    87–88, 99, 108, 111, 117
and Langlais, 3, 83, 162, 165, 170,
    175, 213
and legato, 83
and Lemmens, 75, 76
and Liszt, 70, 75, 76, 85, 99, 214
marriage, 71–72
and Mendelssohn, 75, 87
miscellaneous works, 65, 68, 69,
    70, 73, 79, 85, 108, 109, 140
and National Institute for Blind
    Children, 109, 162
and Notre Dame, 85, 99
and Notre Dame de Lorette, 69,
    72, 73, 76
odes, patriotic, 67
and opera, 73
and organ symphony, 17, 101–03,
    191, 203
L'Organiste, 70
and Paris Conservatory, 49, 66–
    69, 70, 74, 79, 85–88, 108, 109,
    111, 113–14, 196, 217
"Pastorale," 80
and the piano, 16, 65, 66, 67, 69
"Pièce Héroïque." See Franck,
    César, Trois Pièces
and plainchant, 67
poetic spirit, 162–63, 165
"Prelude, Fugue and Variation,"
    65, 80
"Prière," 80, 83
and program music, 65, 214

Index

Franck, César *(continued)*
  recitals and concerts, 19, 66, 70, 75,
    79, 82, 85
  and registration, 6, 16, 36, 78, 81–
    84, 125
  religious faith, 66, 110, 113
  and Rome Prize, 68
  and rubato, 83, 163, 175
  and Saint Clotilde, 2, 3, 4, 48, 77–
    79, 82, 83, 85, 99, 110
  and Saint Eustache, 19, 75
  and Saint Jean–Saint François, 73
  and Saint-Saëns, 42, 55, 64–65, 74,
    75, 84, 85–86, 99, 166
  and Saint Sulpice, 85, 100, 109
  and Schumann, 75, 87
  and self-improvement, 68, 79, 103
  Six Pièces, 2, 3, 42, 73, 79–81, 83,
    85, 88
  and sketching, 68, 214
  and specialism, 73, 101
  style and idiom, 57, 68, 69–70, 73,
    74–76, 79–85, 88, 101–02, 103,
    104, 175
  and the symphonic poem, 214
  as teacher, 49, 68, 69, 71, 72, 86–
    88, 110–11, 115, 117
  and technique, 68, 76, 79, 103
  and tempo, 81, 84
  and timbre, 5, 6, 81–84, 103, 104, 125
  and Tournemire, 83, 88
  and tradition, 83–85, 142–43, 162,
    213
  and Trinity Church, 85, 99
  and the Trocadéro, 40, 82
  Trois Chorals, 3, 70, 73, 81, 83, 84,
    108, 159, 173
  Trois Pièces, 73, 81, 82, 84
  and Vierne, 75, 80, 88, 109–11,
    113, 117, 121, 124, 125, 133
  as vulgar and sublime, 69–70

and Widor, 84, 99, 101–03, 107,
  109, 113–14, 115, 117
Franck, Joseph (brother), 66, 69, 72–
  73, 85
Franck, Nicolas-Joseph (father), 65–
  72, 74, 81
Franck-Frings, Marie-Catherine-
  Barbe (mother), 65, 66, 71, 72
Franck-Saillot, Félicité (wife), 71, 72,
  74, 77
Franco-Prussian War, 38, 67, 86, 100
Free improvisation. *See* Thème libre
Frescobaldi, Girolamo, 130, 163, 178,
  190
Freud, Sigmund, 204

Gabrieli, Andrea, 130
Gallon, Jean, 184
Gallon, Noël, 184
Garcia-Viardot, Pauline, 53, 54, 76
Garnier (voicer), 33, 138
Gigout, Eugène, 158–60, 162, 163,
  164
  and Saint-Saëns, 54, 56, 156, 158,
    159
  and Vierne, 132, 157
Gilbert, Alphonse, 69
Girschner, Christian Friedrich Jo-
  hann, 92, 96, 217
Glazunov, Aleksandr, 151
Glock (voicer), 33
Gluck, Christoph Wilibald, 10, 28,
  42, 61, 75, 182, 183
Gounod, Charles, 32, 50, 54, 59, 98
Grandes lignes, 122, 126, 141. *See also*
  Style(s), and acoustics
Gregorian chant. *See* Plainchant
Grétry, André Ernest, 70
Griepenkerl, Friedrich Konrad, 90
Grigny, Nicolas de, 163, 190
Guide-mains, 45–46, 56

(232)

Index

Index

Kant, Immanuel, 68
Karg-Elert, Sigfrid, 104
Kittel, Johann Christian, 90
Koussevitzky, Serge, 199
Krebs, Johann Ludwig, 130

Lacombe, Louis, 94
Lacroix, Sylvestre François, 23, 24
Lamoureux orchestra, 113, 144
Landowska, Wanda, 7
Langlais, Jean, 3, 10
  and Aeolian-Skinner organs, 16
  "Arabesque sur les flûtes," 17
  and the avant-garde, 178
  "Ave Maris Stella," 173
  blindness, 161–62, 173, 174
  and Boys Town, 179
  carol settings, 174
  and Cavaillé-Coll, 36, 79
  "Chant de Paix," 175
  character and mien, 161, 162, 163,
    171, 173, 178
  childhood and schooling, 161–64
  as choral conductor, 172
  and church music, 175, 176–77
  death, 179
  De Profundis (Op. 157), 17
  and Dukas, 173, 175
  and Dupré, 3, 161, 164–67, 168,
    169, 170, 171–72, 174, 175, 213
  First Symphony, 174, 175
  and folksong, 161, 175–76
  and Franck, 3, 83, 162, 165, 170,
    175, 213
  and Guilmant Prize, 172
  Hommage à Frescobaldi, 174
  hymn settings, 174, 175
  and improvisation, 165, 171, 172,
    173, 179
  and legato, 163, 166, 174, 175
  and Lemmens, 163

  and liturgical reform, 176–77
  and Mahaut, 162
  and Marchal, 162–63, 168
  marriage, 172
  and Messiaen, 176, 178, 180
  miscellaneous works, 172, 173, 174,
    177, 179
  and National Institute for Blind
    Children, 162, 164–65, 171, 172
  and neo-classical movement, 177–
    78, 221
  and Paris Conservatory, 164–72,
    173
  and the piano, 162, 170
  and plainchant, 161, 172, 173, 175,
    176, 177
  Poèmes évangeliques, 172
  Prelude and Fugue, 171
  "Prélude sur une Antienne," 171
  recitals and concerts, 3, 163–64,
    174, 176, 179
  and registration, 16, 36, 174
  religious faith, 161–62, 176–77
  revising, dislike of, 174
  as romanticist, 15, 175, 178
  and rubato, 162–63, 175
  and Saint Clotilde, 16, 79, 83, 162,
    173, 176, 179, 213
  and Saint Etienne du Mont, 163
  and Saint Germain des Prés, 163
  and Saint Pierre de Montrouge, 173
  "Scherzo Cats," 173
  and Schola Cantorum, 178
  and Schumann, 164
  sense of humor, 161, 173–74
  Six Préludes, 171
  and Société des Amis de l'Orgue,
    172–73
  style and idiom, 17, 57, 162, 163,
    173–76, 178
  Suite Médiévale, 174

Index

recitals and concerts, 194
and registration, 16, 36, 184, 189–91
religious faith, 182–83, 184, 186, 192, 196, 198, 201
and rhythm, 184, 185–86, 191, 194, 197–98, 199, 202, 203
as romanticist, 15, 193, 202–03
and Rome Prize, 184
and Saint Ouen, 189
and Saint-Saëns, 191
and Saint Sulpice, 189
and Schola Cantorum, 194
and Schumann, 197
and serialism, 197, 199
and Shakespeare, 182, 183, 185
and Sophocles, 182
and stained glass, 185
style and idiom, 2, 16, 57, 185–86, 186–89, 198, 202–03
as teacher, 194, 199
and tempo, 2, 185
and Tennyson, 182
and timbre, 189–203 passim
and time, 185, 186, 192, 195
and Trinity Church, 189–90, 197, 201, 222–23
and unity out of diversity, 192
"Verset pour la fête de la Dédicace," 200
and Vierne, 191
and Wagner, 184, 201
and Widor, 203
Messiaen, Pascal (son), 194, 200
Messiaen, Pierre (father), 180, 182
Messiaen-Delbos, Claire (wife), 194, 200
Messiaen-Loriod, Yvonne (wife), 200
Meyerbeer, Giacomo, 23, 32, 70
Michel, Charles-Marie, 123
Michelangelo, 134

Milhaud, Darius, 143
Mixtures. *See* Cavaillé-Coll, Aristide, and mixtures; *individual composers*, registration
Modes, 154, 184, 186, 187, 191, 202, 203
Monet, Claude, 151
Montalembert, Charles, 75
Montgolfier, Jacques-Etienne, 92
Montgolfier, Joseph-Michel, 92
Morelot, Stephen, 75, 91
Mormon Tabernacle, 176
Motion, needless. *See* Deportment
Mozart, Wolfgang Amadeus, 7, 11, 13, 14, 47, 69, 74
and Dupré, 141, 168
and Messiaen, 182, 184, 188, 197
and Saint-Saëns, 42, 44, 45, 46, 61, 63
and Vierne, 112, 126
and Widor, 116
Müller, Christian, 178
Music. *See also* Style(s)
as adjective, 127
as language, 119, 200–01, 202
program, 15, 65, 95, 127, 191–92, 193, 196, 198, 201, 214
and words, 18, 127
Mutations. *See* Cavaillé-Coll, Aristide, and mutations; *individual composers*, registration
Mutin, Charles, 156

Napoleon (Bonaparte), 15
National Institute for Blind Children, 109, 110, 112–13, 162, 164–65, 171, 172, 218
National Shrine of the Immaculate Conception, 179
Notre Dame, Cathedral of, Paris, 19, 32, 34, 35, 41, 82
and Dupré, 146

Index

Index

Index

Index

Stream of consciousness, 127
Style(s). *See also individual composers*
  and acoustics, 56–57, 81, 122, 126,
  129, 141, 170, 175. *See also Ca-*
  vaillé-Coll, Aristide, and
  acoustics
  classic, 11, 13, 14, 22, 42, 47, 82,
  90, 94, 118–19, 153
  dignity and solemnity as elements
  in, 9, 17, 47, 81, 102, 104, 118
  fidelity to, and technique, 56
  Impressionist, 13, 49
  legato, 9, 16, 56, 96–97, 115–29
  passim, 152, 153, 170, 175, 203
  neo-classical, 12–13, 103, 158, 177–
  78, 189–90, 210–11, 221
  Realist, 13
  romantic, 13, 15–18, 22, 28, 202–03
  "Symphonic," 103, 150
Symphony, organ. *See* Form, organ
  symphony

Tchaikovsky, Peter, 44
Technique, 16, 47, 56, 118, 202. *See*
  also Deportment; Pedaling; Piano
  vs. organ; *individual composers*
Teilhard de Chardin, Pierre, 183
Tempo, 8, 9, 57, 81, 90, 96, 118, 119,
  170, 175. *See also individual*
  composers
Tennyson, Alfred, 182
Théâtre des Champs-Elysées, 193
Thème libre, 87, 142, 171–72
Thomas, Ambroise, 32, 86, 94, 98
Thomas, Saint (the Apostle), 30
Thomas Aquinas, Saint, 183
Tilborghs, Joseph, 217
Timbre, 9, 15, 28, 81–82, 104, 203.
  See also individual composers
Tolstoy, Leo, 68

Tone color. *See* Timbre
Toscanini, Arturo, 6, 84
Tournemire, Charles
  and Franck, 83, 88
  and Langlais, 83, 172, 173, 176
  and Saint Clotilde, 79
  and Saint-Saëns, 56
  and Vierne, 115, 120, 160
  and Widor, 115, 120, 160
Tradition, 2–3, 6, 84–85, 91, 95, 157,
  176, 177
  and Bach, 90–91, 98, 169–70
  and Franck, 83–85, 142–43, 162,
  213
Trinity Church, Paris
  and Franck, 85, 99
  and Guilmant, 83, 130, 158, 189, 222
  and Messiaen, 189–90, 197, 201,
  222–23
  and Saint-Saëns, 61, 99
  and Widor, 99, 158
Trocadéro, Palais du, 32, 40, 61, 82,
  106, 149
Turgenev, Ivan, 54

Varèse, Edgard, 143
Ventils. *See* Cavaillé-Coll, Aristide,
  and ventils
Verdi, Giuseppe, 10
Viardot, Pauline, 53, 54, 76
Victoria, Queen, 39
Vierne, André (son), 146
Vierne, Henri (father), 111, 113
Vierne, Jacques (son), 146
Vierne, Louis, 2, 10, 15, 191
  afflictions, 111–12, 113, 145–46
  and art secular *vs.* religious, 125
  and Bach, 2, 110, 126
  and Cavaillé-Coll, 16, 36, 120, 122,
  123, 125

Index

character and mien, 109–10, 112, 120, 121, 128, 176
childhood and schooling, 109, 111–14
children, 131, 146
death, 157
and Dupré, 75, 133, 137–38, 142, 144, 146, 149, 153, 160
and Fauré, 126–27, 156, 157
Fifth Symphony, 125
First Symphony, 124
Fourth Symphony, 125, 163, 173
and Franck, 75, 80, 88, 109–11, 113, 117, 121, 124, 125, 133
and Gigout, 132, 157
and Guilmant, 125, 129, 130, 132, 146, 156
and harmony, 124, 125
and improvisation, 124
and Langlais, 162, 164, 172, 173, 176, 179
and legato, 126
and Lemmens, 95, 110
marriage, 131, 146
memoirs, 156, 157
and memory, 110
and Messiaen, 191
and the metronome, 126
miscellaneous works, 124
and Mozart, 112, 126
and music pure *vs.* descriptive, 127
"Naïades," 16
and National Institute for Blind Children, 109, 110, 112–13, 162
and Notre Dame, 2, 126, 131–32, 145–46, 156, 157
and the organ symphony, 17, 124–25
and Paris Conservatory, 110, 111,

113, 120, 123, 126, 129, 137, 146, 156–57, 160
and the piano, 109, 112
Pièces de fantaisie, 125
and plainchant, 120
and reason *vs.* sensibility, 128
recitals and concerts, 123, 137–38, 157
and registration, 16, 36, 125, 126
and rhythm, 124, 125, 126
and Saint Clotilde, 78, 110
and Saint Ouen, 137–38
and Saint-Saëns, 57, 123–24, 125
and Saint Séverin, 123, 125
and Saint Sulpice, 121–22, 126, 131, 137, 141
and Schola Cantorum, 157, 179
and Schumann, 112, 125, 126
Second Symphony, 125, 128
Seventh Symphony, 125
Sixth Symphony, 125
stage fright, 123
style and idiom, 17, 57, 124–28
as teacher, 120, 123
and tempo, 2, 5, 126
and themes, 125, 127–28
Third Symphony, 144
and timbre, 125
and Tournemire, 115, 120, 160
Vingt-quatre Pièces en style libre, 125
and the violin, 109, 162
and Widor, 114–15, 120–23, 124–25, 126, 129, 131, 137, 146, 156–57
as writer, 127
Vierne, René (brother), 137, 146
Vierne-Gervaz, Marie-Joséphine (mother), 111, 146
Vierne-Taskin, Arlette (wife), 131

Index

Villa Medici, 50, 156
Virtuoso *vs.* interpreter, 5, 147–48
Vivaldi, Antonio, 115

Wagner, Richard, 10, 11, 43, 86, 106,
    125, 126, 169, 188, 201
Walcker, Eberhard Friedrich, 29
Walter, Bruno, 7
Walther, Johann Gottfried, 130
Watt, James, 22
Weber, Karl Maria von, 15, 28, 75
Webern, Anton, 125, 154, 174
Wells, H. G., 185
Widor, Charles-Marie, 2, 10, 12, 15,
    19, 159, 160, 163, 165, 168, 196
    and architecture, 99, 106, 116, 155
    and art secular *vs.* religious, 106–
        07, 159, 196
    and Bach, 18, 35, 91, 95, 97–98,
        102, 106, 114, 115, 117, 118–19,
        156, 158
    and Callinet organs, 92, 216
    and Cavaillé-Coll, 16, 32, 36, 38,
        41, 89, 92, 98–101, 115, 134, 143,
        156, 158
    character and mien, 97–99, 101,
        105, 107, 114–16, 121, 123, 134,
        143, 155–56
    childhood and schooling, 91–
        92, 95
    as conductor, 105
    death, 157–58
    and deportment, 116, 117, 122
    and Dupré, 84, 92, 98, 107, 133,
        134, 137, 143–60 passim, 166
    and Dupré, Albert, 134, 148
    and duration, 56, 115, 116, 119, 126,
        203
    and duty of interpreter, 118
    Eighth Symphony, 102, 106
    and Fauré, 107, 156
    and Fétis, 95, 216
    Fifth Symphony, 102, 106, 117
    First Symphony, 101
    Fourth Symphony, 101, 117
    and Franck, 84, 99, 101–03, 107,
        109, 113–14, 115, 117
    and Guilmant, 84, 128–29, 156, 158
    and improvisation, 49, 114, 117
    and Institute of France, 155, 158
    and legato, 5, 56, 97–98, 115, 116,
        122, 126, 203
    and Lemmens, 35, 92, 93, 94, 95–
        98, 103, 117, 118, 216
    memoirs, 105
    and Mendelssohn, 105, 116, 117
    and Messiaen, 203
    military service, 100
    miscellaneous works, 99–100, 105,
        106, 107
    and Mozart, 116
    Ninth Symphony ("Gothique"),
        102
    and Notre Dame, 18, 99, 131–32,
        156
    and opera, 99, 101, 105, 155
    and orchestration, 104–05
    and, organ *vs.* orchestra, 102,
        103–04
    and the organ symphony, 17, 101–
        03, 104, 124, 191, 203
    and Paris Conservatory, 49, 100,
        114, 128–29, 155, 160
    and phrasing, 56, 119, 122, 126
    and the piano, 99, 140–41
    and plainchant, 106
    recitals and concerts, 98, 106, 155
    and registration, 16, 36, 118–19,
        125, 126
    and rhythm, 2, 96, 119, 122, 126
    and Saint Clotilde, 99
    and Saint Ouen, 106, 134

Index